The Advanced Game Narrative Toolbox

The Advanced Game Narrative Toolbox

Edited by
Tobias Heussner

CRC Press
Taylor & Francis Group
Boca Raton London New York

CRC Press is an imprint of the
Taylor & Francis Group, an **informa** business

Cover artwork created by Ramón Acedo.

CRC Press
Taylor & Francis Group
6000 Broken Sound Parkway NW, Suite 300
Boca Raton, FL 33487-2742

© 2019 by Taylor & Francis Group, LLC
CRC Press is an imprint of Taylor & Francis Group, an Informa business

No claim to original U.S. Government works

Printed on acid-free paper

International Standard Book Number-13: 978-1-138-49963-8 (Paperback)
978-1-138-49964-5 (Hardback)

Visit the Taylor & Francis Web site at
http://www.taylorandfrancis.com

and the CRC Press Web site at
http://www.crcpress.com

Contents

Editor vii
Contributors ix

Chapter 1:   Introduction 1

Chapter 2:   Why Authentic Diversity, Consultants and Research
             Are Needed in Narrative Design 13
             Tanya DePass

Chapter 3:   Writing Romance and Sexuality in Games............... 23
             Heidi McDonald

Chapter 4:   Building A Universe 33
             Danny Wadeson

Chapter 5:   Writing for Nondigital Games (Board Games) 51
             Alexander Bevier, MFA, MA

Chapter 6:   From Novel to Game and Back Again 65
             Matt Forbeck

Chapter 7:   From Movie to Game (and Back Again?) 75
             Craig Sherman

Chapter 8:   Get It into the Game: Writing and Implementation 85
             Tobias Heussner

Chapter 9:   Cinematics and Dialogue 105
             Brian Kindregan

Chapter 10: Get This, Kill That, Talk with ... Mission and Quest
             Design... 125
             Tobias Heussner

Chapter 11: Planning Your Work 145
             Cash DeCuir

Chapter 12: Yes, Videogames Need Story Editors!.................. 159
             Toiya Kristen Finley, PhD

Chapter 13: Freelancing in Games: Narrative Mercenaries for Hire **179**
Toiya Kristen Finley, PhD

Chapter 14: Conclusion **203**

Glossary **209**

Resources and Groups **211**

Index **215**

Editor

Tobias Heussner is a senior game content/narrative designer, producer, and writer. He has been working for over 20 years in the game industry and with his teams; he has successfully developed and published more than 20 titles including the award-winning AAA RPG *Drakensang*, the Action-RPG *Drakensang Online*, and *NBA Playgrounds*. He has worked in various design roles and led teams as a designer as well as a producer. Throughout his career, he has had the opportunity of working with a wide variety of professionals, gaining knowledge and acquiring experience in various project management philosophies and approaches.

He has spoken at game developer conferences various times and likes to share his expertise with fellow developers and learn from their experience and feedback.

In 2015, he published *The Game Narrative Toolbox* with Focal Press, co-authored by Ann Lemay, Toiya Kristen Finley, and Jennifer Hepler. He's currently working on new book projects and supports CRC Press as a series editor for a book series on Unreal Engine 4.

He's currently the production director of Saber Interactive Spain and oversees all projects of the local studio as well as the communication with the other Saber Interactive studios and external partners.

His personal website and resume can be found at http://www.theussner.com.

Affiliations

- Chair of the Executive Board, International Game Developers Association Special Interest Group—Game Writing, Toronto, Ontario, Canada
- Lifetime Member, International Game Developers Association, Toronto, Ontario, Canada

Contributors

Alexander Bevier is a writer, game designer, and design researcher. He has worked on games based on Jurassic World and Jack Ryan for Amazon Alexa. He has also worked on board games with Iron Wall Games and provided preliminary writing for Wadjet Eye's Unavowed. Alexander also serves as a committee member for the IGDA Game Writing group, where he manages and facilitates gatherings of game writers around the world. He has an MFA in Game Design from NYU and an MA in Design Research, Writing and Criticism from the School of Visual Arts. He lives in the Bay Area.

Affiliations

- Producer, Earplay, Boston, Massachusetts

Brian Kindregan has worked in the animation industry for 10 or so years, at a variety of studios, including Sony Imageworks, where he storyboarded the Oscar-winning short film *The Chubb Chubbs!*

Eventually, he switched over to games, working as a writer at BioWare Corp on *Jade Empire* and *Mass Effect 2*, and moved on to Blizzard Entertainment to finish up the writing on *StarCraft II: Wings of Liberty*, as co-lead writer. He subsequently went on to be lead writer on *StarCraft II: Heart of the Swarm*, and *Diablo III: Reaper of Souls*. He is currently a narrative director at Ubisoft Montreal.

Cash DeCuir is a freelance narrative designer, writer, and lecturer currently working with the narrative outsourcing studio Talespinners. He is also the former lead writer of the critically acclaimed *Fallen London* by Failbetter Games.

Affiliations

- Partner, Talespinner, Cardiff, United Kingdom

Craig Sherman has worked as a writer for the last 20 years. His first feature film script was 2002's *New Suit*, which was a lot of fun to make but hardly anyone saw. Craig subsequently wrote feature films for 20th Century Fox, HBO, Paramount/Appian Way, and Sony/Smokehouse. None of them have been made yet, but he got paid, so whatever. As a writer for video games, he's written several projects, including Saber Interactive's upcoming *World War Z*. He enjoys spending time with his family, sleep, and writing about himself in third person.

Affiliations

- Member, Writers Guild of America West, Los Angeles, California

Danny Wadeson is a freelance writer and narrative designer based in Cambridge, UK. At the time of writing, he was working on *Röki, Abandon Ship, Harold Halibut, Neuroslicers,* and *Fusion Guards.* He also hosts a podcast on storytelling named *Uncaring Universe,* mentors young game design students, and is a games journalist published by the likes of Polygon, Kotaku, and Killscreen. He thinks Kentucky Route Zero is really rather good.

Heidi McDonald is a narrative designer, musician, and game designer from Pittsburgh, PA. Women in Gaming's Rising Star for 2013, her work has won recognition from groups including Serious Play, the International Conference on Game Jams, and the IGF. Author and editor of *Digital Love: Romance and Sexuality in Games* (A K Peters/CRC Press, 2017) Heidi has published and lectured extensively on romance and sexuality, and emotional engagement, in games. She is also known for her collection of magnificent hats and for dressing as her pirate alter-ego, Lizzie Bones. She has dedicated her career to the idea that games can do amazing things for human beings.

Matt Forbeck is an award-winning and *New York Times*-bestselling author and game designer with over 30 novels and countless games published to date. His recent work includes the new *Dungeons & Dragons: Endless Quest* books (Candlewick Press, 2018), *Dungeonology* (Candlewick Press, 2016), *Halo: Bad Blood* (Gallery Books, 2018), and *Life Is Strange: Welcome to Blackwell* (Titan Books, 2018), plus work on *Assassin's Creed: Origins* (Ubisoft, 2017), *Ghost Recon Wildlands* (Ubisoft, 2017), and the *Shotguns & Sorcery* roleplaying game (Outland Entertainment, 2019) based on his novels. He lives in Beloit, WI, with his wife and five children, including a set of quadruplets. For more about him and his work, visit Forbeck.com.

Tanya DePass is the founder and director of I Need Diverse Games, a not-for-profit foundation based in Chicago. She's part of Rivals of Waterdeep, the programming coordinator for OrcaCon; and often speaks on issues of diversity, feminism, race, intersectionality, and other topics at conventions. Her writing appears in Uncanny Magazine, Polygon, Vice Gaming, Mic, Waypoint, Wiscon Chronicles, Paste Games, and other publications.

She's also the editor of *Game Devs and Others: Tales from the Margins* (CRC Press, 2018), an anthology featuring stories from marginalized game developers and others adjacent to the industry.

Affiliations

- Member, International Game Developers Association Special Interest Group—Blacks in Gaming, Toronto, Ontario, Canada
- Game Devs and Others: Tales from the Margins, CRC Press, Boca Raton, Florida
- DePaul University, Chicago, Illinois

Toiya Kristen Finley, PhD—a writer, editor, game designer, and narrative designer/game writer—holds a PhD in literature and creative writing (Binghamton University) and is on the IGDA Game Writing Special Interest Group's Executive Board. Some of her published games include *Academagia: The Making of Mages*, *Fat Chicken*, *Verdant Skies*, and *Siren Song*. She has written and/or edited for Chapters and Endless Entertainment, served as a game and narrative designer for Digital Myths, taught videogame writing for UCLA Extension Writers' Program, and co-authored *The Game Narrative Toolbox* (FocalPress, 2015). Recently, she edited and contributed to *Narrative Tactics for Mobile and Social Games: Pocket-Sized Storytelling*.

CHAPTER 1

Introduction

Contents

How to Use This Book. 2

What It Is About 2

Alexander Bevier 3

Heidi McDonald 3

Brian Kindregan 4

Danny Salfield Wadeson 5

Craig Sherman 5

Cash DeCuir 6

Matt Forbeck 7

Tanya DePass. 8

Toiya Kristen Finley 9

Tobias Heussner 10

References 11

> "Once upon a time, there was a little lonely writerling. A writerling, one of those creatures that roam the world armed only with a pen and paper. He wandered through the forest, desert and fields. Lonely, he filled his pages, lonely, he journeyed, until one day he saw a small glimmering fire in the city they called Austin. He walked toward that fire and to his surprise, other writerlings were there, sitting, talking, drinking around this fire that felt like home, like the place to be…"

This is how some of the most well-known tales begin, and, ironically, most careers in writing start in a very similar way. We all started to write one day, by accident or out of pure determination, our first story. We usually did this alone, in front of a piece of paper or our computers, and slowly the worlds in our heads formed into something living and breathing, something that wanted to be shared, something that became a living being on its own. However, the more we worked on our stories, the more we began to understand the difficulties of being a writer and, like the writerling, we felt the loneliness of our craft. It was at this point that we started our quest for help, feedback and a search for others from whom and with whom we could learn and grow.

With this book, we invite you to join us on this journey of constant learning that comes with the craft of being a game writer. The authors of this book gathered to share some of their experiences during their journeys as writers. These experiences may be specific to each author's situation, but regardless of how specific these experiences are, they all convey a piece of general learning, and we hope that these pieces will be helpful on your journey and that one day you'll join us at the campfire, sharing your very own experience so that we can all learn from each other.

How to Use This Book

The aim of this book is to make you *think* about narrative design. Whether you agree with any of it is not an issue, as long as you advance your own thoughts on the subject (based on Bartle, 2004).

This is how we want you to use this book. We can't tell you what challenges your career will bring, but we can share our experiences and hope you think about them and find something useful for the challenges on your writer's journey.

What It Is About

In this book, we talk about advanced narrative design techniques such as how to approach diversity, how to develop believable relationships among your characters and how to work with transmedia sources.

We assume for the content that you have at the very least a basic game literacy and that you are familiar with the basics of writing and storytelling. If not, we recommend that you pick up Robert McKee's *Story* (1997) and one or two books on game writing such as *The Game Narrative Toolbox* from Ann Lemay, Jennifer Hepler, Toiya Kristen Finley and Tobias Heussner (2015) or Evan Skolnick's *Video Game Storytelling* (2014).

Each chapter in this book will end with exercises and sample solutions to these exercises. We hope that this will help you to practice and compare your approaches to the problems discussed in every chapter.

So much for our introduction, but before we jump right into the content, let us introduce ourselves and share what brought us to the writerlings campfire. For this introduction, we asked ourselves the following questions.

- How did you break into the industry?
- What are your fields of expertise? Why?

- What did you study? And what are you learning right now?
- What are two of the most memorable experiences of your career?

Alexander Bevier

My breaking into the industry occurred slowly. I began working as a journalist determined to write about video games. I was a young undergraduate at the time, so I had plenty of opportunities to volunteer for events. Over time, I built a large network of contacts and friends, primarily in game writing, which opened the door to my becoming a committee member for the IGDA's Game Writing SIG. Eventually, I went to graduate school for game design and found a job shortly after finishing a second master's degree.

My experience and expertise are very broad. I'm eager to learn and figure out what I don't know, opening doors to understanding the history of mid-twentieth century board games. I took advantage of my English degree to figure out how to access archives to study Sid Sackson's extensive body of work and have used that to continue to broaden my understanding of design criticism.

One of my great honors is to annually host Write Club during the Game Developers Conference. It's always a wonder to see newcomers rise through the ranks and impress their peers, only to see them again with paid game-writing positions. There have been numerous occasions in my short career where people have told me I opened the doors for them. It's a great privilege to already give back to my community.

Heidi McDonald

I broke into games as a second career, at the age of 41. While studying communications, film, and digital media at Chatham University, I secured an internship with Schell Games in Pittsburgh, PA, as a writer, and upon my permanent hire there after graduating, I worked on nine titles at Schell as a writer and designer. Several of these games are award winning, but the one I'm particularly proud of is the IGF Honorable Mention for Excellence in Narrative for *Orion Trail*, a goofy *Star Trek* parody game in which I gave thousands of players space dysentery. Another highlight was working on *The World of Lexica for Amplify Education*, a language arts curriculum game for grades 6–8 in which I got to write character dialogue for well-loved public-domain literary characters such as the Cheshire Cat, Tom Sawyer, Baba Yaga, and others.

Outside of my day job, I began to investigate questions relating to game romance, simply because I was interested in it and I'm exactly the nerd who likes to write research papers for fun when not going to school. This ethnographic research led to numerous publications and worldwide lectures on the topic of romance in games, culminating in my book *Digital Love: Romance and Sexuality in Games*, in late 2017 (A K Peters/CRC Press, 2017).

Most recently, I worked as senior creative director at an organization called iThrive Games, which advances social and emotional learning using games. This mission helped me to learn more about neuroscience and social psychology and how these sciences can be utilized to produce resources that help game developers intentionally design for positive practices such as empathy, kindness, and optimism. In addition to leading the development of these design resources, I oversaw developer education and outreach and did creative direction on projects that present for subject-matter expertise.

Brian Kindregan

A more definitive answer to this question can be found on my website, briankindregan.com. The short version is that in 2002, I saw that BioWare Corp was looking for writers. They insisted that in order to apply, you had to create a game mod in *Neverwinter Nights*. I knew nothing about scripting or creating mods, but I set out to learn. BioWare had generously shipped the complete toolset with the game, so I was able to dive in and learn very quickly. I submitted a Neverwinter mod, and they liked it. They hired me to work as a writer on *Jade Empire*.

Having been a key writer on character driven role-playing games, real-time strategy games, action role-playing games and a multiplayer online battle arena, I've had to understand and embrace the power and limitations of many different game genres. So, I think my main field of expertise is simply understanding narrative creation in a wide variety of genres.

Beyond that, I have had the opportunity to write a number of very high-profile cinematics.

I studied animation in the film school of the California Institute of the Arts. My main focus was storyboarding.

Creative professionals must always continue to grow, so I'm currently trying to get a stronger command of transmedia.

The opening cinematic of *Diablo III: Reaper of Souls* seems to have made a big impact on many people. We had a lot of exposition to wrap into the package and still be entertaining, even powerful. It is important to point out that I wrote the cinematic, but many other people poured their own creativity into it. It was a team effort.

Beyond that, I've been lucky enough to work on many moments that seemed to speak to people, but one of which I am quite proud is the Biotic God from *Mass Effect 2*. In a deeply silly moment, I added a volus named Niftu Cal to the game, who had chemically induced delusions of grandeur. For some reason, it struck just the right chord, and he became a meme, and even showed up in *Mass Effect 3's* multiplayer mode. Sometimes you've just got to be silly.

Danny Salfield Wadeson

My first foray into the industry was working on its fringes: as a journalist while working a day job in online video and advertising. Eventually I got involved early with a very small, two-man project and ended up quitting my day job to cofound the studio to work on it. A few years after that, having learned a lot and built a small reputation from showing the game's trailer on the Microsoft stage at E3 2017, I went fully freelance as a writer and narrative designer.

It was a slightly tortuous route, but I never once gave up on creating stories for the industry that had so captured my imagination since I was a very young boy.

I'm probably most confident with folding in traditional, immersive storytelling wisdom with the native mechanics and more interactive nature of games. From my fiction writing and time spent in film, I also love creating dialogue that sounds very natural to the ear.

My time in advertising and running a studio has also given me an intimate understanding of how to build efficient working relationships and narrative design pipelines.

I studied literature and film. So, I've gone deep for many years into the differences and similarities, the strengths and weaknesses of the storytelling tropes and mechanics of each medium.

Right now, I'm focused on learning more about the technical pipelines of games, including improving my skills with narrative design and writing middleware. Varied experience never hurts, either.

The first is quite an intimate thing. It was seeing fan feedback about a lore story I'd written for an online multiplayer game: they said reading the story had made them try out a character they'd never wanted to before and end up loving them. The second was seeing the trailer for a game I was doing the narrative design for shown on the Microsoft stage at E3. The reaction to it—to the setting, the story we hinted at—was overwhelming.

Opposite ends of the scale, but both helped me feel like I was on the right path of interesting world building.

Craig Sherman

I was working as an assistant in Disney Television, constantly scheming for a path to become a writer. Part of my job was to provide water bottles to writers

5

who were meeting with my boss, and my initial career goal was to reach a position where other people brought me water. While I was toiling away at the studio, I wrote a screenplay and showed it to my boss. She liked it quite a bit and sent it out to agents. An agent liked it and signed me, and about a year and a half later, the movie got produced as a low-budget feature. That was my foot in the door as a screenwriter. Years and many film projects later, a friend of mine who founded and runs a game studio asked me to work with him, and I jumped at the chance.

I began as a comedy writer. My first two scripts were comedies, but I somehow gravitated to biopics. My cowriter Bob Jury and I sold the story of famous football coach Pop Warner to Fox and wrote the script. I then went on to adapt a script from a nonfiction book about World War II. After that, my writing partner Brian Hecker and I sold a biopic to Paramount about Atari founder Nolan Bushnell and then adapted a book about the Smothers Brothers for Sony Pictures. I'd say, if I have an area of expertise, my experience as a screenwriter would categorize me as a dramatic writer, but I still feel like comedy is in my DNA. As a game writer, I've had the opportunity to write several genres, but I've spent the last year or so writing a dramatic game.

I studied film at the University of Miami. My initial goal was to become a film director, but I soon realized that it was an overcrowded field filled with people who hadn't proven themselves and would probably never have the chance. I decided that I might have enough talent to give writing a shot and I never turned back. I'd say the bulk of my learning happened after I graduated film school and moved to LA. I spent 14 years in the trenches. There's no better teacher than experience. Right now, I'm learning to perfect my craft as a game writer. I can certainly lean on my screenwriting background for most tasks, but the opportunity to write games and then play them provides insights that you can't get any other way.

The first memorable career moment has to be when my screenplay was being produced as a film and I was invited to the casting sessions. I had been trying to write for years, and this was the first time I'd heard professional actors—actors whose work I knew—performing my words. It was absolutely surreal and a joyous moment for me. I'd say the second most memorable career moment was when my oldest friend in the world, Saber Interactive CEO Matt Karch, invited me to join him to create new games. I've known him since I was four years old and the fact that our career paths brought us together was wonderfully serendipitous, and I've enjoyed it quite a bit.

Cash DeCuir

Shortly after graduating college—where, by tremendous fortune, my writing professor encouraged me to study everything except writing, his belief being that it's more important to develop a base of knowledge, since writers can always practice their craft in their own time—I saw that Failbetter Games was looking for a writer. To apply, one had to have two published titles. I spent a full month and a half creating two Twine games. The application process went on several months more before I had the job.

My path was unusually straightforward. It was luck as much as ability and grit. I was in the right place at the right time. What's more, I had the opportunity and the encouragement to dedicate myself to earning the position.

Since then, I've continued to develop myself as a writer and narrative designer. Finding the story in mechanics and the mechanics in story, then heightening both—searching for novel means to more thoroughly intertwine them—is my primary focus. Games offer ways to tell stories as they've never been told before. We're fools if we don't take the opportunity now, while our medium is still so young, to pioneer. To this end, I'm brushing up on my coding skills. The more I'm able to implement my designs, or at least create a base for other team members to build from, the more I'm able to serve the narrative.

I'm proud of the work I've done. One story from my time at Failbetter springs to mind: a premium story from *Fallen London*, called HOJOTOHO!—being the story of a young girl, inspired by an encounter with art to become a hero. It was a deeply personal story. I was tremendously relieved to see it resonated with the public. Another work I think will be particularly memorable—though it's still in production—is *Over the Alps*. It's a spy thriller set at the outbreak of WWII, which delves into similar themes of resistance and resilience, even in the darkest times. Hope is the message I tend to preach, and I think this will be one of my loudest proclamations yet. Art should serve the audience, after all, and the game's message is tragically one we need now.

Matt Forbeck

I broke into the video game industry by knowing people who were already working in games. I started out as a tabletop game designer, and over time, the video game industry raided tabletop games for more and more designers. Some of those folks knew of my skills with both game design and writing and reached out to me for help when they needed it.

Over the years, I've become an expert at both game design and stories. I'm strongest at the intersection of those two skills, which is why I keep winding up writing for video games. Meanwhile, I also design tabletop games and write novels (including ones for both *Halo* and *Guild Wars*), nonfiction books (like *The Marvel Encyclopedia*, DK ADULT, 2009, Revised Edition), and books that blend games and stories (including *Dungeonology*, Candlewick Press, 2016 and *Endless Quest*, Candlewick Press, 2018).

In college, I started out studying both computer science and creative writing. At one point, I had an approved plan to get degrees in both fields. I eventually dropped out of computer science to concentrate on writing, but I still get a lot of use out of those skills. Even when you're primarily a writer, it helps to be able to speak to the coders, the designers and everybody else on the rest of the team in terms they understand.

I've done a lot of wild things in my career. One of the coolest ones was when my tabletop dystopian superheroes role-playing game *Brave New World* debuted at Gen Con (the largest tabletop games convention) in 1999. We set up a huge debut in which we were going to haul in a superhero from the game in chains and then execute him in the center of our booth by firing squad. We had rifles loaded with blanks and even those exploding blood squibs you use in films to simulate gunshot wounds all set up and ready to go.

Sadly, a couple of weeks before that, a day trader went on a shooting spree in Atlanta. After talking with the folks at Gen Con, we realized that shooting off blanks in a crowded convention center could cause a panic, so we changed things around. We threw out the blanks and the squibs and decided to stage a dramatic escape for the condemned hero instead. That actually changed the story I was writing for the game books and affected everything we did with the game from that point out, and it got a huge amount of attention for the debut of the game.

Tanya DePass

I "broke" into the industry by being mad about videogames around six a.m. before work back in October 2014. I'd been a long-time consumer of games but never had knowledge of how they were made or how much work it was to implement a feature, for example. I did know games very rarely had characters like me or my friends. Earlier that year, there had been the ill-fated commentary of "it's too hard to animate women" in regard to a new Ubisoft title due out soon. Also, hearing that they were "inches from playable female characters" in *Far Cry 4* set me on a bit of a rant; throw in the latest wave of games featuring yet more white, scruffy, brown-eyed, blond/brown-haired male leads, and it frustrated me enough to add #INeedDiverseGames to some tweets, and off they went to trend and also get picked up by the unsavory denizens of gaming who were running rampant online four years ago.

My field of expertise, if any, is viewing things via a diverse lens, a.k.a. my life experience. I've no formal training in looking for diversity or not seeing it in media I consume. My expertise is formed around learning to express these inequalities mostly through writing or speaking about it on panels, discussing the games I play while broadcasting on Twitch—the hard-knock life lessons earned through experiencing a lot of vitriol and backlash for expressing a mild critique of a video game for having no people of color, of falling back on tired tropes and surviving the hostile wilds of Twitter, Facebook and comments left on articles I've written.

I've studied various topics throughout my collegiate career, including Japanese culture and language, and dabbled in public service at the grad level, but my degree is in human–computer interaction, with a focus on user-centered design. Right now, I'm learning how hard it is to create when the country I live in is rapidly entering into a dystopian landscape: how difficult it is to get people to actively listen and engage versus throwing up their hands and going "not me!" or "I didn't do/say/think that" when it comes to the current way of life in the United States.

Though things are terrible in the greater world, there have been two bright spots in my career so far that stand out. One is getting to edit the anthology *Game Devs and Others: Tales from the Margins* (A K Peters/CRC Press, 2018), collection of personal essays from marginalized people adjacent to and in the games industry. The other is less tangible, but is every time someone thanks me for what I do, for being present and visible, when I'm at a conference or on a panel or podcast.

Toiya Kristen Finley

Back before I knew anything about getting game-writing jobs, I took to Google and did a search … for game-writing jobs. Black Chicken Studios was working on its first game. I did a writing test for a lore writer (something I didn't know existed), they liked it and they hired me.

I've written and published short stories in just about every genre imaginable, and I've published creative nonfiction, manga and material for RPG supplements, as well as games. Over the years, I've learned the differences between different storytelling media and audience expectations for each. That's important if you're going to tell stories for those audiences that are satisfying. And you can't innovate in these media if you don't understand what's already been done.

I'm also an editor (developmental/substantive, copyeditor and proofreader). Being a writer makes me a better editor because it helps me communicate with writers. Also, reviewing the strengths and weaknesses of other writers sharpens my skills in improving upon the strengths and weaknesses of my own work.

I was a professional student for 8 years. As an undergrad, I got a BA in individualized study at NYU, and focused on psychology, Spanish, Italian and creative writing. At Iowa State, I got an MA in English with a creative writing concentration and a minor in linguistics. For my doctorate, I went to Binghamton University and got a degree in literature and creative writing. Currently, I'm looking to learn some noncoding engines so I can work on my own game projects. I'm looking to develop my own IP and be a content owner, and this would help me accomplish that.

After 10 years of working in games, my most memorable experiences happened fairly recently. I got two of my largest gigs exposurewise within about a month of each other. It's how I got the jobs that makes them memorable. When I first pursued writing for games, I was told that I needed to be on LinkedIn because everyone in the industry used it. I found that to be true. I would meet someone at a conference and, within a few hours, they had looked up my LinkedIn profile. I never got any work through the platform until a few months ago as of this writing. A company was looking for game writers, and a recruiter found my profile. About 30 minutes later, I'd had an interview and been offered a contract. For the second gig, a couple of people recommended me after someone asked if anyone knew of a writer with my expertise. An interview later, I had the job. Referrals are magical, and at no other times in my professional life had I not had anyone else competing with me for gigs.

Tobias Heussner

Officially, I started to develop games when I was in high school and 16, having a small indie development team, talking business and pitching to publishers. Unofficially, it all started a lot earlier, when I bothered my family with self-invented rulesets for *Hero's Quest-like* games and when I wrote my first game concepts for beat 'em ups and adventure games.

It took several years from my first steps into the industry before I released the first game, which was one of the infamous German horse games. By then, I had left my own team behind, as everyone was either going to university, had moved away or was pursuing another career, and was hired by Radon Labs, a company I got to know during networking events and which I had helped to finish one of their games in the past. While it took years to get the first game released, it was the experience gathered on the way to this first release that helped to get it done. Looking back, I think this early time as an indie developer gave me the experience I needed when I later started to work on bigger IPs and for bigger companies where you don't have the same level of freedom but need to excel every day.

I started as a game designer, but my passion for stories and role-playing games was always present and thus I was drawn to the field of content design. Today, my fields of expertise are narrative design, level design and game production, as I also worked as a producer in addition to being a content designer.

When I broke into the industry, no classes for game design and so on existed, so I studied computer science to learn more about programming, and later I studied feature film writing, fiction writing and management. Currently, I spend a lot of time learning game design theory, the internals and effective use of Unreal Engine 4 and leadership principles and approaches from John Maxwell.

The most memorable experience of my career happened at the beginning when I designed the horse games and when I attended GDC, meeting with all the professionals and learning from each other. Yes, it is a great experience finishing a game and finally seeing it on the shelves, but more important is the experience on the way to the final game. During the development of the horse games, games I most likely would never buy, I learned that it doesn't matter what kind of game you're working on; what matters is that you always seek the best experience for your players. Working on the horse games helped me early on in my career to develop this mindset, and it was a great experience, even more so when we, as a team, got to see how our target audience enjoyed the experience we created. When you enter the industry, you may not work on the title of your choice, but don't see your current situation as simply a step toward your goal; take what you can from it and learn to become better. My experience with the horse games helped me further down the road to cut features in *Drakensang* to optimize the player's experience, even though as a fan of the *Dark Eye RPG*, it hurt to see some good rules not making it to the game. In the end, it was the best for the game.

Going to GDC Online or other industry conferences was another key experience in my career. Suddenly, the small world of the studio I worked for opened up to a whole world of developers. Sitting together with Chris Metzen talking about *Diablo* or with Richard Dansky talking about *Vampire: The Masquerade* or listening to Flint Dille talking about transmedia … it was a beautiful opportunity to learn and even more to see that all these people whose names I had read in credits were facing and struggling with the same problems I did when creating the next big game. Remember our writerling? That's how I felt when first arriving in Austin for GDC Online, and it was such a great experience being welcomed like a family member. Ever since, seeing my fellow writers has been like a family reunion, and I hope to welcome you one day at our campfire as well.

That's it for the introduction, and now let's dive into the content and listen to our daily struggles and what we have each learned on our journeys. We hope you'll find something useful in the chapters to come, and don't forget that the only way to become is to practice, practice and practice.

References

Bartle, R. A. 2004. *Designing Virtual Worlds*, San Francisco, New Riders Publishing. Preface, xvii.

Heussner, T., Lemay, A., Hepler, J., Finley, T. K. 2015. *The Game Narrative Toolbox*, Burlington, Focal Press.

McKee, R. 1997. *Story*, New York, Harper-Collins Publishers.

Skolnick, E. 2014. *Video Game Storytelling*, Berkeley, Watson-Guptill Publications.

CHAPTER 2

Why Authentic Diversity, Consultants and Research Are Needed in Narrative Design

Tanya DePass

Contents

Authentic Diversity 14
Examples of Failure to Have Authentic Diversity in Games. 14
You May Wonder: Why Not Stereotypes? 17
Before You Get a Consultant, Let's Talk Research 17
Conclusion 20
Exercise 21

We always hear the words "diversity" and "inclusion" around gaming, technology and media. They've almost become meaningless buzzwords that get lip service, if anything, in response to critique about a game's setting, characters or world-building instead of them becoming benchmarks for the industry to improve upon and to realize players are not the 18–35-year-old white male demographic we're often told is the audience for games, despite statistics that prove otherwise.

In this Chapter

- We'll look at diversity both in the general sense and in defining authentic diversity
- We will give resources for diversity consulting
- We'll explore ways to research experiences outside our own before putting them into our content

What is missing is authentic diversity in all aspects of game design, but especially narrative design. When a character is written, what comes out of their mouth and what we learn about them via the story and the world informs how they are introduced to the player. When there is a lack of authentic diversity, it can harm players that the character may represent in that world. We can easily find a definition of diversity, which Merriam Webster defines as:

> the state of having people who are different races or who have different cultures in a group or organization

That's a simple definition, good for everyday use, but it does not deal in authenticity or inclusion; it's a simple way to give a definition to have on hand rather than addressing the issue. But what is authentic diversity?

Authentic Diversity

How does one define this? It's a little more difficult than you'd think to find a commonly used and accepted definition of authentic diversity. There's a lot of discussion and definition of just diversity or just authenticity in the workplace, but nothing combining them. Here's a shot at giving you a small tool for your kit in bringing this to your projects.

Authentic diversity (AD), for the purpose of this chapter and going forward, is defined as:

> Representation that does not fall back on or rely on tropes or stereotypes. Diversity that is thoughtfully portrayed as part of daily life, not an exception to the rule or an anomaly that needs to be explained, justified or otherwise hand-waved as something other than the regular operation of that media's world-building and the experiences of the characters. Additionally, authentic diversity will be achieved with the work of diversity consultants, in lieu of team members from the group you are trying to represent.

Now that we have defined authentic diversity, let's quickly look at a few examples of inauthentic diversity so you can see the things you should avoid doing as you take on stories, settings and characters that are outside your lived experiences.

Examples of Failure to Have Authentic Diversity in Games

Examples of Inauthentic Diversity

Let's look at a few examples of inauthentic diversity, where games tried to do better but didn't quite make the mark. Note that including games in this section is not indicative of their overall quality; however, I am noting their failure to be authentically diverse.

There are so many examples of this, I will try to keep it brief and not turn this section into a running list of all the ways games have failed to be authentically diverse and inclusive. We can go back to the earlier days of console gaming with Barrett in *Final Fantasy VII*, continuing on to T-Hawke in *Super Street Fighter II*, who hits just about every bingo square possible for a diversity fail. We also have other games such as *Beyond Good and Evil*, with a dreadlock'd Rhino (which also returns for the sequel), *Guild Wars 2* having black hair on nonhuman characters as an option, and the lack of good lighting of dark skin in games. This indicates how game narratives don't address the choices a character makes in how they look vs how the game world and narrative react to the PC.

In *Dragon Age: Origins*, you can make a "dark-skinned" Warden as a human noble, but your family is always white. It got slightly better in Dragon Age 2, where your family's "genetics" did try to match your Hawke, as noted in a piece I wrote for *Offworld*, "In Fantasy Worlds: Historical Accuracy Is a Lie." This isn't a factor in Dragon Age: Inquisition, as you don't get to see or meet the Inquisitor's family, though there are party members who are somewhat stereotypical while also managing to be groundbreaking in some areas.

Another example, perhaps the most egregious, is David Cage's most recent release as of this writing, *Detroit: Become Human*, a game that uses androids as stand-ins for the civil rights struggles of black people unflinchingly, including having Markus, an android played by Jesse Williams, have to stand in the back of the bus in an "android only" section. Yet Cage tried to claim there is no message in the game while using actual quotes from Martin Luther King and evoking imagery of the Shawshank Redemption and marches at Selma, or, if you take Markus on the aggressive route open to him, you can get Markus killed along with his android followers, giving an unconscious confirmation that attempting to free yourself via any means necessary will cost your life so it is better to not resist your lot in life.

There are plenty more examples to give, as both tabletop and video games have decades of getting it wrong under their belt, but rather than belabor the obvious, let's briefly go over why diversity, especially authentic diversity, is still needed in games.

Why do we need diversity of any kind? Well, because representation is important, especially when you realize that who gamers are has changed from the assumed demographic of 18–35-year-old white males to the average gamer being reported as over 35, with women 18 and over making up a majority of those playing games, per the 2017 Entertainment Software Association (ESA) report.

Knowing this, you must be wondering why diversity isn't a bigger priority in narrative design. Good question, and one we'll give you some tools to help with in this chapter and the rest of this book. So how can developers get past this lack of diversity, inclusion and, more importantly, authentic diversity in games?

The obvious answer is to get more people of color (POC), queer and other folks into the industry so studios aren't so homogenous and designed around what has always worked and fit instead of getting more talent at the table. Another option is getting diversity consultants, so representation isn't done by people with no experience with being queer, a person of color, a woman, mentally ill or disabled, for instance. Telling stories outside your experience is a minefield, one that well-meaning developers often fall victim to. They don't mean to offend or harm, but they do through failure to understand the stories they are trying to tell without being part of that group.

Diversity is having people of various backgrounds, ethnicities, economic statuses, gender identities and cultural backgrounds present, but also actively involved. It is having more than one person of a marginalized identity so that one character does not have to represent that identity for everyone and all experiences, which leads to tokenization rather than representation as intended. Often, when people try to have diversity in games, they have one character who is black or brown, female identified or queer and maybe, just maybe if they are really thinking about it, they'll have a character with a physical disability or mental health issues.

There are several problems with this, and that inclusion of one character who is supposed to represent a marginalized identity or identities is why help is needed by developer teams. There're several ways in which to get help for this that go beyond reading a blog post, an article that yet again rehashes introductory-level concepts of diversity or a half-hearted internet search for all the wrong things. This lackadaisical "research" will often yield results that are as bad or sometimes worse than not paying attention to these issues at all. We'll delve into research and ways to have a baseline of where to start a little later in this chapter, but for now, let's talk about bringing in the experts after you've done your initial research.

Why Do Development Teams Need Diversity Consultants?

Because a consultant on the lived experience you are trying to bring to your game can help steer you clear of harmful tropes and stereotypes (hopefully!), avoid cultural faux pas and help you course-correct if you have already started down that path toward poor representation.

Why do dev teams need diversity consultants? It's not because we just want money—though money is a requirement for the labor involved in diversity consulting, it's not the motivating factor. Dev teams need diversity consultants to have that authentic diversity we talked about earlier. It's because telling a story outside your experience leaves room for mistakes, unintentional ways to reinforce racism, homophobia and other biases. Since dev teams are more likely to be majority white men, or in some cases mostly white women, it's very easy to fall back on stereotypes and tropes when creating characters outside your experience.

You May Wonder: Why Not Stereotypes?

After all, it's easy to write what people think they know, but falling back on those causes more harm than good. When you portray a black male character as a thug or a drug dealer, for instance, that's a reliance on a harmful stereotype. It's easy and, some would say, lazy storytelling. It is the same as if you had a female character who was only there to be rescued, or fridged to advance the plot and give the assumed male player character a motivation; again, it's relegating a character to a prop instead of part of the story. Those are just a couple of examples of why stereotype usage is harmful. Devs can avoid this by reaching out to diversity consultants.

While there is the temptation to use the grain of truth that is often embedded in stereotypes and tropes, the reality of subverting a stereotype and making it somehow work is a nuanced operation that requires more work, diligence, research and cultural understanding, and even an experienced diversity consultant may not be able help you achieve this goal. It is a rare narrative designer who can twist these tropes to their will, and because that is such a fine edge to walk and will often open the door to a failure, it is something to be undertaken with extreme caution.

If you can make this happen somehow, it should be reviewed at least twice, and by members of the group that the stereotype applies to. For instance, if you wished to subvert the trope of a black male assumed to be a gangster by creating a character who looks and sounds like a stereotypical thug, but have him be a pillar of the community, someone who does not fall into the column of what players assume a character like him would act, dress and speak like to break the stereotypical assumption, you must have black men read over the script and review the concept art, and keep them involved until everything is locked in.

Before You Get a Consultant, Let's Talk Research

So why do research if you're going to hire a consultant, right? Well, it will make the consultant's job easier in the long run, cost you a little less money and show that you have a better idea of what you are looking for from them besides, *I screwed up; fix this please*. This is often the case for jobs that I've taken, or the other side of it will be, *I have barely done anything, and I am terrified of messing up, so hold my hand so I don't wind up doing something terrible.* Or, in some cases, you come into a project so late, even when you have feedback, it's far too late for your changes to be implemented except at great cost and a delay to the project.

So, the question is: *How* do I research this? Assuming that research into the topic for which you are bringing in a consultant isn't your everyday thing to do, I'll walk you through some steps. Depending on your current job level and what you've done educationally and in the scope of other jobs, this may be something you already know. If you already have a handle on researching, feel free to skip ahead.

One: Note that doing a few searches does not excuse you from getting a consultant, but this will help you set a baseline. Use Google as a starting point, and have a short list of keywords to search on. For instance, if you wanted to have a fantasy game set somewhere besides faux medieval England, you could look up terms such as *Moors during the middle ages, black in medieval times* or *Nigeria in the middle ages/medieval times,* and add date ranges to get more specific results. From there, you could dig into specifics like the Benin Empire and drill down from there.

Two: Make notes on specific things you want to incorporate into your project, such as if there are names and locations you want to use, including notes on the appearance of people in the era in which you wish to set your project. In this example, let's say you're setting a game in the early 2000s in Chicago. You'd search neighborhood names, politicians, major news events. You've already done the initial search and now you have notes that you can take to your writers, artists and possibly your voice actors so they have an idea of the time period, slang, etc. they are going for.

Three: Now that you've gotten all this information together and you've got your initial concepts, your sample dialogue and how you want this character to look as well as sound, you should collate these notes into a format that will make it easy for your consultant to read over, assess the project and start their work with you.

To help you with this, I've provided a simple outline that I've put together for myself based on client-provided materials. Doing this has helped me stay organized and keep a clear goal of what the client needs from me when doing diversity consulting.

Synopsis: Paragraph or two of what the project is about.

Research already done by the client: Broken into person, place, things.

What they are seeking feedback on: Dialogue, concept art, setting, all of the above?

What kind of feedback they want: Written, a follow-up meeting (Skype, Hangouts, Discord if the client isn't local to me) or do they want both kinds of feedback on a project?

How do you find a consultant? Well there is the internet, and our friend Google. The other way a lot of people find consultants is by asking outside their usual networks and on Twitter. For all that it can be an instrument of evil, Twitter is often a great space for collaboration outside your usual circles. There's also everyone's nonfavorite place to network, LinkedIn. That's likely your best place for reaching out to folks you may not know personally, but whose profiles can show you if they fit what you're seeking. A simpler way to do this is to reach out among colleagues to ask if they've ever used a diversity consultant and if they can connect you for a project.

I will advise against using Facebook to reach out to potential consultants, as many people maintain their Facebook presence as a personal, friends- and family-only place separate from their professional spaces, especially marginalized people who may not have other places to speak freely or about the many issues in their daily lives. At the end of the day, someone you are calling on as a consultant is a person, not merely a resource. Remembering that will help in approaching them to collaborate and in receiving their feedback.

While writing up this section, the few resources I wanted to link to are no longer available due to the misuse and lack of payment many sensitivity readers encounter in this work. The fact that it is hard to find an easily searchable listing of who does this work online, and that a great resource was misused to the point where it had to be shut down to keep people offering this service safe, show that the service is both needed and also needs to be set up in a way that works for both prospective clients and consultants.

Once you have a consultant, you'll have to figure out the best ways to utilize their skills so that you're getting what you need for your project and your consultant is not having their time or skills wasted such that you wind up back at step one.

A Short How-To on How to Utilize a Diversity Consultant

There are many ways to utilize a diversity consultant once you have brought one onto your project, which we'll cover in this section. Other than compensation, the biggest way to utilize their expertise and not waste their time or yours is to listen to their feedback and implement it.

Congratulations, you've hired a diversity consultant for your project, but now what? Well, aside from making sure you have a signed NDA and contract for their services, you should prep a document outlining what work you've already done to research what you need their expertise on and set aside time to have a meeting with them if needed to get them on-boarded.

There're some high-level issues that would need a consultant, such as the development of characters, how the main character and NPCs look and who the voice actor is, including the character's speech pattern, dialect and, if applicable, their accent, as well as their backstory. These are critical elements that are hard to change after a certain point in development, so it's best to bring someone in at the beginning of development to avoid getting to a point where things can't be changed without a release delay and significant cost to a project.

At this point in the project, your consultant should be giving feedback on character concepts, both visual and text. This can be on their backstory and, if possible, their dialogue. Even when a character may look fine, what they say is as important as how they look. For example, if your lead character is a black female from a major metropolitan area, such as Chicago or New York, and doesn't use regional slang or phrases, that could be a thing that players pick up on if they are from that area.

In the middle of things, one thing you'll want your consultant to give feedback on (if possible at the point at which you've brought them onto a project) is the voice actor for the character(s) they are reviewing. Oftentimes, a minority character is voiced by a white actor or a person of color, but not someone of the same ethnicity as the character players will encounter in the game.

On the other end of the spectrum, there are low-level issues that should be considered when creating a character or world: this is where your consultant can help you decide what can be let go, what is not a make-or-break aspect of the game in regard to diversity and representation. It will be easy to try to be all things to all people, but no one game can do that. This is also a good point to review your world-building and make sure that your idea of diversity is not "The Only One," where there is one queer character, one brown character, one female character and so on. That way, those non–white dude characters don't shoulder the burden of being all representation to all players who may identify with them.

The last thing to consider is when it's too late for a diversity consultant to help with your project and when that consult becomes more about learning lessons for the next project versus what you are currently working on. If you are already at a point where assets have been built, art done and voice work done, you may be beyond where a consultant can help your game not fail in terms of representation. Or, if it's past the point of no return, you may be looking at a significant cost to go back a few versions and course-correct where you failed.

Conclusion

After reading this chapter and going out and talking to people, and hopefully getting a consultant for your next project and game, I hope that you'll remember that while getting a diversity consultant is great, it doesn't replace doing your own research before even calling in a consultant. Yes, we just spent all that time explaining why they are great and why you should use one.

You might wonder why you need to do all this just for a game. Because nothing exists in a vacuum, and representation matters. If you need convincing on why this is important, see responses to films and games like Marvel's *Black Panther*, Disney's *Moana*, Hangar 13's *Mafia III*, or Blizzard's *Overwatch* as a start.

If you want to set a game outside medieval England and, say, put it in ancient Egypt or on the continent of Africa, occurring during a certain time period, you'd research the clothing, history and locations you'd want to build a world in, so why not do the same for the characters the world inhabits? Failure to research and falling back on tropes or stereotypes will send a message to the player that the studio and developers didn't truly care about diversity but completed a list of checkboxes to avoid being called out by those who do care about such things. All in all, I hope this chapter helped get you on the path to research, knowing why a diversity consultant is needed, and how best to utilize their time as well as their expertise while they are on your project.

Exercise

Write and develop a female character for a medieval game setting who struggles with the limitations given by this setting, not wanting to fit into the typical role society gives to women in this era.

By the time you complete this exercise, you should have a female-identified character who is good with weapons, has educated herself by alternative means and does not use the equivalent to modern-day African American Vernacular English (AAVE) to express herself or her concerns with being taken seriously as a fighter or perhaps academic.

Now, try to develop a character of color in a low-income, modern-day city without falling into the trap of using stereotypes.

CHAPTER 3

Writing Romance and Sexuality in Games

Heidi McDonald

Contents

What Is a "Romance Game"? 23
Satisfying and Dissatisfying Romance 26
The Workflow of a Romance 29
Representation and Sexuality 30
Exercises 32
Reference 32

Video games have come a long way from a time when Mario rescued the princess and Ms. Pac Man chomped across an interlude screen to kiss Pac Man. There are whole games now made about romance and sexuality. Some of these are done well. Many of them are not. This chapter does not discuss hentai and adult/sex games, mostly because players who enjoy those games are seeking a specific experience, with little nuance, when they play games of that type. A game with romance in it, to be done well, usually requires subtle differences in approach. This chapter will offer practical tips on how to write game romance and how to best represent various sexualities.

In this Chapter

- Different ways that romance is typically presented in games
- Considerations for what makes a satisfying or unsatisfying romance
- Suggested workflows for romance writing in a video game
- Thoughts about writing romances for characters with different genders and orientations to your own

What Is a "Romance Game"?

In the Eastern market, romance games popularly take the shape of otome, or dating sims. The object of such games is singular and related to the romance:

for example, to get a date to the prom, get married, or end up with one from a group of potential romantic partners (with the fruition varying from getting a date, to having a first kiss, to having sex, to getting married). These games are often targeted to young women, though people of all ages and genders enjoy them. Japanese roleplaying games (JRPGs) often include romance as optional content, which doesn't usually go too deep into the particulars of the relationship but might add a particular flourish to the story's ending.

In the Western market, at this writing, nobody seems to know what a romance game is—not players, scholars, or game developers. What's exciting about this is that the current generation of game developers gets to decide what "romance in games" looks like for the Western market. Typically, romance in mainstream Western AAA roleplaying games (RPGs) presents as optional side content that may or may not offer gameplay benefits such as a buff, an ability, or a piece of equipment; players are often rewarded for their efforts at romancing their nonplayer character (NPC) of choice with a cutscene in which consummation of some sort occurs. In the independent space, romance presents in ways as wild and varied as the landscape of independent games themselves.

There are three ways that romance is typically integrated into the gameplay of a game:

Mechanical: The romance happens through one or more game mechanics.

Example: *Give an NPC enough of a certain object so that the character will love you and marry you.* In *Stardew Valley*, if you decide to romance Elliott, you learn about his favorite gifts and monitor his schedule and moods, then bring him plenty of Crab Cakes, Duck Feathers, Lobsters, Pomegranates, and Tom Kha Soup, and he will fall in love with you if you've given him the right gift at the right time, enough times.

Story: The romance happens through the story, or making the right choices in dialogue options. There are generally two types of game dialogue, branching and nonbranching. In nonbranching dialogue, the only choice the player really gets to make is whether to talk to the NPC, because you are essentially clicking through that conversation without making any dialogue choices that alter the conversation. In branching dialogue, the player gets to choose how to respond at different points in the conversation, and choices will alter the outcome of the conversation. Most romances that depend solely on story do so with the use of branching dialogue, and depend on the player's response choices.

Example: *You choose the "romantic dialogue" in every case when speaking to a specific NPC, and end up in a romance with that character.* This is how romance operates in most otome, visual novel, and dating sim games. Sometimes, romance dialogue is highlighted visually with a heart or some other cue to identify it as the romance choice. Other times, it's just "whatever sounds the flirtiest." In *The Sims*, the player gets to choose what to say to an NPC according to topic, so the romance options are clear.

Mechanical and Story: Some hybrid of the two. The romance happens through a combination of game mechanics and dialogue options.

Example: You choose the correct dialogue to move the romance with the character ahead, and the romance happens either based on an affinity mechanic or results in some sort of gameplay benefit like an ability, bonus, or item. In *Dragon Age II*, the player chooses dialogue options tied to an affinity system, and once the affinity level under the hood hits a certain point, the romance engages, and at various points during the progression of the romance, there are upgrades given to a specific ability you gain for being in a romance with that particular NPC.

Typical presentations of romance in games include:

- *Player character and NPC*. This is where the player character romances a nonplayer character in the game, following one of the mechanical configurations above. This can include something where there is not much interaction or choice at all (even forced romance that needs to occur to advance the story), something where there is minimal choice (like giving them cookies for sex or marriage), something where dialogue choices trigger and continue the romance, or something that combines dialogue choices with a gameplay element, such as in the *Persona* series, where your character relationships also depend on how much time you've spent fighting with, talking to, or traveling with an NPC.
- *NPCs only*. This is where NPCs have a romance that is with other NPCs, independent of the player character. This can be presented as a storyline about a relationship in the world that the player possibly has to help in some way (getting them together or saving one of two characters as part of a quest), or simply as flavor for the world or lore.
- *Player character and another player character playing together in an MMO*. While this is not covered in this chapter because writers don't have any control over this type of romance, players can meet and have relationships with other players in an MMO. This can be roleplayed in the game, as well as something that bleeds over into real life. There are many married couples in today's world who initially met playing *World of Warcraft*.

These are ways in which romance is typically presented in games, which constitute options for how developers can integrate romance into their games. What this does not tell you, however, is how to write a successful romance.

Satisfying and Dissatisfying Romance

Looking to the movies, one example of a romance done exceptionally well is Indiana Jones and Marian Ravenwood in *Raiders of the Lost Ark*. When the pair meets in the movie, it's clear that they have some shared history and things in common; that some conflict exists or has existed in the past; that Marian is an independent, smart woman who is no shrinking violet or damsel in distress; and that they have an air of competition and ongoing tête-à-tête— they are equally matched in intelligence, wit, and resourcefulness, but also in stubbornness. They appear to be in conflict when they appear to be at cross purposes or when there has been a misunderstanding, and there is obvious sexual tension between them, punctuated by moments of genuine sweetness and vulnerability between them. We never see Indy and Marian consummate their relationship, but it's safe to assume that this happens at some point. What we do see between them is more fun and more interesting than what we don't. This is a relationship between characters who are equally matched, borne of mutual goals, friendship, and respect rather than of lust.

While there are cases in video games where a player can choose just to have sex with a character and not take the relationship any further (e.g., in *Saints Row 4*, where it's literally "press X to have sex," or in *Star Wars: The Old Republic* MMO, where it's possible to have one-night stands with characters), sex is often the culmination of the game romance. While watching the consummation cutscene can feel satisfying, emotions can quickly turn to dissatisfaction for players when there's nothing left of the relationship after the two characters have consummated it. One way writers can make the relationship more satisfying for players overall is to have meaningful interaction between the characters after consummation has taken place, for the rest of the game, and with some sort of payoff at the end of the game that acknowledges the characters' relationship, what experiences they have shared, and what they mean to each other. Decide in the beginning about what you want the ultimate goal of your romance to be and what experience you want the player to have: Is it flirtation? Sex? Marriage? Will the romance change the world or the characters in some meaningful way? Will it be happy ever after, or will there be heartbreak or something bittersweet about it in the end?

Think about your romances in the larger context of the game world and how the conditions in that world may affect romance. Are there families, tribes, races that hate each other, or socioeconomic differences between characters that would make romance riskier and more difficult, like in Shakespeare's *Romeo and Juliet*? Are there cultural traditions and rules that your characters can follow or break, such as arranged marriages? Is there lore that might influence how your characters feel like they need to act, and do they long to disrupt it, such as a prophecy that says something specific? Are there rules you need to make in your game about who cannot romance whom, based on how the game world works, such as one specific character being royalty and not being able to marry a commoner? Are there things about the world that you can use to up the stakes in romantic relationships, such as the Nazis on the rise in *Raiders of the Lost Ark*?

According to a 2012 article in *Well Played Journal* (McDonald, 2012), when a group of players was surveyed as to qualities in an NPC that are most attractive, some of the top responses were humorous, fun, strong, adventurous, brave, communicative. The same group was asked to share qualities in an NPC they found most unattractive, and the top responses were religious and childish. Therefore, if you're going to use a less attractive quality, perhaps make that something rooted in conflict, something to be negotiated or overcome. In that same journal article, the survey found that male-identifying players tend to experiment wildly with their own characters' attributes (i.e., they are stronger, braver than they are in real life) but romance in a similar way to how they would in real life; female-identifying characters tend to experiment wildly with their romance options, but often play as characters who are close to who they are in real life. Therefore, it's possible that a game aimed at women should have a wide variety of romance options to experiment with, and that a game aimed at men should have more traditional romance choices. Most players in that survey overwhelmingly said that they play the romance because of the story—to see what effects it has on the rest of the world and on the characters, and because it's additional story content. Fewer players, mostly male-identifying, said that they play the romance because of gameplay benefits that result from doing so.

Things to Avoid:

- *Forced romance*, or a specific romance that must be played out in order for the game to advance. This has a way of alienating players who don't like the character they have to romance, who would prefer to have more choice in their actions, or who are of a different sexual orientation than the romance they are being forced to enact.
- *Rigid gender roles* within relationships are also becoming less appealing to audiences as they expand to include people along the gender and sexuality spectrum, and people who are polyamorous or asexual.
- *Graphic depictions of domestic abuse and rape*, especially if there is no trigger warning or if the game is not required to be ESRB-rated. Rape is often used in entertainment media as a reason to justify revenge; it acts as a plot device or becomes the reason to be sympathetic to a female character. Tread very carefully here. While there can be cases where such storylines are compelling if done respectfully and not in a sensationalistic way, you don't want to add to toxic culture or traumatize your players. This is a case where playtesting will be very important.
- *Bad dialogue*—such as cheesy pick-up lines or conversation that comes across as canned and insincere, or dialogue with bad grammar and

spelling—is one of the quickest ways to turn off your players. Add some depth. This can be difficult to do when there are character limits imposed by screen space and localization, but the creative writer will think about how to get around this.

There could conceivably be cases where the world itself sets some boundaries that would conflict with these points to avoid. For example, a world that does have strict gender roles bears the expectation to represent an authentic, historic scenario. In such a case, the way you handle this will depend on whether you yourself are in charge of the world-building or whether you have a content bible you are required to follow, provided to you by someone else. You may want to think about stories that seek to disrupt the status quo, because these stories have existed even in historical times with rigid gender roles.

Women did dress up like men to sail as pirates, to practice as medieval doctors, to fight in armies, and homosexuality and bisexuality have existed for thousands of years (Alexander the Great was married to a man!). If the world is yours to describe and change, look for historical examples of these real life "disruptive" stories to inspire you. If the world is someone else's to define, perhaps talk with that person and see what their receptiveness is to telling other stories within the world that run counter to the rules of the world, as a means of representation that will appeal to a larger audience, and as a commentary on whether bucking the status quo in the ways the characters will is ultimately wise or unwise. Joan of Arc dying in battle after leading an army can have emotional impact, and so can a character who makes emotional decisions that carry particularly high stakes in the world. If there is a content bible, talk to a lead about what stories you have in mind to find out what your parameters truly are.

Tropes. Players might actually enjoy romances based on common themes such as friends or enemies becoming lovers, soulmates and fate, a second chance at love, unrequited or forbidden love, etc. If you are going to use a popular trope, think about how you can make it fresh and interesting. Rather than avoiding tropes, do them thoughtfully and well so that it doesn't feel cookie cutter. For example, "second chance at love" could be interpreted in any number of ways. How can you make it new?

Romance vs. Friendship. The difference between writing romance and friendship is going to be the romantic/sexual component, which will be missing in platonic friendships (unless your storyline is about a friend wanting there to be more to the friendship). The relationship, even without sexuality or romance, should still involve elements of give and take, situations where there are decisions that have consequences for the relationship, and how commonality and differences are negotiated between the two characters.

The Workflow of a Romance

The workflow of a romance is going to depend on whether the romance is central to the story and is the thing that changes the world and the overarching story (like in a dating sim where your job is to find a prom date), or whether the romance is optional side content in a larger story taking place in the world.

Workflow 1: Central Romance.

- Decide the three-act character arc of the romance.
  - First act, meet and establish mutual attraction and connection (or a question about whether this exists).
  - Second act, have there be some sort of conflict or obstacle to overcome between the characters in the romance. Think about personality differences between the characters and whether these create conflicts, or whether different approaches to circumstances in the world create conflicts, or whether there are outside influences creating conflict (like the king wanting his daughter to marry someone else).
  - Third act, resolve the conflict. Will it be a happy ending or a sad one?
  - Write the outline, and then you can fill it in with story beats, decision points, and eventually dialogue.
- Note that you should pay attention to what's going on in the world, and that should affect the romance to a point, but the romance ultimately is the focus in the world, so the world won't necessarily change based on how the romance resolves.

Workflow 2: Ancillary Romance.

- Decide the three-act character arc of the romance (as above).
- Do extra writing and preparation around what's going on in the world as this romance plays out. For instance, make a timeline of how things unfold in the world at large, and fit your romance into that to determine how the larger story beats of the world impact the romance and how escalations in gameplay in the overall game will work with the romance.
- Do extra writing and preparation around how this romance is ultimately affected by the world. For example, will they fight the final battle side by side? Will they both live? Will they get separated? Will there be a compelling choice that forces one or both characters to sacrifice in order to be together, or will one or both characters have to sacrifice themselves or the relationship to something else that's more important?

Questions to ask yourself about any romance you create:

- Why are these characters inherently attracted to each other? Are they very alike, or is it a case of "opposites attract"? What will those factors mean for their relationship? How are they alike and different in terms of personality, and how does that play out in the relationship (e.g., one character is a massive extrovert, while the other is shy, and that could cause tension)?

- What would each of them live for, and what would each of them die for, besides each other? How will we see that, and how will it affect what happens to this relationship?
- Are there secrets that one is keeping from the other? Will these ever be found out or shared, and how will that play out?
- How will the characters stay engaged with each other over time? How will we know that the relationship is progressing? What small moments can you create between these characters that are loving, kind, memorable, and special (the kinds of moments that will inspire fan fiction)?
- Are there any power differentials in play between the characters that should be addressed and would affect the relationship? Racial, socioeconomic, or other differences that must be overcome? How do these affect the way the characters relate? How will they overcome these, or will they?
- What is the end point for these characters? Sex? Marriage? Heartbreak? Will those things happen before the end of the game, and if so, how will you give the relationship a satisfying ending if the zenith has already been reached?
- If you're representing abuse in any way, will it be triggering to players, and how can you handle that responsibly? (The suggestion here is to talk with a mental health clinician about how to accomplish this.)
- What is the ultimate goal of this romance? Entertainment? Overall story service? Gameplay considerations?
- If you're representing a sexuality or a gender other than your own in a relationship, are you doing it in a realistic and nontoxic way?

Representation and Sexuality

Until relatively recently, most romances in video games were heterosexual, which is to say that a male character would only romance a female character, and vice versa. This is increasingly no longer true, as social norms are changing and as developers understand the value of making their games accessible to wider audiences. Games are alternatively criticized and praised for including noncisgender and nonstraight content; it's not merely important to have representation, but to do it right. If you are straight and cisgender, what are some good ways to go about writing asexual, gay, lesbian, or bisexual content in a way that's respectful and avoids insulting tropes?

Examples of problematic sexuality tropes:

- Mental illness going hand in hand with alternative sexuality (i.e., "the crazy lesbian," "the tortured, broody bisexual")
- Trans people always being male to female

- Butchy lesbians, effete gay men
- Bisexuals who are only there so that a threesome can happen
- The female prisoner who falls for her male captor, or the woman as a trophy that awards male achievement
- The prude or the slut

Developers might hire a diversity consultant, which is a person or firm specializing in helping content creators negotiate the inherent issues in representation. They will alert you to mistakes you may not have been aware of in how you are coming across to your player base. Hiring the diversity consultant is a positive step toward pursuing representation in a positive way, and it speaks well of you to be able to say that you included one; however, equally important is following the advice of that consultant. Another way that you can address representation respectfully is to include members of the community you are writing for in your focus groups and playtests. Perhaps you donate to an LGBT charity in exchange for a group of members playtesting your queer content and giving you their thoughts. Again, when you are given advice about representation from a diversity consultant or a member of the community you're trying to reach, listen carefully and with an open mind, avoid getting defensive, and take the advice you're given, as it will only make your game better.

One thing to consider about sexuality in your game is: What will the sexuality model be among characters in your game? Will your players get to choose the player character's sexual orientation? In many games, it is assumed that player characters are straight and will only romance people of the opposite gender, and consequently, the nonplayer characters are also all straight. In some games, the nonplayer characters are of a sexual orientation that's jokingly referred to as "playersexual," meaning that any NPC can be romanced by any player. While this does allow for more kinds of romance, that is not the way things work in real life. Games like *Fable 3* and *Dragon Age: Inquisition* present NPCs with their own unique sexualities for the player to discover, which mirrors the way things are in real life. There really are just going to be some people who aren't attracted to you, and that's okay. It's realistic to reflect this.

Polyamory, or multiple simultaneous romantic and/or sexual relationships (not to be confused with polygamy, which is being married to more than one spouse simultaneously, which is illegal in most countries) is something that is becoming more common and accepted, but there are still many misconceptions about it. If you want to include it in your game, realize that there are few game examples that handle it correctly and well, and that you may be opening yourself up to a scope issue (with all of the different relationship configurations and conversations that would need to take place). There are many good resources on the internet with more information about polyamory, but here are a few important things to keep in mind, should you decide to include it:

- *There is no one correct way to represent polyamory.* Each group of people defines their own situation for themselves. One group might consist of someone with two partners who are not involved with each other, where another situation might be a three-person relationship where all three people are equally involved with each other. It is up to each person to decide on their own boundaries and expectations in polyamorous relationships.
- *Polyamory doesn't automatically involve group sex.* While in some situations there are instances where this occurs, it's not automatic. Many polyamorous (or "poly") people only sleep with one partner at a time, even though all other partners are aware of who is with whom in general and, often, specifically.
- *Polyamory is about relationships, not just sex.* There is a difference between swinging and polyamory. Swinging is an open relationship where the people involved have sexual relationships with other people besides their partner, with the full knowledge and acceptance of everyone. Polyamory involves actual relationships and is more than just sex, and everyone knows and accepts this. Navigating this correctly requires a lot of honest communication between all the people in the group.

However writers choose to craft their romances, representation is becoming more important in the gaming landscape, so this should happen with thought, care, and respect.

Exercises

1. Take a familiar romance trope, such as "second chance at love," and write out all the ways in which that phrase might be interpreted as a situation. For each one, come up with three fresh, original ways to present that interpretation of the trope.
2. Write a "meet cute" scene between two men, or two women, who will eventually become a couple. Then, find an LGBT person and get their feedback on the conversation.
3. Analyze the romances in three games you have played to determine how the romance is presented. Is it mechanical, story based, or a hybrid between the two? Note and describe the interaction between the dialogue and the gameplay, if any.

Reference

Heidi McDonald. 2012. NPC Romance as a Safe Space: BioWare and Healthier Identity Tourism, *Well Played Journal*, Vol. 1, No. 4. ETC Press, Pittsburgh, PA.

CHAPTER 4

Building A Universe

Danny Wadeson

Contents

Introduction: Why World-Build? 34
First Principles 34
    Authenticity 35
    Immersion 35
Theory Crafting and Headcanon 35
The Worst Case 36
    Nomenclature 36
    World-Building 37
    Lore 37
    Storysense 37
    Environmental Storytelling 38
My World-Building Toolkit 38
Toolbox 39
    Economy and Dominant Forces Within It 39
    Flora and Fauna 39
    Pantheons and Belief Systems/Mythology 40
    Social Hierarchy (Class/Caste) 40
    Sport and Recreation 41
    Conflict and Arms 41
    Language and Communication (Including Proper Nouns!) 42
    Factions and Geopolitics 44
Workflow 44
On Creating and Deploying Mysterious Lore 45
Some Practical Tips 46
    Go Offline 46
    How Much Is Too Much? 46
    Don't Build an Ivory Tower 46
    Pick Your Battles 47
    Document Sparingly, Effectively 47
    Beware Stealth Exposition and Other Warnings 48

Conclusion 48
Exercises 48
Special Thanks 49
Reference 49

Introduction: Why World-Build?

World-building is often framed as an iceberg, with a small visible tip. That metaphor doesn't sit right with me. It's not a question of deciding what is and what isn't visible. Better, I think, to borrow Philip Pullman's analogy of narrative being a path through a forest. A symbiotic relationship—without the narrative path, you are lost. A path with no forest surrounding it would be functional but utterly transparent, devoid of any context rich with texture or mystery.

As with most game design disciplines, world-building is alchemy: part science, part art, and plenty of random, dumb luck. That spontaneity is half the fun. Knowing how to ensure a solid foundation is the other.

In this Chapter

- In this chapter, we'll address the creative and technical sides to crafting immersive, inspiring worlds. We'll explore how to communicate world-building to your players, but also to your team.
- We'll grapple with broad commercial considerations and some nuts and bolts.

This chapter also includes some world-building exercises to get you thinking outside the box and help get you into some good habits.

First Principles

Before we examine my World Builder's Toolkit more closely, let's attend to first principles. Why world-build in the first place? After all, it's a time-consuming exercise and chances are it'll fly completely under the player's radar.

Done well, neither of those negatives need apply.

The best world-building is efficient and informs and/or provides a useful framework for developing the narrative and the entire visual design of the game, and can soak nourishingly into the player whether they realize or not. It can evoke delight, and, most importantly, it can create opportunities for them to exercise their own imaginations. It can create parallel narratives that unspool based on player participation.

It can create new worlds that players will come to love the tastes, sights, textures, and smells of. Then you have helped the player lose themselves—a lofty goal.

Authenticity

Perhaps most importantly, world-building will make your world feel authentic. *Dishonored 2*, for example, is mechanically *non pareil,* but its A–Z narrative thrust has been criticized as unoriginal. Yet it remains one of the most evocative game universes in recent memory. Why? It's because the space in which the mechanics exist along with the player-adjacent narratives and the emergent gameplay are all lent gripping context by the world-building itself.

Immersion

Enabling a flow state is one of the most sought-after achievements for a game. There exists plenty of documentation on how to engender it, centering around the balance of challenge and progression. I'd like to argue that there exists such a thing as "narrative flow": that feeling when, despite the gameplay not challenging your reflexes and showering you in digital dopamine hits, you are utterly absorbed and invested in the detailed textures of a game world.

CREATING FLOW—FURTHER READING

- "When a skill is too low and the task too hard, people become anxious. Alternatively, if the task is too easy and skill too high, people become bored. However, when skill and difficulty are roughly proportional, people enter Flow states": https://www.gamasutra.com/view/feature/166972/cognitive_flow_the_psychology_of_.php
- Toward an Understanding of Flow in Video Games: https://dl.acm.org/citation.cfm?id=1371223
- Flow and Media Enjoyment: https://onlinelibrary.wiley.com/doi/epdf/10.1111/j.1468-2885.2004.tb00318.x

We could also call it "deep immersion." A gripping narrative is always going to be the driving force in this pursuit, but it's world-building that will make it believable and keep the set-dressing interesting, too. Deep lore can imbue player character and NPC actions/interactions with a greater sense of agency and consequence, which in turn can make a player increasingly invested in their in-game decisions. Put simply, having to choose which of two characters will stay and sacrifice themselves would be arbitrary if all you knew about them was their name.

Deep immersion and narrative flow, then, do not rely on effective world-building but are greatly aided by it.

Theory Crafting and Headcanon

Stephen King famously said that "description begins in the writer's imagination, but should finish in the reader's."[1] To some extent, this is generally fantastic advice for the world-builder, but I want to highlight an unexpected corollary to the principle: parallel narratives. As much as this chapter is about helping developers to world-build for their players, it's also about giving the players the tools to do it for themselves.

While theory-crafting can often refer to players discussing strategy, it also often applies to metadiscussions of lore, characterization, and unfolding episodic narratives. This is where theory crafting and headcanon begin to overlap heavily. So long as your objective is not to lead your players deterministically to one set conclusion, fans developing headcanon is a fantastic outcome. It means your players are so invested in the game or IP/wider universe that they are establishing and holding true to a conclusion they've parsed out and developed themselves.

What really happened to Commander Shepard in the *Mass Effect 3* end game? Who is the *true* or *right* romance for the player in each of the *Persona* games? What the hell was really going on with Laguna in *Final Fantasy VIII?!* Whether there's actually a canonical/authorial answer is beside the point if you've managed to make your players care enough to argue about it.

The Worst Case

So, at the risk of preaching to the converted, what if you don't world-build thoroughly? The likelihood of your game being riddled with internal inconsistencies and stereotypes increases dramatically—to say nothing of increased difficulties in the narrative development/pipeline and fewer guidelines for the artists.

Less critically, *Warcraft*, for example, has struggled through a number of continuity issues, not least of which is "Azeroth," denoting the human kingdom, then the continent, and eventually the world itself. It often attempts (for better or worse) to fix or "retcon" these in subsequent releases.

Frankly, you risk a stale IP. Unless you're gunning for a multiplayer franchise like *Call of Duty*—for everything else, effective world-building now can become an even better investment one or more future games in the same world/universe down the line.

Nomenclature

Before we move on to the world-building toolkit, it's important we get on the same page in terms of nomenclature. Accurate/consistent terminology is essential to communicating your world-building vision to a team. Even if you're working solo, understanding the distinctions is important to unlocking new ideas and clarifying your implementation. Talking cross-purposes with your team can cost many hours of confusion.

Please note, these definitions aren't set in stone, and you can reword and apply the terms as you see fit, bending them to your own style—the important thing is making the distinctions and keeping them consistent in your thinking and written communication. The story is a subtle thing, prone to miscommunication, so make sure everyone on your team is using the right word-bricks if you don't want the world-house to fall down.

World-Building

The all-encompassing term for creating functional, fictional worlds. It absolutely does not denote "the parts that are explicitly visible in the finished product." It can also apply to a "universe," that is, spanning multiple games, and equally can be as specific as some character-specific inventions without worrying about the entire apparatus they operate in.

Lore

Often used (erroneously) interchangeably with world-building, lore is probably better defined as specific events or truths within a world. Lore is composed of traditions, knowledge, and beliefs as held by a particular group. So, of course, there is overlap, but lore skews more heavily toward narrative.

Example: The economic hardships of *Final Fantasy VII's* Midgar fall under world building, but the details of its best-loved and hated inhabitants—the legends and deeds of Sephiroth or the AVALANCHE members—count as lore.

Storysense

A term popularized by game and narrative theorist Tadgh Kelly, story sense can be loosely summarized as the story details as intuited by the player, not explicitly shown or told—it's about putting control into the player's hands. This is why world-building could be said to be more important than linear narrative to player agency.

The *Zelda* series is a prime example. None of the games have much narrative thrust beyond "save Zelda from Ganon," but the way players can unearth details of the world—the story sense, the narrative ambiance, is richly underscored through the item design, NPCs, and metanarrative discussions around the different games in the series and any links between them. Like *Zelda* and of course *Dark Souls,* storysense is often thematic rather than prescriptive.

And it's not to be confused with another term often influenced by world-building—which leads us to…

Environmental Storytelling

This much-maligned term is often satirized as "finding a skeleton in a toilet stall." Yet it can be a powerful tool when used well—as again with the *Dishonoured* franchise—to evoke the world-building and to tell non–player driven narratives. These parallel or tangential narratives can be visual, which is an economical way of communicating them to the player, and/or verbal (usually epistolary). A mix will cater to a broad range of players and allow them to better make sense of their character's motivation.

My World-Building Toolkit

How to Use

Liberally, in effect. Most of the below will be self explanatory. It's important to remember while crafting a world to be judicious. Unless you're doing it purely for fun as a hobby, or you have the luxury of a long preproduction period, the likelihood is you're going to need to target the elements of world-building that offer the best return on your time investment. We'll go into more detail on production pipeline impacts later, but as a quick example:

OFTEN SEEN

Language
Folklore
Dress
Food
Weapons/conflict
Prejudice
Hierarchy/class/caste system
Aesthetics
Politics
Inequality
Race

RARELY SEEN BUT STILL INFORMATIVE

Family roles
Superstitions and traditions
Medicine
Infrastructure
Gender roles
Justice

Attitude toward the environment
Holidays/festivals
Child-rearing
Gestures
Recreation
Economy

VERY RARELY SEEN (THEREFORE, OPPORTUNITY!)

Beauty ideals
Manners
Sport/spectacles
Education
Evolution

Toolbox

Economy and Dominant Forces Within It

Economies are at the beating heart of most worlds. In *Grand Theft Auto*, various methods of making cash outside the system are usually the central motivation of most characters, including the player. In Seth Dickinson's novel *The Traitor Baru Cormorant,* the protagonist is sent to root out insurrection as a bookkeeper. The way in which the geographical and political landscapes are revealed as she traces the lines of power back from the money is exemplary.

That's the micro view, but the macro is just as important. For example, the faces on currency can succinctly say a lot about the power structure, hint at historical figures, and more. And what of the currency's name? To drill down further: without any exposition, you could price bread in your fantasy RPG at 1000 *dînera* to communicate the realm is suffering from inflation.

The economy obviously bleeds into things like your world's class system, common professions, and political situation, some of which we'll go into more detail on below.

Flora and Fauna

Flora and fauna are a huge part of any world. Many games are almost totally defined by their plant and animal life—look at *Horizon Zero Dawn's* (admittedly nonbiological) mega-fauna, or at the scanning gameplay of the *Metroid Prime* trilogy. The question is: How deep do you want to go? Will your F&F have discrete impacts on your feature set and character progression? Or is it immersive set-dressing? Where possible, it should be both. In the former, the 'fauna' is more of a visual cipher for the narrative, whereas in the latter series it's much more detailed and central to the gameplay.

In *The Witcher,* having Geralt (and the player by extension) read up on the requisite lore when hunting a monster provides insight into its weak points. Of course, you're then required to harvest the flora for mixing into the relevant potions or oils. It's an elegant system that makes studying the F&F both totally diegetic and a source of in-game benefits.

Monster Hunter World, on the other hand, is mechanically elegant in teaching players the link between F&F but focuses on a much more visual (and cat pun–reliant) kind of world-building. Flora have certain amounts of relevancy to surrounding fauna: creatures called Mosswine exclusively found patrolling near mushroom patches, for example. There is a player's handbook, but it's less background lore than behavioral detail. Either way, creating compelling and believable F&F requires at least a cursory understanding of how real-world eco-systems work, a study that will no doubt provide plenty of inspiration at the same time.

Pantheons and Belief Systems/Mythology

Given the huge reliance on Norse and Greek mythology throughout gaming (and wider) history, one would be forgiven for continuing to cleave close to it. However, creating your own pantheon and/or belief systems, secular or otherwise, can be tremendously rewarding for players.

In *God of War,* the mythos is shorthand for getting into the action, and it's also fascinating to see how the mythical figures are represented, whereas in *Dragon Age* and *The Elder Scrolls*, there's huge satisfaction in learning about the pantheons and factions around them, and in both, they're painstakingly fleshed out.

This means that a player can either join the dots between a certain god and its gameplay associations (Mara, god of healing; therefore, an amulet bearing her name will increase healing magic, for example) or they can intuit deeper lore about the world's structure and the relationship between the deities themselves and their followers.

And if, especially as with Skyrim, you get to actually meet with a few of said pantheon? Even better. One must beware, however, of letting mythos stand in for actual narrative or established mythic character tropes replacing three-dimensional characters.

Social Hierarchy (Class/Caste)

Social structures and class systems are hugely important but often underexplored facets of world-building and character motivation. The pitfall of explaining social hierarchy is usually that you end up with either the stilted, repetitive dialogue of classic JRPGS ("Oh, I heard that Jen, the Mayor, is suddenly raising taxes because of an ancient curse on her family!") or that it becomes a moral binary. These usually revolve around whoever is blatantly and/or ruthlessly oppressed/oppressive, along with interminable *cui bono* debates. It's important to remember that the fabric of society is just that—it effortlessly binds things together, but is likely to have a few wrinkles. And tears and stitches, but rarely huge schisms that are remarked upon casually in passing.

When designing the social fabric for your game, then, it's another case of synecdoche. Let a few pertinent observations stand in for the wider sentiments. And remember to present multiple perspectives.

On that note, I was recently impressed with a Singaporean indie game entitled *Masquerada: Songs and Shadows*. It was one of the freshest game settings I've experienced in a long time, At a glance, the game feels like a cross between the geopolitics and the Imperialist "Masquerade" of *The Traitor Baru Cormorant*, the aesthetics and complex social hierarchy of Val Royeaux from *Dragon Age: Inquisition*, and the pseudo-Italian nomenclature of *The Lies of Locke Lamora*. And it *works*.

Sport and Recreation

Often and sadly overlooked in games, sport and popular forms of recreation, along with their assorted physical and cultural accoutrements, are hugely telling and evocative. For my money, *Final Fantasy X* is the best example of a protagonist drawn directly from a fictional sport. The predictably (given Supermassive's pedigree) rich and inventive *Pyre,* however, goes a step further by baking the mystic sport of "The Ritual" into every facet of the gameplay, narrative, and lore.

Conflict and Arms

Although one of the most ubiquitous aspects of world-building, it's still important to consider how conflict and the arms involved can be more than a power-fantasy visual hook.

To some extent, war never changes. The exact motivations and morality of a game's white knights usually wiggle only a little. All told, it's usually a two-dimensional motivational backdrop and narrative thrust than a cauldron of interesting world-building—*but it doesn't have to be.*

The *Destiny* series suffers from what seems to be an acute case of "pantsing," (flying by the seat thereof), and the devs themselves have disappointingly admitted that they never actually knew what the big bad "Darkness" was. However, when it comes to the story sense provided by the *excellent* flavor text—penned in part by the aforementioned Seth Dickinson—and visual design of the weapons, it stands as best in class.

Take the exotic weapons "MIDA Multi-Tool" and "Crimson" and the exotic armor "Shinobu's Vow." The synergy between their implementation, actual lore and visual design, and gameplay function is remarkable:

Each exotic in *Destiny* has a perk that is totally unique to the weapon, one usually referenced by the short line of flavor text positioned just above the weapon's statistics and a close-up of the weapon itself—and then by holding down another button, one can read a slightly more detailed account of the item's lore.

This is an inspired marriage of UI and gameplay design. To change the effects of the weapon is also to bask in the awesome design and to take in the flavor text virtually by accident—all on the same screen. This is also where the *Destiny* writers shine—the name of the weapon reliably evokes the unique perk, the lore text situates it in the fictional context, and they're always either funny or imaginative.

This helps create a mental connection to the lore each time you use the weapon, cementing immersion.

A Quick Analysis of the Flavor Text for Each

MIDA Multi-Tool (scout rifle)—Select application: Ballistic engagement. Entrenching tool. Avionics trawl. Troll smasher. Stellar sextant. List continues.

Shinobu's Vow (Hunter class gauntlets)—"No supplies. Armor in tatters. But the refugees had asked for help. And she had given her word." —Tale of the Six Coyotes.

Crimson (hand cannon)—"According to official Vanguard policy, this weapon does not exist."

In MIDA's case, it's a light-hearted whiz through *Destiny*'s flavor of language; Shinobu introduces an in-game legend or myth, and Crimson raises a few interesting questions/mysteries around the world's/Guardian's rules and conventions.

For all the game's many failings, the way it weaves together lore, UI, gameplay, and exotic weaponry is exemplary.

Language and Communication (Including Proper Nouns!)

Creating a new language isn't just reserved for the Tolkiens among us, nor would anything of the depths he went to for Middle-Earth be worth it for a game. However, as plenty of recent titles have memorably demonstrated, there's absolutely a place for both unique visual language and some semblance of a true verbal one.

Some games, such as the forthcoming *Heaven's Vault,* build deciphering language into the gameplay itself, and in doing so flip the usual method on its head, creating a loop that makes gameplay immerse you in the language, and around again. Others, such as *Journey* and its aquatic cousin *Abzu,* transmuted their civilizations into runes, line drawings, and glyphs. They're not necessarily meant to be deciphered, but both are nevertheless committed to total nonverbal storytelling, and so create the illusion of fallen civilizations in the same visual style as the gameplay.

Creating jargon and slang, and even going as far as creating a pidgin for your text- or dialogue-heavy game can be a powerful world-building opportunity. Pidgin (a.k.a. lingua franca) is different from slang or argot in that it evolves from a mix of dialects and slang into something supposed to be "universal" to allow the most people to be as understood as possible.

And this is where Proper Nouns come in. Proper Nouns, that is, Your Cool Name for the Thing. Done well, they can be a litany of world-building, a mantra for immersion. I'm talking *Transistor's* Camarata, *Command & Conquer's* Tiberium, *The Witcher's* Wild Hunt. However, it's easy to get carried away—making every noun in your world proper in the hope of setting it apart can just as easily part your player from your game. Imagine being asked by an NPC to take the Mag-Wave to the Nexus to pick up some ProTEEN from the Hexchange before you set off on your Pilgrim-AGE in hope of finding not just the source of the Murkiness, but also yourself. Lots of made-up terms do not a brave new world make.

Giving the appropriate number of things appropriate names is crucial. It shows care and gives depth to your universe, and can communicate subtle information about the society. If it ain't broke, though, don't fix it. *Mass Effect* can't resist the stereotypically enigmatic Element Zero but sensibly refrains from making the Council something like the PanCitadellion. *BlazBlue* has perhaps some of the most egregious Proper Nouning in any franchise: from the GuardLibra system to the Huge Pentacle Sightings, to NOS to the Murakumo Unit and beyond, it veers from an interesting backstory to impenetrable jargon quicker than you can say Astral Heat.

When actually deciding on the name to give something, it can be useful to give yourself a checklist, depending on the genre of game you're working within, the functionality of the dialogue/writing, and your desired style.

For example, do you want to give the impression of a stifling bureaucracy, full of almost nonsensical acronyms? When naming sci-fi corporations or Wipeout-esque manufacturers, consider either making them simply sound good and satisfying to say (Feisar, Qirex, Auricom) or reinforcing said organization's philosophy or niche: Umbrella Corporation (*Resident Evil*), the family-owned Mishima Zaibatsu (*Tekken*), Shinra Electric Power Company (*Final Fantasy VII*), Versalife (*Deus Ex*).

Factions and Geopolitics

Humans are social animals, and we love making groups. However, groups need to be easily identifiable and distinguished from one another if they want to attract a membership. They need to stand for something. And this is something that games ignore at their peril. Most RPGs and shooters and a host of other genres rely on faction identities to convey the stakes and positions of a conflict, and often task players with joining one to affect the outcome of it or the wider world.

The key to creating great faction identities and the geopolitics that shape and become shaped by them is granularity. Put simply, "The Anarchists" of our fictional game *Faction Wars,* who attempt to sign the player over their arch-rivals "The Peacekeepers" aren't going to have much luck while everyone involved has a spiky mohawk and a manifesto that reads "Our plan is to have no plan!"

Well, I guess it depends on how lame the Peacekeepers sound. Anyway, a good faction has an interesting motivation and, like so much of effective narrative, promotes player and faction agency. They want, and maybe even *can* enact change in the game world's geopolitics, micro or macro. They will have in-fighting and colorful characters who signed up for a variety of reasons, and their *raison d'être* will very much reveal the issues of the world around them.

Workflow

How one goes about applying this can change dramatically from project to project. Knowing what to build, and when, takes experience, but starting with first principles has never led me astray yet. It is, within reason, always better for your team to agree on the fundamentals as early as possible—the economy, factions and geopolitics, and perhaps the social hierarchy.

Usually, game design will more heavily affect the secondary world-building concerns as you flesh out characters, what they need and can do, etc.—conflict, nomenclature, and flora/fauna.

It's somewhat inevitable that details will be constantly tweaked as production goes on, but that's just it—if you're tweaking what something is called, fine, but if you need to rethink the entire social structure, you might risk invalidating hours of hard-fought design decisions and causing knock-on effects because some things no longer make sense. That way loose ends and madness lie.

On Creating and Deploying Mysterious Lore

There is always going to be overlap between world-building and narrative design. Both sides of the coin would be failing if there wasn't. Perhaps one of the greyest cross-hatched areas, and also one of the most important and powerful, is creating mysteries. And for the world-building narrative designer, inventing and deploying them properly must go hand in hand.

The imagination of a player is like nature: it abhors a vacuum, and will desperately attempt to fill it. I need only utter the name *Dark Souls* as proof of this concept. The series leaves breadcrumbs of lore hints for the player to put together a rough patchwork of conclusions about the heroes, villains, and even whole civilizations that underpin the various games.

Lest we lionize *DS* too much, you might also say the *lore* is fantastic, but the implementation is lacking. Why is the player/character able to "read" lore descriptions for each of the items they pick up? What happens to your understanding of the game's universe if you accidentally miss a key lore item? Does anyone know if any of it actually makes sense!?

Omnipotent lore whispering aside, once you create your mysteries, you must decide whether they have an answer, and if yes, how much will be communicated to a player, and why. And if not, then why not?

One categorization depends on whether you want to engender theory crafting (i.e., meta/crowdsourced lore sleuthing) or individual "a-ha" moments, something that can deepen an individual's understanding of the game world around them. The "itchy, scratchy" revelation in *Resident Evil 4* is memorable, epistolary lore that anyone can figure out from paying attention to the notes lying around, whereas *Silent Hill 2* has engendered many fans comparing notes to figure out the real meaning behind the various endings.

As world-building übermensch Tom Toner (of *The Amaranthine Spectrum*) says: "If you're going to hint at a mystery, you should have the answer squirreled away somewhere, or at least ticking over in your mind" (personal communication). The reason is simple: a lack of closure can be incredibly frustrating.

An unconsummated cliffhanger is not a mystery, it is a terrible tease. However, where the events are concrete but the meaning is fluid, then we have a psychological mystery, which is more of a fine balance. Take the ending to *The Last of Us*. It is successful because the player is allowed closure by enacting a dramatic rescue. Yet, as Joel drives Ellie away, it's left ambiguous whether she believes him or realizes the full truth. Where the excellent narrative ends, the subtle world-building begins or exists, allowing players the context to make their own minds up and to understand the stakes of either conclusion.

"World-building generates world-building," Toner continues, "but it's also essential for the simple reason that you're writing within a dramatic framework. Everything should have a resonance, but it's up to the writer to decide the correct place to reveal those answers. Sometimes that means resisting the temptation to air things out early" (personal communication).

Let's come back to efficiently creating a sense of mystery. Amnesia is the easy way out, but the galling thing is that it often still works. On the other end of the extreme is something like *What Remains of Edith Finch*, which is incredibly sensitive with how it shows the player plenty of mysteries and legends surrounding the ill-fated family, then slowly doles out most of the answers.

Environmental storytelling often abuses this idea—often the most satisfying examples make you work to figure out the answer, but, crucially, there is one.

Some Practical Tips

Go Offline

It's not guaranteed to work for everyone, but starting freeform on a nice blank space can work wonders. It can free up creative associations, and there seems to be a natural limit to sketching in the broad strokes of a concept/world/ technology/society before it feels like critical mass and the time is right to get started.

That leaves room for exploring all the smaller details with spontaneity, hopefully in line with the development of gameplay and other systems. A combination of notebook, laptop, and probably some combination of apps (there are so many—whatever works for you is valid) is essential in really exploring an idea because your thoughts act differently in each medium.

How Much Is Too Much?

Our minds have to have something—even if it's tiny—to latch onto that's familiar. Otherwise, it's all too abstract to describe and too foreign to generate a sensation (and impossible to come up with without drugs).

Also, there comes a time when you must trust your instincts. If you're having to work too hard to fit something in—chances are it doesn't belong.

Don't Build an Ivory Tower

Not unlike in literature, good world-building means nothing without proper implementation. And proper implementation usually means communicating your world-building effectively to a team. A busy team. One that probably isn't down for reading a 20-page document just to find out what kind of clothes a character should be wearing. Just like, coincidentally, your players not wanting to "play" through an hour-long treatise on the respective political machinations of the Strong Empire, the Sneaky Cabal, and the Downtrodden Collective.

Pick Your Battles

Not only must you be ruthless with yourself about the parts of your world-building that really influence the game itself, but you must also be doubly ruthless with what you present to your team. And let's be real—the reality for many of us writers/narrative designers is that ours is not the final say.

So it's fine for your cyberpunk game that you become an expert in neural nets, blockchain, and biochemistry. However, if you're going to waste weeks arguing with your team over the exact economic vicissitudes of an analog vs digital currency? Then your world-building may be in danger of becoming game-razing. One needs to remember that world-building *has* to feel believable but does *not* have to necessarily detail the future or a fantastical political system with perfect accuracy.

Moreover, something you *want* might not be possible, or may conflict with what the game design *needs*. Navigating this fine line is difficult, and it's a skill that applies to many areas of writing for a team. World-building is, arguably, even lower down the ladder of imperatives than dialogue or key character arc beats.

Document Sparingly, Effectively

It's also crucial to remain flexible and get your documentation in order. Technical roadblocks or new gameplay features—or worse, misunderstandings between team members—may mean you can no longer include a meticulously researched and fleshed out character or location. And frankly, it can be hard to kill your darlings, and it could mean reimagining/ factoring a lot of other elements.

You need a system. A Google doc is collaborative, which is good, but to be remotely readable, you're going to need to pay close attention to the outline sidebar, highlight the important parts carefully, think about color-coding relevant sections to corresponding departments/team members, etc.

If all this sounds more like advice on producing or project management, well, that's because it is.

World-building is, at the last fact, a complex set of rules. And the more rules you have, the greater the complexity involved in changing one of them— it's pure chaos theory/butterfly effect. The more complex your model is (and games are *such* complex models), the more likely a small change is apt to have knock on effects to the rationale of everything else. This is why sketching things out roughly as a whole first, and committing as much as you can to the key tenets of your world is important, before you flesh out the connective tissue. When you create a world, be careful, lest it truly take on a life of its own.

Beware Stealth Exposition and Other Warnings

- Volume does not equal depth. Many open-world RPGs suffer majorly from exposition and epistolary overload, not least *The Witcher 3, Skyrim, Divinity Original Sin*, and, well, most any other you can think of. Neither does obfuscation, that is, making points of lore pointlessly vague. Which brings us to:
- *Trust your players*. Kojima is one of the modern masters of creating speculative near-future fiction, but it's hard to say he's a soft touch with it. The *Metal Gear* series veers from massive exposition to maddeningly vague and opaque references. It's possible to err on the side of caution and simply either trust your players to figure stuff out or to make it so that you don't have to worry if they do or not.

Conclusion

Hopefully, by now, you've got some food for thought and a greater awareness of the potential benefits and pitfalls of professional world-building. Of course, the reality of game development is hectic, whether you're a freelancer brought in to make the shape of things or a studio founder hashing it all out for months by yourself. It may not be possible to methodically go through every step. Luckily, the human mind is adept at filling in the gaps, so it's always important to remember that the whole edifice probably won't come crashing down if you forget a brick, character trait, or economic power structure.

Still, you would always do well to remember the tenets we've discussed. Once you know the rules, you begin to learn when and how to break them. Player expectations can be subverted to great effect, and subtle twists on a trope can open up new creative possibilities.

Ultimately, just remember—your job is to create a world that others want to escape to, without getting lost in it yourself.

Exercises

- (Ongoing) Keep a list in Evernote, Trello, or similar of your favorite proper nouns: concepts, institutions, place and character names.
- Reverse-engineer one of your favorite examples of world-building, be it from a game, novel, film, or otherwise. Deconstruct how the visible and dominant systems work and how they help move the action and characters forward.
- Pick one of the following:
  - Alternative reality city name (e.g., New Vegas, Cyber-Paris, Nega-London)
  - Antihero protagonist or lovable antagonist in a steampunk world

- Biotech sci-fi corporation name
- Fantasy kingdom/dynasty name

Now write 30 variations of a name for it. It will be hard, but don't stop short. Then, whittle that list down to your best 10. For each of those, write a line or two of key lore details for it, whether it's a motto or mission statement. Also, try to detail the rationale behind why the name works for each of your top 10.

- Using the toolkit, invent (bullet points are fine) your most nightmarish dystopian and your most perfect utopian country or city-state.
- Describe the most boring world you can imagine playing a game in, in no more than 300 words.
- Pick an existing real or fictional city and write an epistolary description of it, first as though you were one of the elite, living in luxury, then from the perspective of the lowliest worker/laborer or criminal.

Special Thanks

Tom Toner, Keith Lee, Seth Dickinson, Ursula Le Guin.

Reference

1. King, S. 2012. On Writing: A Memoir of the Craft, Hodder Paperbacks.

CHAPTER 5

Writing for Nondigital Games (Board Games)

Alexander Bevier, MFA, MA

Contents

Games Covered in This Chapter 53
How to Embed Narrative Content 54
    Understanding Uncertainty. 55
    Understanding Turn Orders. 55
    Understanding How These Two Will Shape Your Stories 55
Anatomy of a Playing Card. 56
    Card Art. 56
    Flavor Text 56
    Mechanical Function 57
    Storytelling as a Mechanic 57
The Connection of Board Games and Their Narrative Content 57
Successful Case Studies! 58
    Betrayal at House on the Hill 59
    Gloom 60
    Android: Netrunner 60
The Future 62
Conclusion 62

With the rising impact of video games on our culture, it might seem silly to take a step back and provide tools to help design for their physical brethren. While it's true that jobs are increasing vastly for narrative design in video games, board games are themselves finding a comfortable life in homes and bars around us.

In this Chapter

- How narrative content works in nondigital games
- How to approach them as a narrative designer
- How dynamics and mechanics play together to deliver stories

According to a 2015 article on FiveThirtyEight, board games accounted for nearly two hundred million dollars on Kickstarter. This means that people are excited to buy new board games, but people are also able to find the money to create new nondigital games. Additionally, webseries like Geek and Sundry's Tabletop have helped showcase how accessible and social nondigital games can be. These factors have helped foster what board game website Shut Up and Sit Down (https://www.shutupandsitdown.com/) have called a new Golden Age of board games.

For freelance narrative designers, it's important to note that most board games are created by small teams, often a single designer who comes up with the core mechanics and larger systems. They hand it off to a developer, who spends their time playtesting, coming up with cards, and iterating on the design further to make sure it's ready to print. Oftentimes, the designer and developer are the same person. Coming from indie game design, that should not be too surprising. If you find yourself either on a nondigital game team or looking to design one of your own, then it's important to understand the role of narrative design in nondigital games!

As a narrative designer, it's important to understand how your desired narrative interacts with the core systems. With board games, the system and mechanics are where the game's design will thrive. While video games are able to develop methods of other, traditional media to deliver a fulfilling experience, board games must require a tight narrative design in order to tell a meaningful story.

The heart of nondigital games, however, comes from the relationship between the game and player. While video games can function without a player—Mario can easily and quickly be killed by that first goomba, creating an emergent (if simple) narrative—nondigital games are statues. They are static artifacts that have no meaning without players using them, mediated by a designed ruleset. In other words, unless you know how to play the game, the pieces are meaningless, other than for aesthetic beauty.

But deeper at the heart, the heart's heart, is the experience of play between players. While there are single-player nondigital games, which manage to draw evocative play experiences by interacting directly with the rules and components, board games are at their best when they're shared around a table with others. Therefore, no matter how intricate and demanding the rules are, it's not a bad thing to tweak or break the rules for the sake of play. If everyone at the table has a good time, then you'll always have people to play with.

But as game designers, we understand that these objects deserve meaning through play. The core of our intentions is to craft something deep that players can understand through the way we blend theme and narrative into our rules and systems. If you're coming in as a video game designer, you'll leave this chapter with a better appreciation of how board games are able to create an experience equal to anything on a digital screen. Any nondigital game designer will walk away with a new set of lenses to analyze how board games tell their stories, but also with new tools to help develop their own games.

In this chapter, we'll detail some of the best practices for crafting a story in nondigital games. We'll look at some of the techniques used in some of the best recent games, as well as outlining some recent, exciting approaches in the field. This chapter will also highlight the overall ways board games function so that you'll understand the best ways to create evocative narratives in your board games.

Games Covered in This Chapter

Before we dive too deeply into the subject, I want to specify what I mean by nondigital games, because it's as broad a field as video games. Pedantically, a nondigital game would mean any game without a digital component, but that would also include experiences like live-action roleplays and sports. While it would be a fantastic opportunity to discuss how to create a gripping narrative through a game like American football, I'll have to wait until *Even More Advanced Narrative Toolbox* for that. Maybe one that comes with an electric screwdriver.

This is also intentionally leaving pen-and-paper roleplaying games out of this conversation. RPGs are very much their own work of design and have their own multitude of narrative topics to divulge. This is way too large a topic to include in this modest chapter.

For this chapter, nondigital games will refer to board and card games. Broadly, this is looking at experiences like *chess* and *Settlers of Catan*, while also examining the place of narrative in experiences *like Magic: The Gathering*.

Board games have existed far longer than any video game. *Backgammon*, one of the earliest known board games, predates the pyramids of Giza. However, it's not hard to realize that their existence was not established with storytelling in mind. However, much of the play had a thematic and spiritual component. *Senet*, a game from ancient Egypt, is considered a game to summon the will of the gods, for a cosmic force to influence their dice rolls.

Most modern board games are divided into two different styles: Eurogames and Ameritrash. Don't get the latter's name wrong, however. "Ameritrash" has become a term of endearment.

Most players will already be familiar with both types of game, even if they haven't understood the designed underpinnings. The thing about *Settlers of Catan vs. Monopoly* is that *Monopoly* relies on luck, with dice rolls dictating where players can go and, as such, when they are able to purchase and sell property. It's full of flavorful paper money and distinctive character tokens. These tokens become parts of a player's identity for the game, with many electing to play only as the dog, the racecar, the thimble. *Monopoly* ends when only one player remains on the table, having bought out every player from their property.

Settlers of Catan, however, still uses dice, but to deliver a wide supply of resources. The pleasure of play comes from how players exchange resources. The dice are a tool to facilitate the play, rather than the dice directly guiding the play.

These two distinctions are important for understanding how narrative traditionally fits into the play of board games. Story is viewed as thematic flair to a game, while games meant for serious considerations are regarded as story light.

Card games, or collectible card games (CCGs), like *Magic: The Gathering*, tend to be more overt and aware of their narrative, but the narrative still takes an aside for the play. *Magic: The Gathering*, for example, features a new world with every set in order for new spaces and characters for the narrative to unfold, but the narrative itself is focused on the two players summoning monsters to claim victory.

However, it should go without saying that many of these topics bleed into one another. As with any great works of design, aspects of one field will inform and develop toward another, just as there are digital aspects to games like *X-com: The Board Game*. Your narrative design will almost inevitably use techniques you learned while working on video games, and vice versa.

Despite this, many of the highly regarded Eurogames are heavily focused on resource management, meaning that they end up using a theme of colonization. Without claiming any narrative direction, players will have to take the role of having to apprehend unruly slaves, as well as taking ownership of another country's land. This goes to show that all games bear narrative and theme, and therefore must understand the context of the designed play experience. We'll go into this deeper in a future section, but this deserves to be mentioned at every opportunity.

How to Embed Narrative Content

After reading this section, you'll:

- Understand how flavor text interacts with theme, mechanics, and artwork
- Understand how uncertainty affects narrative flow
- Understand turn phases and solutions for creating exciting stories

This chapter will offer several lengthy case studies of what I consider momentous works of board game design narrative. As with all artistic works, it's important to understand the medium by experiencing them at their best. The following games are among the highlights of narrative design, and I hope my explanations of them help inform your thoughts on the nondigital medium. While these components don't speak to all of board game design, they do function as some of the base aspects for understanding a game's design. At the end of this chapter, ask yourself where the uncertainty lay in a game you've played. Additionally, consider how the turn order and phases of play affected the way you made decisions and experienced the game. With these two analytical tools, you'll be all set to begin understanding nondigital game narratives.

Understanding Uncertainty

While most video games have scripted events, there are levels that players can encounter linearly, and there are cause-and-effect scripts for NPCs to react to the player's interactions. The narrative in these situations is what's considered emergent play, and the wonder of this play comes from uncertainty.

Uncertainty allows for the unexpected and surprising moments in the game, and board games are rife with them. All games rely on uncertainty, and games are able to take advantage of them in two key forms: perfect and imperfect information: in short, imperfect information in games exists when something unseen can occur. This can be a player hiding a hand of cards, a deck of randomly ordered consequences, or even a random value determined from a die.

Understanding Turn Orders

The constraints of most games exist in turn orders, while a videogame can exhibit itself in the entirety of the player's actions. Board games, however, are forced to stop at determined intervals.

Board games exist in turn orders and phases. Games are designed with a determined order of actions to help organize what players are expected to do.

As a design constraint, it's important to realize that turn orders are completely under the control of the game's creator. Therefore, you can plan for narrative moments within these turn orders. This is how you control the pacing of the overall experience, and pacing is the key to a strong narrative.

Understanding How These Two Will Shape Your Stories

Both turn orders and uncertainty represent two key facets of game design: control and randomness. Designers will be able to facilitate the steps to create the play experience, but uncertainty keeps the game exciting or provides resistance to the player's freedom. Both aspects are at the heart of why we play games. We wouldn't find much enjoyment if we knew the exact way a story would end, with no potential for being wrong. Additionally, it wouldn't be much of a game without some controlled system, establishing clear ways to interact in the space of play.

There are many other aspects of board game design that are worth knowing, but these two will be at the focus of our game analysis. These are the biggest tools to help us move forward toward understanding how narrative functions in nondigital game design.

Anatomy of a Playing Card

This example looks at the elements found on most cards. These can be for either card games or board games. Regardless, most of the text will be featured on these cards. This means that most of the game's narrative will be delivered through these cards.

Card Art

It doesn't come as a surprise that the card's artwork is among the most eye-catching aspects of a card. The action exists in verbs, but the card's appeal comes from the action depicted in the illustration. Card art often becomes the key aspect of how players remember what the card does.

Flavor Text

Flavor text is designed to have no systemic function but intends to make the card's purpose more explicit. While being noted as flavor, this is the space on a card where worldbuilding text can stand front and center. Flavor text can help mythologize the content on the card or deliver a few clever lines to lighten the mood.

Mechanical Function

The mechanical function is the space where the card states what it does systemically in the game. Every piece of the card, be it the art, title, or flavor text, should speak to the function listed on the card.

Storytelling as a Mechanic

This chapter will detail the breadth of options and place for narrative and character in nondigital games. As with all design, the elements are nearly too broad to name them all. Still, these highlighted aspects will serve as a jumping-off point to help you identify methods to tell a meaningful storytelling experience.

The Connection of Board Games and Their Narrative Content

As I alluded to earlier, board games and narrative have always gone together, but it was often invisible. The importance of theme in board games cannot be overstated. Even *chess*, which is likely considered the most important board game in history, uses the theme of combat to draw meaning between the two teams of 16 pieces.

However, this theming is considered light, and chess isn't appreciated as a deep simulation or warfare narrative. While most narrative experiences of video games are ignored or dismissed, they have tools and devices to demand the attention of players. Noninteractive cutscenes and textboxes allow the narrative designer to guide the experience on behalf of a story. Board game designers don't have this option.

To think more deeply about this concept: imagine *chess* without a familiar symbol. Imagine the horses and queens and kings referred to as Piece A, Piece B, and Piece C. Already, the game is harder to wrap your head around. *Chess* is a complex game, where players must understand the move patterns of six different characters, split among 16 tokens on the table. To make matters harder, players must understand tactical openings, closers, and tactics throughout the experience to be considered skilled at *chess*.

To help with these dynamics of play, we can understand that the King is the most vital piece because the King is at the forefront of the army's command. His Queen is able to reach out to any part of the battle and use her guile to achieve victory. The Knight, the horsebound cavalry, can charge through any piece to get itself into the formation. All of this helps the player understand the fundamentals of *chess*.

Additionally, most board games are overtly designed with the theme as a window dressing. Consider *Settlers of Catan*. The game allows for resource management and political exchanges of goods, but the initial goods are determined by a dice roll. This allows for light elements of luck to guide the guile of players and allows for a recommended and approachable example of what the medium has to offer.

However, light theming often allows for a normalization of stereotypes, which might not be intended by design. Catan's setting has players colonizing an island, creating underlying themes of raiding a previously settled land. The only nonplayer icon, the thief, being relegated to a desert suggests that the players are exchanging goods previously owned by a mysteriously absent people. The conflict here is that these suggestions are subtext. The theme of the game was created to facilitate an exciting and political experience. This play reinforces and normalizes a colonial history of the world. Other games are more overt with this subtext, but seldom attempt to address it outside of the means justifying the ends. *Puerto Rico*, another board game with a theme to support resource management, has the players actively using turn actions to deal with natives, caricatured with lip rings and narrow faces.

Outside of the themes, it's important to understand how the systems of the game affect the experience. The first aspect to understand is randomness. These are the uncontrollable elements in a game. These can be the hidden top card on a deck, the uncertain number on the face of a die, or any other form of uncertainty not controlled by any player.

While some players prefer games without any form of luck or randomness, it's often an equalizer. It also adds excitement to a game. Randomness can thwart or support skill, allowing for unpredictable events to occur in a game. Unpredictability is a source of drama and can be used in great design.

Alongside luck, there are politics. Politics in game design are mechanics that feed the drama between the players. This often comes from games where players must negotiate with others, be it because they're trying to exchange resources or two players trying to achieve different goals. Politics are often exciting because they allow power dynamics between players to rise and fall as the play unfolds. This is such a strong element that these feelings often last after the game is played. There are some people who refuse to talk after playing highly political games like *Diplomacy*.

Politics allows for inner conflict to rise and allows personal feelings to swing play. This isn't a bad thing and is inherently dramatic, leading to thrilling narratives. With intelligent design, political elements allow for play experiences that will remain for years to come.

Successful Case Studies!

The following section will use three games as case studies in excellence in narrative design. We will examine what they do from a play perspective while highlighting how the narrative affects the experience.

While games like *Monopoly*, *chess*, and *Settlers of Catan* have been mentioned, it's important to look at games with narrative design at their core. The following three games are what I'd consider masterworks of game design and have storytelling at their core.

Betrayal at House on the Hill

Betrayal at House on the Hill is a game where players spend half of the game exploring a haunted house. Designed by Bruce Glassco, with additional work by experts Rob Daviau and Mike Selinker, players spend their turns venturing into new rooms, drawing cards that detail their spooky encounters.

Betrayal is designed entirely for its narrative. The player's health can be divided between four different stat perimeters, allowing for players to fidget their way to survival. To help deliver the horror feel, players won't know how to finish the game until halfway through. The first part of the game is about exploring the new rooms and resolving cards, each one delivering a narrative feel before mechanical instruction. Once enough "omen cards" are drawn and the players fail to pass an omen check, a dice roll that becomes harder to pass with every omen card drawn, the second phase begins.

The second phase is determined by the last omen card drawn and which room the player was in. One player is dictated to take the "traitor's tome" rulebook and leave the room, while the others read through a prescribed page in the "survivor's guide." In each book, there are 50 unique ending scenarios, detailing the horrific fates of those in the mansion. Some scenarios include characters being buried alive by the traitor, and others have the traitor secretly being an alien and the mansion a secret spaceship. The surviving players and the traitor player must follow the victory condition outlined in this book in order to win, usually by rolling dice in a specific room with a specific item.

At least half of *Betrayal at House on the Hill's* text is in service to the narrative. The long card shape, as well as the flavor text presented before the mechanics, encourages players to dive into the theme and read every detail out loud. This is a game to be played vocally, which helps counterbalance the second half when the traitor player skulks to another room to learn how to win. It creates an experience that often surpasses the overall systems design of the game. While the game delivers 50 different end states, it offers that variety in place of systemic depth.

The largest design flaw in this game, however, is that the latter half can be considered flat. The semirandom ending means that perfect conditions for an exciting playstate may not occur. As such, the latter half can occasionally end as a dice-roll contest, which isn't particularly exciting.

Gloom

Gloom is a simple board game in a small box. Designed by Keith Baker, the cards are all clear plastic, allowing for players to place new cards on top of others, with transparencies allowing players to see the previously covered information.

Taking advantage of Addams Family–style aesthetics, the game uses the expected game conventions in support of its narrative. Instead of players with the most points winning, player's families are supposed to die horrific deaths, meaning that the winner is the one with the lowest point value.

This game uses its cards to determine the flow of the narrative, which is led by the players. *Gloom*, like several others, is considered a "storytelling game" because storytelling is the core mechanic. Players engage in telling the story in order to play the game.

Unlike *Betrayal at House on the Hill*, where the narrative is written on cards, the titles of the cards guide the narrative experience, leading players to fill in the gaps. The memorable experiences come from players delivering touching and macabre monologues about the tragic fates of their family. It allows for grief to become playful as sadness begets goofiness.

Now, many other storytelling games exist, particularly *Once Upon a Time*. The design challenge for this game, however, is how to engage players who don't enjoy telling a story. A noncreative player can drive the play experience down for others. *Gloom* manages to avoid this by giving each card a point value. Even if the player isn't focused on storytelling, they can find value in the structural components of the game.

Android: Netrunner

Android Netrunner (A:NR) is the redesign of a card game originally released in the 90s by *Magic: The Gathering* designer Richard Garfield. It is an asymmetrical card game, meaning that the two players have different victory conditions. Published by Fantasy Flight Games and design-led by Lukas Litzinger, one player runs a corporation in a cyberpunk dystopia. Their goal is to push and fulfill their dark agendas at the expense of the world. The other player is a runner, a hacker trying to push through servers and archives, trying to unearth the agendas before the corporations are able to finish achieving their ends.

A:NR was released with four corporations and three runner factions, each with its own identity. NBN represented the news and entertainment media, running propaganda and global surveillance. Hass Bioroid promised better living through robotic efficiency. On the runner side, there were Shapers, experienced criminals looking to make money. Additionally, there were the Anarchs, firebrands fighting for their rights against the dominant class. All these classes had individual character cards and corporate branches, allowing players to have an even more personal touch as they interacted in the world.

Additionally, the game was released as a living card game, meaning that cards were released in sets with predetermined cards. Unlike the original *Netrunner*, which used random booster packs, A:NR packs meant that players knew what they were getting. Additionally, packs were released in cycles, with six packs per cycle. This release system allowed for deeper worldbuilding than previously seen in *Magic: The Gathering*. The control allowed for each card in the pack to feature controlled aspects. In the fourth cycle, the SanSan Cycle, each pack detailed a unique area in the San Diego/San Francisco supercity.

The game also took full advantage of its cyberpunk aesthetics, which allowed it to represent gender and race in posthumanist ways. In a future where characters in the universe would be able to give themselves robot arms, it stands to reason that anyone would be able to represent themselves as they wish. As such, the characters in lore represent this diversity.

Additionally, while runners were using viruses and breakers to tear through corporate servers, the defense would install ICE to protect themselves. The art on the cards was often high-concept illustrations, detailing what the code would see themselves as if they were a physical being.

The Future

The future of board games looks bright and has shown a lot of potential for new and exciting narrative techniques. One of the latest trends has been for legacy games: games designed to be played a certain number of times with the same group of people. What this design affords is a sense of permanence and meaning through controlled changes in the play experience.

Common features of legacy games include writing your names on character cards or the board. They often feature stickers to permanently note significant changes onto the board. They include boxes containing hidden pieces, with labels spouting "don't open until game six!" All of this creates an intentional pacing on the narrative designer's behalf. They're able to decide when the stakes of the play changes for the sake of developing a story. One of the most recent legacy games, based on Matt Leacock's *Pandemic, dubbed Pandemic: Legacy*, was subtitled Season 1. Each game represented a month out of the year (with players allowed to attempt a single replay for each lost game), escalating a conflict of global disease. While playing the game with a small group in a graduate school, my cohort would regularly talk about the game starting with the phrase "where are you in it," revealing a spoilerlike discourse for the events of the game. Never have I seen a board game discussed the same way as an episode of *Game of Thrones*.

This, and many other legacy games, reveals a wonderful new space for storytelling in board games. Despite board games being around for millennia, designers are finding new ways to create meaningful nondigital experiences.

Conclusion

Board game narratives require a cohesive touch. The theme and story must intersect completely with the play experience, which requires a strong grasp on uncertainty and turn order. Deeper narrative themes will be developed through the art and flavor text of the experience.

What's important in designing narrative board games is understanding how your system controls the experience; how your use of theme, art, and flavor text guides the players into a feel; and how to foster your designed play experience around the table. While balancing these three things isn't easy, a clever nondigital design often becomes a person's favorite game.

The range of board game experiences is expanding and new approaches to design are being shown constantly. Game designers constantly experiment with the dynamics of how players interact with rules, with victory conditions, even with the objects themselves. All of these narrative techniques help turn the static game objects into deep, meaningful pieces of play.

It's also important to echo that board games tend to be much shorter than digital games. The experiences range from 15 minutes to several hours and require the cooperation of other people. As such, the stories and experiences drawn from sitting around a table can often be the apex of the experience, rather than the designed narrative. Millions of people have stories of playing *Diplomacy*, and it would be folly to ignore it in place of one's own narrative. However, the greatest narratives come from blending player action with the designed narrative. Don't be afraid to discover new ways to give players something they'd never expect.

CHAPTER 6

From Novel to Game and Back Again

Matt Forbeck

Contents

Getting the Rights Right 65
Dive In 67
The Heart of the Matter 68
Consult the Creator(s) 69
Approvals 69
Making a Game. 70
Writing a Book 71
Taking Criticism 72
Exercise 73

Over the years, several games have been made out of novels, and even more novels have been written for games. The two media share a strong affinity for vivid characters, solid action, and intriguing explorations of various kinds of ideas, so it's only natural that people want to tap successes in one medium into sources for success in the other.

In this Chapter

- How to approach adapting a novel to a game
- Considerations for when adapting a game to a novel
- What the important steps to consider are

Here's how that happens.

Getting the Rights Right

The first step in turning a book into a game is securing the game rights to the book. In most cases, the developer approaches the author (who usually, although not always, controls these rights) and offers them a deal. This normally involves a royalty on the game's earnings, as well as an up-front payment, known as an advance.

It's called an advance because it's an advance payment for expected royalties. Once the game earns enough in royalties to burn through the advance, the developer issues the author regular statements that hopefully come with a check attached.

Lining up the rights properly requires a contract and the help of a couple of attorneys, but you need to make sure you do this correctly. Never develop a game based on a book (or any other property) for which you do not own the rights. If you do that and you're lucky, you'll wind up getting sued for a good chunk of the money you make off the game. In the worst-case scenario, the author can file an injunction to stop production and sale of the game entirely.

The only exception to this is if the book in question has fallen into the public domain. That means that the rights to the book have lapsed and anyone's allowed to do whatever they want with it—including make games based on it. Since the default length of copyright now extends 70 years past the death of the author, only books that are several decades old are likely to be in the public domain.

The older the book, the more likely it's in the public domain. You can bet, for instance, that *Assassin's Creed Odyssey* isn't going to have to cut a deal with Homer's descendants. The works of authors like H. P. Lovecraft or J. M. Barrie are on the edge of such lines. In short, if you don't know for sure if you're working on something in the public domain, hire an attorney who specializes in intellectual property. If you want to negotiate a contract with someone, you're probably going to need one anyhow.

Much of the same advice applies in the reverse direction. If you want to write a book based on a game, you need to secure the literary rights for that.

This is, by the way, almost always done by a book publisher rather than an author. Most game developers would rather deal with someone who has the proven ability to get their stories into bookstores, and it's a rare author who can manage that on their own. Once the publisher secures the rights, they then find authors who are interested in writing novels based upon the game, and they hire to them to do so.

Games are young enough that few of them have fallen into the public domain, although some have been voluntarily released that way or published under a Creative Commons license. Again, if you don't know the game's status for sure, assume someone owns it and that you can't have it for free.

Some eager writers have been known to sit down and write an entire novel as a means of showing off their talent and their familiarity with the game the book is based upon. Don't do this.

If you're just doing it to practice your craft and expect to do nothing more than post fanfiction online, go ahead, but there's almost zero chance that a publisher would want to purchase that book from you and publish it. Even if the publisher has the rights to that particular setting, they usually already have plans in place for their line of books. On top of that, the game developer may have all sorts of ideas about what's going on in their game's world that they haven't shared with the public yet.

In both cases, you have no chance of knowing what those obstacles are. If you write a book blind, you should expect to stub your toes on a crushing amount of disappointment.

If you want to write tie-in novels or books based on games, the best way to go about it is to write a book of your own first—something original that you yourself own. The main reason for this is that you can then prove to a prospective editor that you're capable of finishing a novel, a skill that the vast majority of people don't have, no matter how much they might wish it.

If you can finish a novel—and, better yet, find someone to publish it—an editor in charge of a licensed line of novels is going to feel much better about hiring you to write a book for them. No one wants to give an advance and stake their own reputation on a writer who can only claim to be a novelist but has no actual proof. If you write your own novel, you have that proof.

Better yet, you then also have your own novel that you can sell or publish on your own. Maybe someone might even want to make a game out of it someday, too.

Dive In

Once you get the rights all sorted out, it's time to figure out how to make a game out of that book—or a book out of that game. In both cases, you should start out the same way: dive into the source material until you know it as well as you can.

If you're making a game from a book, then read the book. If there are several books in the series, read them all. If you can find articles or books of criticism about the books, grab those, too.

If you're writing a book, play the game or games the book is based on. Take your time and make sure you see everything. Explore bits that you might normally breeze past or skip over. If you're an accomplished player, you should even play the game badly, on purpose, just to see how every sort of player experiences the game.

If you're a rotten player, get someone who's good at it to play the game for you: a friend, a son or daughter, a niece or nephew, a spouse—whoever. If you can't get someone to help you out like that, check out Let's Play videos of the game on YouTube or Twitch. In some ways, these can be even better, as you can pause, rewind, and advance the gameplay as you need, and you can go back and consult them once you're done.

Take notes as you go. Better yet, build a wiki to store your accumulated knowledge about the books. If the book or game you're studying is popular enough, fans may have already done a lot of this work for you. Hunt down a public wiki on the subject and make liberal use out of it.

Be cautious, though, of trusting any public wikis entirely. Fans sometimes mix their own theories or artwork in with the facts. While such wikis can be a great resource, you should always double-check details by consulting original sources.

The reasons for this are twofold. First, you want to get things right. The fans out there who love the original are going to judge you on how well you adhere to that original—as will the people who control the original property.

Second, you don't want to accidentally copy the work of something you don't have the rights to use. If you mistake fan work for something created for the original property and incorporate that into your work, you might be violating that fan's copyright. At the very least, it's sloppy work—and at the worst, you might get sued.

The Heart of the Matter

While you make this deep dive into the material, don't just take notes about the facts of the game. Analyze it as well. What is it about that original that resonates with people? What is it about it that makes its fans love it?

Drill down as hard as you can into the core of the original. Peel back the layers and see if you can find its heart, the thing that you can love about it, too.

Once you have that, post it someplace in big, bold letters. That's your lodestone for the entire project. Your north star. Use it to guide you whenever you have a question about which way to go with your project.

Many times, you're hunting for the emotional center of the original. Is it about the power of friendship? Love? Family? A thirst for money? Power? Revenge?

Since most books and games have functioning stories in them, figuring out the heart of the original's story can guide you on your project. This is the easy (well, easier) way to go, and you should never ignore it. After all, the stories in both should dovetail with each other, complement each other, and even expand upon each other.

However, don't ignore other central traits of the original that can transfer over to your project—and always take care to avoid going in directions that clash.

For instance, if you're creating a game based on a regency romance fantasy, it's probably not going to make a fantastic first-person shooter. Similarly, if you want to write a novel based on a first-person shooter, you probably shouldn't make it an epistolary story that unfolds over the course of a series of lovingly crafted, handwritten letters.

On the other hand, writing an action-packed novel based on an action-packed game makes perfect sense. The people who come for the action in one will stay for the action in the other. Novels of political intrigue probably aren't going to resonate as well with the same crowd.

Consult the Creator(s)

If at all possible, consult with the people who worked on the original project. They're going to have insights into that project that even the most attentive reader or player isn't going to be able to manage. They'll be able to pull back the curtain and discuss exactly why they made certain choices for their project—and what kinds of things might be happening in the setting, away from the main things they focused on.

As part of your project, you're going to have to build out this expanding context, and there's no better source for your research than the original creators. If you can manage it, talk with them regularly and respectfully. Ask them questions about what they were thinking and run your own ideas past them for feedback.

Besides which, it's the right thing to do. Show the original creators the respect they deserve for coming up with this thing that you're now going to be riffing off of. If not for the sake of your own love for the project, do it for the fans you're hoping will follow you from the original project to the one you're working on. If you don't show the original creators the respect they're owed, it could well get back to those fans, and they might decide to have nothing to do with your project.

Approvals

Most of the time when you're working on a licensed project, you don't own it, and you don't have control over it. In some cases, when you're working on a video game, the developer will purchase all nonliterary rights to the property by paying a (hopefully) exorbitant amount of money. In exchange for that, the developer will get to call the shots on the game (at least) from that point on.

More often, though, the owners of the original project have rights of approval over everything on your licensed project. Because of that, you need to be in regular and constant contact with them at every stage of your project's development.

It's important to establish channels of communications straight away and to know exactly when something is official or not. That usually means that someone has to be officially put in charge of the licensor's approvals for the project. Sometimes that's the person you deal with most often, but not always. Either way, it's the person who gets to make the final decision about what you can accomplish with your project.

Good approvals people can be hard to come by. In some large companies, it's one of the lowest positions, a place where someone can get a start and prove their skills and their passions. This means that if someone's amazing at that job, they can get promoted out of it right away—and if they suck at it, they might stick around until they do something stupid enough to get fired.

This happens less often with partners that care about the stories they're working on. If your licensed project is going to be part of the official canon— and that's something that matters to the licensor—then the licensor usually puts someone competent and helpful in charge. Otherwise, they're certain to wind up making everyone involved miserable.

Either way, you get to deal with them. Make friends with them if you can. Ideally, you all want the same thing: to make great projects happen based on this common story that you love. Keep that goal in mind, even if you have to explicitly remind each other of that from time to time.

Making a Game

When you're making a licensed game, your contract usually states when you have to submit your game for approvals. If you're lucky, it states that you have to do this regularly and that the licensor has to give you the thumbs up or thumbs down in a timely manner. Otherwise, you can wind up waiting weeks for approvals that you need, and since time is always short, you wind up charging ahead and hoping that you've gotten things right.

If it turns out you don't, you have to go back and do everything over again. That can be a huge loss of staff-hours on a project—which means a loss of money. Avoid this if you can at all manage it.

If the contract doesn't require you to check in regularly, do it anyhow. There's little worse than getting to the middle or—worse yet—the end of a project and discovering that the licensor hates everything you've done. That means you've wasted all that time. Maybe even enough to put your company entirely out of business.

Start by showing your licensor your initial concepts. The art. The design doc. The models. Everything they're likely to be able to care about and understand.

Most licensors aren't going to want to look at your code, for instance, or care about which engine you might use in the game. They just want to know how the game plays, what it looks like, how cool the story is, and if it all feels true to the original.

It's your job to explain everything to them in terms they can understand and to keep them happy.

Never ignore your responsibility to get the licensor to sign off on what you're doing at every step along the way. Make sure you get it in writing if at all possible. At the very least, have an email trail so if there are any troubles or bits of confusion in the future, you can go back and refer to your discussions and agreements in writing.

There are many ways for people to misinterpret each other, and people often have different memories of the same conversation, especially if it happened weeks or months ago. Having things written down helps everyone. Stick to it.

Writing a Book

Once you're asked to write a book based on a game, the first thing to do is agree with your editor on what the book is about. There are two ways this normally happens.

In the first, the editor says, "This is the book we want. These are the characters to use. This is the plot. Go write it."

This most often happens with books that are novelizations of an already-existing story. The basics of the tale are already set in stone. It's your job to flesh them out and make a novel out of them.

While games are great at presenting intriguing choices and showing action, novels are even better at digging into a character's inner world and motivations. Lean on that a bit, showing those internal monologues and peeling back bits of the characters' histories to give their actions more context and meaning.

The second kind of novel is an original story based upon a game. With these, the editor may come to you with the rough idea of a story already prepared. It's just as common, however, for the editor to ask you for ideas for stories.

You can tackle story pitches in whatever depth you like, but it's often better to shotgun a bunch of ideas rather than try to snipe with one or two notions developed in better depth. There are countless reasons an editor might reject any particular pitch you come up with, most of which you can't possibly know about ahead of time. It doesn't really matter how much time you spent on an idea if something basic about it knocks it straight out of the running.

Sometimes the editor picks one of your pitches and tells you to run with it. Sometimes they ask you to develop two or three of them in a bit more depth instead, perhaps a page or two each. Then they take these to the licensor and decide on which one they like best.

Once a pitch is settled on, the editor often offers you a contract. This comes with an advance and (hopefully) a royalty. Many editors will point out that they're already paying the licensor a royalty, so they don't have a lot of extra money to throw around on a royalty for a writer. They should be able to give you a little something, though, even if it's as low as 1%. It'll take forever to earn out, but if the book sells like crazy, at least you'll have something extra to show for it.

Assuming you can settle on the contract's terms, it's time to break down your pitch into an outline. This can be as in depth as you like it. At the very least, you should break the book down by chapters and describe in a few sentences what you plan to have happen in each. Notes about the main characters, overall plot ambitions, and how it all fits into the greater universe can help as well.

Some people like to write outlines that are 10,000 words or more, and you should do whatever works for you and makes it easiest to work with your editor and the licensor's approvals person. As long as you're all confident that you're headed in the same direction when you set to doing the actual writing, you should be fine.

You can turn the novel in by chapters or chunks if you like, but most editors would prefer to get it all at once. You only get one chance for a first, cold reading of a book with fresh eyes, after all. Some authors don't like to show their work to anyone until it's done, too. Works in progress are just that, and they can be messy and unrepresentative of the writer's best work.

Taking Criticism

No matter if you're working on a game or a novel, you need to do your best to take criticism professionally. If you're working with good people, criticism is never intended personally but directed at the project instead.

Ostensibly, you all want the same thing: to make the best project possible. Any criticism leveled at the project is meant to improve it, so take it with that in mind.

One mistake that people giving feedback make is to only point out the mistakes in a project. If all you, as the creator, get is negative feedback, you're inclined to change everything about it in an effort to make things better.

A wise critique, though, also tells you what you're doing right. That way, you don't mess with the parts of your project that are working well. On top of that, it helps you figure out what the critiquer likes and appreciates so you can bend your solutions to your mistakes in that direction.

Remember, in the end, the licensor has final say about what goes into the project. That doesn't, however, mean that you're powerless as the creator. You can discuss points of contention intelligently and politely. You can push back and explain the reasons behind your choices.

With luck and persistence, you may manage to prevail in such disagreements. You should also be prepared to lose some of them and do so in a collegial way.

If you do find yourself in a position in which you cannot stomach making a change—because you can't bear to have a project you think would be substandard out there with your name on it—you always have the option to walk away from the project. This is the nuclear option, though, as it may prove the end of the project. In addition, you may have to pay back some or all of the advances you've received, depending on the contract. So, only turn to this as a last resort.

With hard work, open communication, and a contractual relationship built on a common vision and trust, you can conjure up a project of which everyone involved can be proud. Keep an open mind and your love for the original property in your heart, and it can even be a fantastic amount of fun.

Exercise

Pick a chapter from your favorite novel and try to make it an interactive scenario for a game fitting the general tone and theme of the novel. Then, pick a game and try writing a short story using your gameplay experience and parts of the lore you're familiar with.

CHAPTER 7

From Movie to Game (and Back Again?)

Craig Sherman

Contents

Movie to Game 76
Game to Movie 80
The Takeaway 82
Exercise 82
References 82

While the ultimate goal of any mass-produced media is to turn a profit, a pure cash grab has a distinct odor, and consumers have become acutely adept at picking up the scent. The infamous business of video game/film crossovers is teeming with these stink bombs. Films and games are two distinct industries that both rely on the unpredictable task of trying to pick hits, so when one of them strikes gold, it's no surprise that the other attempts to board the gravy train. The problems, and subsequent flops, arise when content producers disregard their own medium's strengths and differences and simply attempt to duplicate the project they've licensed. This happens for a number of reasons—scheduling, budget, inexperience, arrogance—but the outcome is consistent: they fail because they cannot stand on their own.

In this Chapter

- The relationship between movies and games
- How writing a movie differs from writing for a game
- Why it's hard (*impossible?*) to adapt a game to a movie

Of course, there have been successes, or, more specifically, there have been successful games based on movies. For example, *GoldenEye 007, The Warriors,* and *The Chronicles of Riddick: Escape From Butcher Bay* are renowned for both their quality and popularity. These are games that are enhanced by their licenses, not restricted by them. As writers, understanding and embracing the advantages and limitations of both art forms puts us in a position to produce better work.

Before we begin, I'd like to address two questions that we hear often: "Why did this game get made at all?" and its close cousin "Why did they make this movie?" Let's take these questions off the table. They got made and will continue to get made because the people who make these decisions believe these projects are the most likely to make money. There's nothing wrong with that; it's why video games and movies exist. In hindsight, it's easy to snicker about a studio's decision to make an *Assassin's Creed* movie, but it's not an artistic decision. *Assassin's Creed* is a widely recognized title and, at least on paper, less of a risk than releasing an unknown title. The same can be said for something like the *Wayne's World* video game. Movies and games are expensive to produce, and any steps that can be taken to mitigate that risk will always prevail. "Why" they're made isn't our job and it's not the subject of this chapter. As writers, our responsibility is often to work miracles with what we've been given, and it can be done. Don't believe me? In 2014, Warner Bros. released a film written and directed by Christopher Miller and Phil Lord and based on a license for plastic interconnecting toy blocks. *The Lego Movie* has a Rotten Tomatoes score of 96% and has grossed over $450 million. Miracles happen, and what appear to be ill-advised licenses can be spun into gold; let's figure out how.

Mobile Games

To clarify, when I speak of video games, I'm referring to console or PC games, not mobile games. In terms of writing, mobile games are a completely different animal.

Movie to Game

In my opinion, when it comes to adaptation, the path from movie to video game has the advantage. We've seen this play out in both critical reception and sales. The reasons are twofold: the inherent freedom of the format and economic success's effect on storytelling.

The process of adapting a movie into a video game is all about expansion. Since games generally range from a four-hour experience on the very low end to over 100 hours for the deepest RPGs, even the shortest games are longer than an epic film. While the majority of this time in a game is not spent on storytelling, video games provide a writer with room to work. Fortunately, this latitude to invent results in exactly what players most enjoy. The best games based on movies begin with the film as the seed of an idea and grow the story in new directions. Fans of a particular movie who play the corresponding licensed video game are fans of the movie universe. They want to explore this world beyond the specific story told in the film. Film novelizations and film-to-television series adaptations operate under the same principle; they provide more depth to a proven concept. Video games that truly take advantage of this principle take on a life of their own, can be enjoyed without having seen the film, and even spawn sequels. (e.g., the *Star Wars* and *Lord of the Rings* series of games).

Video games are more profitable than movies—a lot more—and that financial superiority has led to a decreased dependence on film licenses and bolder storytelling. In 2008, video game revenue first surpassed that of films, and the gap has widened ever since. Video games earned $30.4 billion in 2016,[1] while film box office revenue was $11.6 billion.[2] These days, with over 40[3] video game films in various states of development, movies are much more likely to attempt to cash in on a game's success than the reverse. Twenty-five years ago, game developers clamored for movie licenses. The industry was young and, in theory, games would benefit from the association with films. In many cases, what actually happened was that game development cycles were extremely rushed in order to coincide with a film's release. The result was poor-quality games (as in the famous case of *E.T. The Extra-Terrestrial*). They were seen as cash grabs, because they were cash grabs. Consumer dissatisfaction and ultimately falling game sales followed, but the video game industry has learned and adapted. Developers have grown into their position as the world's leading content providers. Most current hit films do not have corresponding big-budget games. The license fees, rushed development, film studio interference, and potential backlash from lackluster films just don't make sense. Often, even when a game is based on a film license, the game's release does not correspond with the film's release; they share little more than a title and perhaps the rules of a universe.

As the audience for major motion pictures has begun to stagnate and costs have increased, studios have reacted by taking fewer risks in terms of concepts and storytelling. While this has somewhat stabilized the health of the movie business, it's a short-term strategy. At some point, audiences will tire of sequels, remakes and comic book films. These greenlight decisions are coming from a place of caution and risk management. Game developers, on the other hand, are more often swinging for the fences. Of course, a fair share of new games are sequels, but, for the most part, each new edition of a video game series improves on the concept, not just technologically, but in terms of world-building and story. Look at the *Grand Theft Auto*, *Tomb Raider*, and *Mario* series as examples; every follow-up pushes the title in new directions. Gamers have come to expect more and developers deliver. This isn't something we can say about most movie sequels. With the meteoric rise of game sales, developers' decisions are inspired by confidence and a resulting willingness to take risks. For writers, this is always an advantage. The gaming industry is in the midst of a creative expansion, much like the movie industry of the 1970s. The rise of independent game development has served to push the entire industry even further in this direction. We've got indie narrative trailblazers like *What*

Remains of Edith Finch and AAA mindbenders like *BioShock Infinite*. It's truly a great time to be creating video games.

I am currently at work on the video game adaptation of the film *World War Z*, which, in turn, is an adaptation of Max Brooks's best-selling novel *World War Z: An Oral History of the Zombie War.*[7] The experience has been illuminating. Instead of utilizing the film's protagonist, Gerry Lane, portrayed by Brad Pitt, as the vessel for our expanded *World War Z* experience, we follow the stories of several characters coping with the aftermath of the zombie war in far-flung locations, in much the same way as the book. The game shares the film's universe; our zombie hordes terrifyingly sprint and climb rather than lumber, and we use several of the film's locations, but we weren't confined by the film. My co-writer, Oliver Hollis-Leick, and I were given leeway to work with the game designers and artists to create characters and storylines that, for the most part, we felt were engrossing. (More on "for the most part" later.) The resulting game will, I hope, succeed on its own merits.

Having come from a screenwriting background, I can say that game writing differs in key aspects on a daily basis. I immediately noticed the responsiveness of the process. Screenwriters working on films in development typically work in near-total isolation, perhaps with a partner, but almost completely cut off from other elements of filmmaking. There's the occasional call or meeting with a producer, studio executive, or attached director to check on the script's progress, but there's no contact with a cinematographer, set designer, or anyone else on the production side. Because a large majority of films don't begin any sort of production activity until a script is complete, the procedure is split between a routinely lengthy period of script development and everything else. It is not uncommon for a screenwriter to spend much of his or her career working on projects that never advance past the writing stage. Due to the nature of their development, games don't work that way. Games are collaborative from start to finish. A AAA game title can take anywhere from two to five years to complete, with all departments working nearly every day in synchronization. In the earliest stages of writing the *World War Z* game, I can remember discussing character ideas with the designers and I was shocked to see rough artist renderings the next day. Games are developed *as you're writing*.

This responsiveness is a double-edged sword. While it's exciting to see instant results, there isn't much time for experimentation. When writing a screenplay, it's not uncommon to write a scene, decide it's not working a few days later, and rewrite it. In games, that idea you had a few days ago may have already been worked on by a team of artists, designers, and programmers. Rewriting may be costly and, in some cases, not even an option. Collaboration with developers during the writing process is usually exciting and useful, as passionate team members sometimes introduce ideas that the writer may not have considered, but it can be frustrating for the same reason. As I mentioned above, "for the most part" my co-writer and I were free to create on *World War Z*, but gameplay is still king in most games, and game designers sometimes make choices based on playability with no regard for story or character. This is an instance of making the best of a situation, and writing films also includes its share of compromises. A film writer has many masters, from studio to director to actor, and many of those masters are not nearly as familiar with the story as the writer. It's frustrating, to say the least. My feeling is that in games, at least the people I'm collaborating and sometimes disagreeing with are as knowledgeable about the project as I am, and in some cases are more familiar with it than I am. Their contributions come from a place of understanding.

Movies are at their best when a great film involves the audience both emotionally and intellectually. Not every film succeeds. In fact, I'd argue that most don't. Master filmmakers have earned this distinction because they understand how to skillfully draw audience members into the film's world and the journey of its characters. A clear example of this is James Cameron's *Titanic*. Every audience member was aware (spoiler alert!) that the ship would sink at the end, yet moviegoers were spellbound for over three hours. Like it or not, it worked. People cried, and it broke records and won an Academy Award. Only the most expertly crafted films can truly pull off the magic trick of manufactured empathy. Beyond all logic, and knowing that the outcome is beyond our control and totally predetermined, we become invested in the odyssey. On the contrary, video games are designed to be influenced by the player. They are fully interactive empathy machines. Whether the game's world is open or not, gamers control the narrative. They discover the universe on their own, at their own pace. We identify with the protagonist because we control his or her fate. Even a poorly designed game has this feature built in. A well-made game based on a film can exploit this dynamic in a way that a game-to-film adaptation cannot. In games, we are the story's hero. In movies based on games, we're forced to experience the game's world through someone else's eyes.

While modern video games have made great strides in the delivery of emotional storytelling, as game writers we cannot rely on the traditional narrative tools utilized in films. Embracing this fact is key to creating effective drama in a game. Just as screenwriters writing a game-to-film adaptation would do well not to try to recreate the full game experience, game writers adapting from film should resist the urge to lean on filmic tools. Have you ever been in the midst of exciting gameplay only to be interrupted by a cinematic that felt like it would never end? That's overreaching. It's the game writer leaning on traditional storytelling that feels obviously out of place in a video game. Simply put: games are not interactive movies. The reality is that few video game genres even allow for dedicated story moments. The *World War Z* game I'm currently co-writing is a story-based shooter, but we don't have the luxury of in-game cutscenes. It's not that kind of game; its focus is nonstop action with high replayability. Stopping to reveal background would only hurt the game. Our story must be conveyed in short prelevel and postlevel cinematics and through in-game dialogue. It's surely a challenge, but my co-writer and I have found that if we accept the rules and work within the game's framework, it can be done effectively. The designers have repeatedly asked us to squeeze in story dialogue during gameplay, and we've tried, but it simply doesn't work. It stands out and breaks the reality of the game. It feels like exposition, and obvious exposition, whether in film or games, is deadly. A filmmaker has the luxury of total control. As game writers, we relinquish this power in exchange for interactivity.

Game to Movie

In 1993, when the *Super Mario Bros.* film crashed and burned both critically and financially, gamers and moviegoers could reasonably assume it was simply a failed first attempt at a crossover. Twenty-five years and 35 movies later, video game films have earned a reputation for consistently subpar filmmaking. Browse the web for the history of video game film adaptations if you dare and you'll find that the most critically acclaimed effort is the most recent one (at the time of this writing), with *Rampage* scoring a 53% Rotten Tomatoes score. This bears repeating: that's the *highest* score out of 35 films. What's going on? Why can't Hollywood crack this formula? How can it be cracked? Let's take a detective's eye to critical darling *Rampage* to find out what went right. The first thing we might notice is the fact that hardly anyone remembers the 1986 video game it's based on. Another detail: most people don't even know the film is based on a game. And the biggest hint of all: the movie's story has almost nothing to do with the video game. The filmmakers were not beholden to a horde of perpetually triggered fanboys. Nobody was expecting the *Rampage* arcade game movie experience. Even the game's monsters' origin story of humans being turned into giant animals was thrown out for—wait for it—something that the filmmakers felt would work better for a movie.[4] The screenwriters were empowered to write a giant monster movie that works on its own as a giant monster movie. Novel idea.

Let's get through the bad news first: the odds are severely stacked against the success of a movie based on a video game. The main reason is fairly simple: *movies are short.* Games are a particularly difficult transition, but a feature film adaptation from almost any other medium must cope with the same restriction. Books to film, television series to film, games to film—they're all a process of cutting and condensing. I've never adapted a video game to film, but I have had the pleasure of adapting two books for the screen. My most recent attempt was David Bianculli's brilliant *Dangerously Funny: The Uncensored Story of the Smothers Brothers Comedy Hour* for Smokehouse Productions and Sony Pictures.[6] Mr. Bianculli's book is an extensive and thoroughly researched account of the fascinating journey of Tom and Dick Smothers. This story could easily have filled several seasons of a television series. My co-writer Brian Hecker and I were tasked with fitting it into two hours. Movie adaptation is a painful process of deciding what material is absolutely necessary, determining which of your favorite elements will never been seen by moviegoers, and gutting the careful work of the book's author so the whole thing can be squeezed into a 120-page screenplay. It's really no wonder that most of the time readers prefer books over their film adaptations. Books are designed to be books; book-to-film adaptations are a distorted version of the same material.

Video game film adaptations are an even more fraught scenario. The worlds of many modern video games are enormous, and players take great joy in exploring every detail. Understandably, when filmmakers adapt a video game into a movie, they endeavor to appeal to fans of the game by including elements of the source material, but it's generally a fool's errand. Gamers who invest a lot of time into their favorite titles tend to feel a sense of ownership over them. What do film versions have to offer fans of these games? A more narrow perspective? Less depth? Zero interactivity? What diehard fans of a particular game really want is the game, not a movie, and they won't be satisfied. Paradoxically, the more filmmakers strive to recreate the game in movie form, the more it detracts from the movie. Of course, the much larger segment of the moviegoing public who have never played the game must also be catered to, and game elements included in the film have no value to them. Filmmakers who adapt games are tasked with obliging both groups and usually alienate everyone. An example of this is the movie based on the game *Doom*. Toward the end of the film, in an attempt to simulate the game's first-person shooter perspective, the camera assumes the point of view of one of the characters on a killing spree. Gamers weren't impressed, nongamers were simply baffled, and the movie bombed. The immortal Roger Ebert stated it best in his review: "No, I haven't played [the game], and I never will, but I know how it feels not to play it, because I've seen the movie. *Doom* is like some kid came over and is using your computer and won't let you play."[5]

For an example of another potential pitfall of video game-to-film adaptation, let's look at *Tomb Raider*. Since 1996, the video game series has provided consistently breathtaking action-adventure. As a film, the title has been popular enough to spawn a reboot, but has never fully hit its stride. Why? Because regardless of the high budgets and the star power of Angelina Jolie and Alicia Vikander, the *Tomb Raider* films feel like *Indiana Jones* knockoffs. Much like the *Uncharted* game series (which is also being developed as a film), the *Tomb Raider* games were obviously inspired by the *Indiana Jones* films. Both game franchises are legendary for their quality and inventiveness, but turning them into films only calls attention to their lack of originality. They're not great games because they were inspired by an esteemed film series,* they're great games because their developers took the care to make them

---

* I'm going to ignore *Kingdom of the Crystal Skull*.

81

great games. Strip away the gameplay and you're left with nothing but a seemingly unoriginal concept.

The Takeaway

Regardless of their checkered past, game/movie crossovers aren't going anywhere. History has provided us with clues as to how we might successfully navigate these waters. While games based on movies have found limited success, and movies based on games have yet to crack the formula, the key to adaptation in both directions is the same. Consider the popular and well-regarded *Spider-Man 2* game, which was officially based on Sam Raimi's film of the same name, but actually drew much more from the rich world of *Spider-Man* comics. The game was "inspired" by the movie, and did include some movie elements, but it would have worked just as well if it had no relation to the film. Since the field of successful game-to-movie adaptations is basically empty, let's briefly reconsider the reason for *Rampage's* relative triumph: it essentially had nothing to do with the game. I'm not suggesting that film-to-game and game-to-film adaptations should have no connection to the original titles, but the efforts that have been most successful have worked on their own regardless of the original title. There's the lesson. *As a writer taking on one of these projects, you're never going to satisfy everyone. Don't bother.* If you're writing a film based on a game, make it a great film first. Critics will judge it as a film and audiences will see it based on its merits as a film. If it's a really terrific movie, even if it's not entirely faithful to the game or missing game elements, you've done your job. The same can be said for a film-to-game adaptation. Write a great game. Explore the world of the film, not necessarily the film itself. Films have unique, enchanting features that cannot be duplicated in a video game, and vice versa. Attempts to capture every element will invariably fail. Focus on your medium's strengths. Create a project that stays true to the *spirit* of the source material but stands on its own and you may forever be known as the writer who cracked the crossover.

Exercise

Pick a scene from a movie and try to adapt it to a scene in a game, making it as interactive as possible, allowing the player to have agency over the action. Afterward, take a scene from your favorite game and try to condense it to a three-minute short movie. Note the difficulties and challenges you encounter during your adaptation attempts.

References

1. "U.S. Video Game Industry Generates $30.4 Billion in Revenue for 2016," Entertainment Software Association, http://www.theesa.com/article/u-s-video-game-industry-generates-30-4-billion-revenue-2016/

2. "Box office revenue* in North America from 1980 to 2017 (in billion U.S. dollars)," Statistica: The Statistics Portal, https://www.statista.com/statistics/187069/north-american-box-office-gross-revenue-since-1980/
3. "40 Video Game Movies Currently in Development," Den of Geek, http://www.denofgeek.com/us/games/video-game-movies/170757/video-game-movies-in-development
4. David Crow, "Rampage Filmmakers Reveal Reason for Major Change from Video Game," Den of Geek, March 19, 2018, http://www.denofgeek.com/us/movies/rampage/271523/rampage-filmmakers-reveal-reason-for-major-change-from-video-game
5. Roger Ebert, *Doom* review, October 20, 2005, https://www.rogerebert.com/reviews/doom-2005
6. David Bianculli, 2010. *Dangerously Funny: The Uncensored Story of the Smothers Brothers Comedy Hour*, New York, Touchstone.
7. Max Brooks, 2006. *World War Z: An Oral History of the Zombie War*, Crown Publishers, New York.

CHAPTER 8

Get It into the Game: Writing and Implementation

Tobias Heussner

Contents

The Lack of Common Formatting 86
Implementing Your Work 87
A Word on Scripting 89
How to Learn Scripting and What to Learn. 89
Talking Art 93
Getting Things Ready. 98
Get It in the Game 102
Conclusion 102
Exercise 103
Reference 103

You have your script, 300 pages, written in perfect FinalDraft script format. You have your compendium of the world, *only* 2530 pages … and you're only getting started.

Even if you did all of a writer's work in game development, the job is only done if what was designed and developed is playable and shippable. This often means that you, especially as a narrative designer, must work on the implementation of your writing.

In this chapter, we'll discuss what this means, what you should learn, and how you can turn your traditional writing into a playable experience.

In this Chapter

- How to get from the written word to the playable
- What you need to know to work on the implementation
- Why implementation skills matter

The Lack of Common Formatting

The first and most common problem you'll run into is that there is no common format for game scripts and no common ruleset for how things should be written so that the game engine understands them. Top this with the fact that every type of professional (artists, programmers, etc.) in the game industry has their own language with their own "secret" words.

Welcome to game development.

If this didn't scare you, then I hope you're up for the challenge you'll face every day as a narrative designer and game writer. It will not always be easy, but nothing is more rewarding than seeing your words come alive on the screen.

So, what should you do? How should you format your script, if there aren't any rules?

First, learn to be a good communicator. It sounds simple, but most of us writers are introverts who enjoy the silence of the creative chamber to hammer out all these engaging storylines; thus, we're up for a challenge here. You don't have to become a public speaker, but train, for example, in front of a mirror or with friends to present your ideas. The goal is to stay focused on the idea you are trying to share and not to drift into all the side information you could share as well. Try to grab your audience's attention within the first 30–60 seconds and only share what needs to be shared. Keep in mind that you want to sell your idea and encourage people to read what you wrote. You don't need to tell them everything, especially because if you do, they most likely will have forgotten 90% by the time you finish.

Second, worry about the content, not the format. As the format changes from studio to studio and can even change from project to project, don't waste your time looking for the perfect format; look for the great stories you want to tell. At the end of the day, you are working on a game that should be sold and not in a format that only you and your teams see. Setting the priorities right can free you from tasks that are unimportant. Also, most likely, your format will be defined by the technology you'll use for a specific game and, as we'll discuss later in this chapter, this can look quite different.

Third, be a team player. Game development is a team effort and only teams that work together can achieve great results. The best writing is nothing without a programmer bringing it to the screen with the game engine. The best writing will remain unseen without an artist who creates the assets needed to bring it to the screen. Also, working as a team benefits your skills as a communicator and helps you learn all the different languages spoken by the different professionals, helping you ultimately to become a better game developer. Your most important tool is to have an open mind and to be willing to adapt and use whatever format is required to tackle a specific project or situation.

Implementing Your Work

And now, after we've gotten the formatting issue out of the way, we're ready to seize the script you wrote and bring it to life in a game. But before we talk about specific tools and approaches, let us talk about some core principles and terms when it comes to implementing your work.

The key concept behind all game development is that we're delivering an interactive experience. "Play, don't tell" is the key, and just like "Show, don't tell," it needs to become your core concept when approaching writing for a game. In very much the same way you try to deliver experiences with the written word when writing a novel or via cinematography when writing a film script, you want to deliver experiences that are experienced while playing the game. This usually involves all kinds of disciplines, not just writers, and listening to each other, learning from each other, and working together is key to a great experience. We all only have one piece of the puzzle, and the whole picture can only be seen if everyone contributes.

During implementation, a lot of time is spent bringing all the expertise together. Content designers, and as such writers and narrative designers who belong to this group, as do level designers, are usually at the center of bringing all the pieces together. Here the assets from the art department are integrated and combined, here the code is used in specific situations, here triggers ensure that everything happens when it is supposed to happen according to the design documents (Table 8.1).

And no matter what the content is and how it was prepared, the key principle from here on, if it hasn't been so thus far, is "Play, don't tell." During the implementation phase, if there is one important task for a narrative designer, it is to cut the fat from all the narrative elements that were developed before now and transform them into a playable experience.

The backstory you wrote … is it needed? How can a player experience it? Does the game world have a library or books? Can this specific element be shown by the design of the environment, the sound?

These and more are the questions you need to ask yourself at this point. On the way to this point, you may have used various forms of writing, such as dialogue writing, script writing, prose or fiction writing, wireframing, etc. You may look at a wealth of documents, yet all this means nothing if the players can't experience it. It is time to kill your darlings and those of your fellow writers. It is time to think about how you want to tell your story with the constraints provided by all the other departments. In the end, for a story, no matter how well written, if it is not experienced, it doesn't exist.

Another important question to answer is the form or forms of storytelling you'll use for this specific game. This is not just the decision about whether the plot is organized in a linear or nonlinear fashion—this decision should have

TABLE 8.1 Sample Domains of Content Designers

	All Three	Writer	Narrative Designer	Level Designer
Overall story/plot development	X			
Iteration response		X		X
Iteration tracking			X	X
Establish/watchdog tone	X			
Writing content	X			
Planning and implementing content			X	X
Environment design and prototyping			X	X
Environment implementation				X
Script prototyping			X	X
Scripting				X
History and backstory development		X	X	
Mission flow design			X	X
Story-related VO writing		X		
Story-related VO/MoCap planning, data preparation, casting, and participation			X	
VO implementation/verification			X	
Narrative tool planning			X	
Narrative scope tracking/scheduling			X	
Edit/polish written content		X		
Narrative submissions/approvals			X	

been made long before the first written line—no, this is about how the game interacts with the players to tell its story. Is it via cutscenes? Is it via NPCs and dialogues? Is the overall progression structure of the game story- or quest-driven or not? How important are the plot and each narrative element for the essential experience (Schell, 2010. *The Art of Game Design*, "Chapter 2—The Designer Creates an Experience," p. 20) of the game?

This phase, especially in the beginning, will feel like an endless flow of questions, but once you make it through these questions, the vision and goal of the narration will be set and you'll be ready to set sail to see your content coming alive and hopefully becoming the experience for the players you had in mind.

From now on, your tools will normally be more than just word-processing programs, as you'll start dealing with scripts written in some form of a programming language, with assets made in a graphics program and potentially with level editors to bring all the content together. Learning these tools may not be essential for you to become a better storyteller, but they will help you to get your story told and understand the people you'll work with on your journey to the finished game.

A Word on Scripting

Should you learn to program in a scripting language or even in a programming language? I can't tell you that you should, but I think it will be beneficial for you to do so if you want to make a career as a narrative designer. When I joined the industry, the design department was not as diverse as it is in today's industry, and usually a game designer had to write the story just as much as to integrate it with the game's tools and script language. Later, as a level designer, it was part of my responsibility to bring the planned quest and stories into the game using an in-house tool that resembled a kind of programming language.

Whether designers and writers should script (or even touch programming code) is passionately discussed in the industry, and you will find people who will say that a designer never should touch any code as much as you will find people who say that everything should be scripted by designers. The truth is most likely somewhere in the middle of these two extremes. If you see yourself mainly as a writer, you may never need to touch a script, and that is fine. If you would like to explore the field of content design, then you most likely will not be able to avoid learning the basics of programming.

Personally, I would recommend you learn the basics of programming, as, even if you don't write scripts yourself, it will help you communicate with programmers. It also has the added benefit that you will be able to prototype your ideas and try things before you pass them to the other departments to make them fully work. Seeing something in motion is so much better than the concept alone. It can even serve as a source of inspiration.

How to Learn Scripting and What to Learn

Well, let's assume you decided to learn to script, but where should you start and what should you learn?

First, and what hopefully comes as a relief, you don't need to learn everything a programmer should know, so you don't need to learn memory allocation, memory management, or regular expressions. You can, but you don't have to. What is more important than any high-level concept is that you understand the basics, such as conditional loops, conditional execution, variables, and basic algebra. In most cases, it is enough to understand object abstraction (or, in other words, the basics of object-oriented programming), variables, functions, and their use and declaration.

Where can you learn all this? The easiest way to explore this is by picking a class on Udemy or a similar platform. You can also get apps from Solo Learn for your phone or watch YouTube tutorials. Your goal is to learn the basics and fundamental concepts; thus, most of the free material is enough and no university courses are required. Whatever medium you use largely depends on your personal preference when it comes to learning a new skill. All in all, learning the basics of programming may take a month and now and then afterward to keep your skills sharp, but it will be worth your time, as you will find it easier to talk to programmers, and nothing is more rewarding than to see your own ideas become reality when you write your first prototype.

Key Programming and Scripting Languages

You may be wondering what programming or scripting language will be worth your time when learning one. While in the end it really depends on your individual circumstances and your passion for learning a new way of writing, I recommend learning at least one of the following languages. Again, your goal is not to become an expert but to understand enough to use them to prototype and communicate with other developers.

C++ is the most used language in the game industry, but it is also the one that is hardest to learn due to its highly technical structure and vocabulary. It clearly is meant to be used by programmers and engineers who understand and have studied underlying concepts such as memory allocation and object abstraction. While you may be able to learn basic concepts relatively quickly, it will take a long time before you can write your first game (except for a text-based console application); however, learning some C++ will help you talk with your programmers and, as it is such a common language that has in turn inspired many other programming languages, understanding its syntax will help you understand other languages such as C#, Python, Java, Visual Basic, etc.

C# is not the next C++ and doesn't try to be so. It is easier to learn, as it automates a lot of the low-level stuff that needs to be considered in C++ (even if these are things that you shouldn't worry about). It has a very similar syntax to C++ and is one of the possible script languages used by Unity3D, which makes it a perfect entry-level C-type language for game developers. You should be able to find a lot of tutorials for the language itself as well as for its use in Unity3D. With C#, it shouldn't take long before you have your first game developed.

Lua is a scripting language that is, unlike C++ or C#, not compiled but interpreted during runtime. It can be changed without the need to rebuild the entire game and thus changes can be made quickly. Sometimes, depending on the implementation, scripts can be even changed with debug commands from within the game. Lua uses a C-like syntax and is widely used in game engines. It is not the only script language, but maybe due to its popularity, it is the easiest to learn due to the vast amount of learning resources. Lua is used by engines and games such as Civilization 6, World of Warcraft, CryEngine, and many more.

Blueprint/Visual Scripting is something that has become more and more popular in scripting and prototyping in recent years, especially with Unreal Engine 4 (but there are implementations for Unity3D as well). Unlike former script languages, visual scripting tries to visualize programming logic as flow charts. It is usually easier to understand and, if kept clean, easier to read, but just like any scripting language requires learning the underlying functions and syntax. As great as it is to have a visual representation, it can also become quite messy if too much functionality and too many connections are made within one graph, not considering common programming practices such as modularization and the use of custom functions. Besides its implementation in leading game engines, visual scripting to a certain extent can also be found in writing tools such as Twine and Articy:Draft, which use the flow chart visualization to visualize the journey throughout a plotline.

Writing and implementing a prototype should be your next step once you have studied the basics. Nothing helps you learn and sharpen your skills more than getting your hands dirty and doing some programming or scripting yourself. Unreal Engine 4 and Unity 3D are two excellent engines to start with if you don't work in a studio that has its own accessible engine to try your skills. You can also try to use the editor tools from other games to take your first steps in scripting and implementation. Using one of these tools or engines will help you understand how basic concepts are implemented by programmers, and it will help you to see how programmers organize functions and objects to get them ready to for specific implementation in a concrete project.

Interview: Tips to learn programming by Marcos Falcon (Technical Director, Saber Interactive Spain)

- What is the easiest way to approach programming for a nonprogrammer?

    Nowadays, starting programming is relatively easy. The use of visual programming tools is widely extended. Those tools offer sets of actions represented by shapes that can be connected to each other. A program in these applications is formed by a sequence of connected shapes (actions) in a sort of flow diagram. Even the most advanced gaming middleware, such as Epic's Unreal Engine, offers solutions to prototype games without writing a single line of code. There are also tools for bringing programming to children. Scratch is a clear example of these kinds of tools. Scratch (https://scratch.mit.edu) is a web-based application that offers a visual programming language for children in an intuitive way.

But if someone wants to start programming with the target of becoming a professional programmer, I would recommend starting with a managed language such as Java or C#. The two main concepts that a programmer wannabe must understand deeply are the concept of a program as a sequence of instructions and the concept of a variable as data storage. Everyone can become a programmer. The hard thing is to evolve towards software engineering, where understanding the ways to prepare applications to grow and evolve is capital.

- What do you consider the essential elements every game developer needs to understand about programming?

The design must be well documented and must be accessible to all the team. The specification of a feature must be clearly written and shared among all team components. Undocumented changes always lead to confusion about the behavior of features. Besides, chains of undocumented changes end with situations where nobody knows how a mechanic must work. Programmers often fill the holes of the specification. If you don't want the programmer to be "creative," do not leave room for interpretation in your documents. Just be clear and concise.

Another consideration about feature design is that the paper supports everything written on it. Usually, all features are possible, but they take time and resources. Think about time and resource constraints before making a design. A good idea could be writing the "best possible feature" and then writing the agreed or affordable solution. If there is time enough for revisiting the feature later, it can be improved towards the ideal solution.

Design (think) twice, implement once (a.k.a. changes are costly). I always like to compare programming to the construction of buildings. Once the design is finished and plans are drawn, when the workers are working in the fourth-floor ceiling, you cannot decide to move some pillars to make the living room wider. Changes in the design of applications when the implementation is in an advanced stage can end in lots of changes in code. While writing code, programmers do make assumptions and choose the algorithms to solve the problems raised by the design based on the specifications. This is even more noticeable when developing games, where the performance is always an issue.

Sometimes, even minor changes in the specifications lead to major changes in code. Of course, the experience and knowledge of the programmers in the field of application can anticipate changes, but consider that ad-hoc solutions are faster in terms of developing time but less tolerant to changes. On the other hand, more general solutions are better at dealing with changes but require more time to develop and test. Consider that changes in requisites do not only imply that new features must be implemented, but also all existing ones must work as before.

Programmers cannot replace QA. Programmers do test our code, but many times, the daily workflow leads us to create "habits" to test features and we can easily forget use cases. Users (gamers) exploit features in unimaginable ways. Always plan the appropriate time to perform a good QA phase. Take into account that coders tend to reuse (and it's good to do so) pieces of code for multiple features. Changes in that common code often lead to forgetting a particular use of that code in some forgotten feature. Do not assume that a change in a feature does not affect other areas of the game.

- What do you wish every developer would know when working with programmers?

Programming is a complex and a brain-struggling task and yes, we make mistakes. At the end, coders are ultimately responsible for ensuring that everything works well. The pressure on programmers caused by time restrictions is huge sometimes. Overtime causes stress and loss of efficiency in written code and is a very common mistake. It is well known that long periods of overtime cause coders to make mistakes and write code that is less robust and oftentimes needs to be revisited. A fresh and rested mind gets creativity to flow. Also, do not blame programmers for the bugs. Major bugs that reach users are often the result of a poor QA process. Relying on tools of static code analysis is a good idea to catch mistakes caused by a lack of attention.

Talking Art

Congratulations: if you made it this far and mastered the basics of programming, you can pat yourself on the back. One thing you may have realized (or already knew) is that scripting is only one side of content design. Without assets, the best script remains invisible or is just a line of text. Don't worry; you don't have to become an artist to implement your ideas, but you should understand some art language so that you can request from artists what you need to implement your stories.

Most assets for computer games are currently made in 3D programs from Autodesk. The most famous is Autodesk Maya. These programs are very expensive (but more affordable indie, feature-reduced versions exist) and not less complex. If you thought learning programming was a complex task, then you'll find yourself in another jungle of complexity when opening one of these programs for the first time. Their complexity is a result of the many areas of art they cover, from modeling (creation of 3D models out of simple basic shapes and polygons) to texturing (adding color and material attributes to plain surfaces) to rigging (adding virtual skeletons and movement constraints) to animation and rendering: everything is covered. If you really want to sneak-peek into these programs, you can either use the trial versions or Blender, a free, albeit harder to learn, alternative.

As a writer and narrative designer, it is not important that you master these programs, as this is the responsibility of artists. It is enough that you understand what each of the different steps means and how they affect you when implementing your work. For example, you may need a specific object modeled and textured to guide players to your objective within a quest; thus, you may need to speak with a 3D modeler and a texture artist to get what you need. Or you need a specific animation; thus, you need to talk to an animator and maybe a rigger to make it happen.

If you really want to, you could also learn to model 3D models, a skill that can be helpful if you quickly need to create dummies during the implementation and to avoid waiting for the results from the art department.

Finally, the two art skills you really want to learn are to change the position, rotation, and scale of 3D objects, which usually takes place in a level editor, and drawing simple, designer art like 2D sketches for maps, object ideas, etc. Drawing can be done in whatever program you like or on paper. A good tool is Adobe Photoshop or its excellent free alternative, GIMP. For maps, a vector-based tool such as Campaign Cartographer or Inkscape can be an excellent solution.

In the end, no matter what tool you choose or learn, your main goal is to learn to express your needs and communicate with the professionals whose job it is to create the final assets and develop what you need to get the narrative elements implemented.

Interview: Tips to learn art by Antonio Alonso (Former Lead Artist, Saber Interactive Spain)

- What is the easiest way to approach art for games for a nonartist?

  In approaching art, we must first know what we are looking for and, more importantly, where to find it.

  No doubt most people relate art to the graphics of a game, and although it is not inaccurate, it is not entirely correct either.

When I think of art, I always think of a magic trick where a magician for a few minutes makes us believe things we know are impossible and yet our eyes are fixed on the show, amazed. So long as we do not know the trick, that feeling of awe lasts, and that balance, that deception, is what I call art.

This kind of deception is not only visual, it is also narrative. We find it in novels where the writer, without describing how a character feels and with barely three or four words, makes us know not only how they feel but also draws us into the plot, feeling afraid, sad, or intrigued. The author knows just the right notes to play and with the right tricks they get us to buy into the deception that, from that point on, you will also call art.

No doubt right about now someone may be thinking, "Is all of this really necessary to make a videogame?" No, not at all. If we want the player to walk to the right, all we have to do is show them a sign that reads: "Please walk to the right," but surely it is far more interesting and less intrusive to trick the player into walking to the right on their own, be it through the composition of the camera, the lighting, or by varying the colors.

For all of you out there who think you lack the resources or technical knowledge to identify or generate these sorts of actions, know that you already possess half of the required information, you just may not know it yet. Most techniques are based on studying stimuli and the natural reactions of human beings. My advice for anyone interested in attempting the adventure of art is that you analyze all the games, films, and books you can get your hands on. Don't focus only on what you like. You also must know what you don't like and why. Little by little you will draw your own conclusions and generate your own tools to create games that are more interesting for the player.

- What do you consider the essential elements every game developer needs to understand about art?

Though I am tempted to talk about art theories and even difficulties when creating designs, I will focus on the five most significant points.

1. *It's not pretty, it's coherent.* One of the most common mistakes is to confuse our personal tastes with what we consider a good design. My advice is to avoid using terms such as "pretty" and "ugly" when analyzing the art in a game, as these are subjective terms that actually have nothing to do with the suitability of a design.

   No doubt very few people would say the designs of monsters in horror videogames are lovely and pleasant. If something is unpleasant, it doesn't mean it can't be likable. The same could be said for games with more experimental aesthetics or less common ones. These designs may initially make you feel uncomfortable given how different they are, but generally speaking, people are more open to forgiving these sorts of designs than incoherent or inconsistent designs.

When defining the central style of a game, the most important issue is to have a clear idea of the limitations, as well as the target audience, not your personal tastes. The only personal aspect you should apply to art is your own judgment when deciding if all of the elements of the game are coherent and consistent.

2. *Rules are meant to be broken.* When I think of artistic rules and techniques, I always think of the rules for color combinations. In most cases you can take them as recommendations, but there are those who state that combining one color with another specific color is tantamount to failure.

   While it is true that there are myriad theories and techniques that facilitate the design of elements, it is equally true that for every artistic rule that says that something should not be done, there are a hundred artists that have done it successfully. At the end of the day, anything can be done, it's a matter of the right set of criteria and a lot of work.

3. *If it's not adding anything, it's taking away.* Oftentimes, especially when we design scenes/settings, we feel the need to clutter them with elements until all occupiable space is filled. This creates in most cases a lot of visual noise for the player and therefore more confusion. That is why we should carefully review each and every element we will show on screen. If you're not really sure it's adding value, then for sure cut it out from the scene.

4. *Not all game art makes it to the game.* Remember, during production there are two kinds of artwork. There is the first and clearest art, which is the final art—that is to say, all of the artistic elements that make it to the final product and are focused on the target audience.

   On the other hand, there is concept art or prototype art whose sole objective is to evoke sensations with which to foster the creativity of all departments. This kind of art does not always make it to the game, but it is essential in developing the central imagination and responsible to a large degree for everything we end up seeing.

5. *Interaction between departments.* Art is omnivorous; feed from other departments. We oftentimes forget the importance of

interacting with other departments and I don't just mean the necessary interaction in carrying out joint tasks but the ongoing enrichment of the product whereby there is "interdepartmental inspiration."

Without it, there would be no music that would evoke settings, nor settings that inspire music. Don't forget it!!

- What do you wish every developer would know when working with artists?

Most developers try to narrow down all of the areas as much as they can to channel the work of a whole bunch of departments, thinking that with that information they will facilitate and ensure a better development of the product. When an artist takes on the design of a character, he or she does not need to be told if they are short or tall, fatter or thinner. What the artist needs is to be told what makes that leading character who they are, and how the players are supposed to see them.

If you had to design a character and if you were responsible for creating that character, I would ask you about their past, what they like, their concerns, where and how they've lived. Perhaps all of that information is never revealed explicitly in the game, but because it is a part of the creation of the character, we can tell their concerns, their past, and what they are like through their posture, their complexion, their outline, garments, color, shape, and expression on their face. But we are not just talking about the character; with the character we also include the color and lighting of the scene, and we can also discuss how our character feels at a time like this or even how we as players are supposed to feel. All of these details tell the story in a much more immediate way. An image can tell in seconds what it would take cinematics minutes.

That is why it is essential that the developer know exactly the feeling they want to convey every step of the way and if there is more than one, which are more important than others. If you want to convey agility, it will not depend entirely on the mechanics, but also the form, animation, and even the music must reinforce that idea.

When working with artists, remember that they can do more than simply execute ideas. They can also help you evoke and strengthen the information that is not explicitly displayed in the direct storytelling of the game but that is essential in improving the experience of the player.

Getting Things Ready

Finally, you have learned all the things you need to know to get started with the implementation. You're ready and waiting for the go, just to realize that there is one more step to take before you should get your material into your game: the step to prepare your material for the actual implementation. The amount of work in this step largely depends on how well you prepared your material in the first place and what tools you used to create it. If you created your script in Microsoft Word and Final Draft, then you'll most likely have a lot more work ahead of you than if you created it with tools closer to the ones you use for the actual implementation. While you could decide to skip this step, doing so will most likely slow you down later and will give you more than one headache.

Preparing your material … what does this mean?

It means that you lay out your plan stating how the elements will be implemented. It means creating flowcharts and preparing character sheets and conditions required to ensure the intended flow. A script like this …

A branching script

… would turn into a graph like this

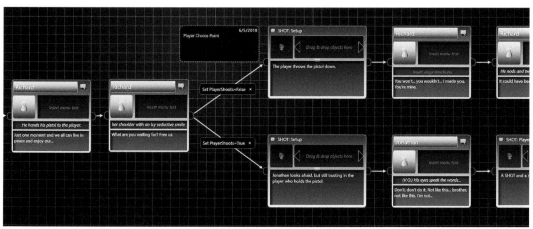

The script turned into a graph

Also, at this stage, you may want to draw some maps to visualize the flow of the individual elements and create a list of things, such as characters, items, functions, etc. you need to implement each element of your material. To a certain extent, this is your final check of whether what you planned to do will be possible and if it can be added to the game in the way you wanted it to appear.

Various tools that also make use of the skills you learned earlier in this chapter will help you to get your material prepared. We won't have the time to cover all of them, but the ones I found most useful are Articy:Draft, Twine, Inkscape, Campaign Cartographer, and YEd.

Articy:Draft, Twine, and YEd are great to create plot graphs and dialogue trees, seeing how each element is related to others and how the player would progress from one step to the next. I personally prefer Articy:Draft, as it includes features to manage backstory and lore-related items and is tailored toward narrative design. It also has the functionality to export data in a format that can be used within a game engine, so your preparation step can also become your implementation step to a certain extent. Combine this with the ability to define variables and conditions and simulate the flow through the nodes and you have a solution that can help you to prepare your content in a Choose Your Own Adventure–style fashion. It has a bit of a learning curve, but once you've worked with it for a day or two, you'll get the hang of it and things will become a lot easier.

I use Inkscape and Campaign Cartographer to create maps for the zones, lands, etc. I use in my stories. Inkscape has the benefit of making it easy to draw simple, vector-based outlines (remember, the goal is to communicate ideas, not to create a beautiful artwork), while Campaign Cartographer, as a tool made for pen-and-paper RPG developers, gives you a lot more tools to create nice-looking maps but requires a bit more time to learn.

All in all, this step is very similar to the preparation of a pen-and-paper roleplaying session and the steps you would go through when preparing to lead a session as dungeon master. If you've never played a pen-and-paper RPG, now would be the perfect time to do so. Also, many books have been written for dungeon and game masters, all including valuable information regarding how to organize and prepare narrative elements for a play session. The only thing you have to keep in mind, unlike a pen-and-paper session, is that you won't be able to adapt the content once it is published (unless you patch the content, but this can be a long and difficult process), and you won't be able to react to the players' decisions, so you have to keep all possible paths in mind when you prepare your content and implement it.

A great way to test if your material is ready is to play it with your co-workers. Most narrative elements don't require a game engine to work and can be tried out with dice and a piece of paper. This is another point where pen-and-paper RPGs can be handy. The longer you're in the industry, the more you'll start to prepare your material directly as outlined here, and this is part of developing a narrative designer's mindset. The important thing here is not to forget where you started as a writer, as backstories can be just as important as the narrative elements that make it directly into the game. One helps you to define your universe, whereas the other makes it possible that your universe can be experienced.

Finally, during your preparation, don't forget that game development is a team effort. Don't forget to prepare your material together with the other professionals involved, or else you will find out maybe too late that no one prepared the assets or code for the awesome story you had to tell. Meet often and in a productive fashion (a.k.a. try to avoid meetings that are unorganized, and set goals for each meeting if you're the organizer) to get things together. Often, other developers can give you just the idea you needed to polish your idea beyond what you ever imagined. Also, keeping everyone updated about your ideas and listening to theirs is the only guarantee that you have that you're all working together on the same game. Communication is the most important ingredient of game development and essential when you prepare your material for implementation in the final game.

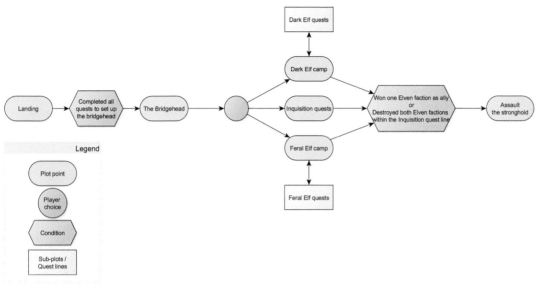

A sample map flow

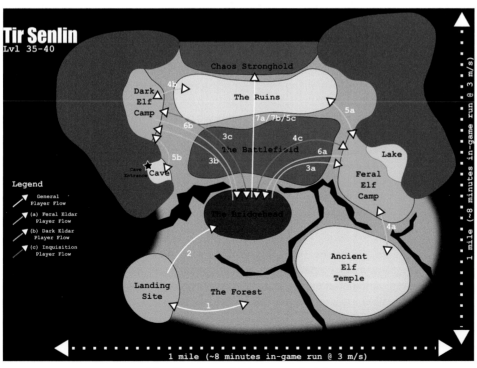

Map flow turned into a map sketch

Get It in the Game

You learned to script, you learned some art and prepared your material, and you're ready to implement it in your game. And yes, you're ready; however, I won't be able to tell you the exact steps you'll have to take to get it into your game, as every engine and game are different.

In some cases, you'll use Excel tables with custom macros to implement your material, in others you'll use an in-house scripting language or an in-house editor, and again in others you may not even be the person to implement your narrative elements. Especially in this case, it was great that you prepared everything well and that you prepared with an understanding of what language the people who will implement it speak.

But what if you are currently not working on a specific game or you just want to quickly prototype an idea to pitch it or to develop your skills?

Well, in this case, you can select an engine like Unreal Engine 4 or Unity 3D and look in their marketplaces for additions that add the features you need. This will help to work with code from another developer, which is close to what you would have to do in a development team. Besides, using one of these bigger and slightly harder-to-learn engines, you could also choose a game that comes with an editor and tries to add your content as a mod. Neverwinter Nights 2, even if it is quite old, comes with an editor that defined narrative tools back in its day. Also, StarCraft 2 comes with a powerful editor, and a lot of things can be done with it. And besides these two, there are hundreds of games out there that come with editors as well. The benefit of writing a mod is that you won't have to worry about creating any assets, as all is already prepared for the base game; also, the turnaround times to get your first element working are usually shorter than starting from scratch with one of the big engines. Yes, these games will have constraints in the form of the features they support, but working with these constraints is not much different than working on a real game where constraints come from all departments involved in the development, and often the writer is one of the last ones coming to the project (yes, we wish this would change) and thus is subject to all the decisions made before and the constraints that result from this.

If you decide to get your feet wet writing a mod or your own game, then enjoy each step you take, seeing your elements becoming part of the game, and analyze what you can learn from each of them, as this is, together with communication, the set of skills that truly will help you to implement whatever story you write into the game you're working on.

Conclusion

In this chapter, we talked a lot about what you need to know to get your stories and narrative elements into the game you're working on. We looked at the challenges of implementation (and the challenges of sharing how to do it) and the benefits of preparing your material correctly. I don't know what the most important lesson of this chapter was for you, but I hope it was that making a game is teamwork. While I may not be able to show you the steps you need to implement your material in your game, I hope I could help you understand what you can learn and do to make the implementation of your material as smooth as possible and to reward you with the great experience of seeing your content coming to life after hours of working together with your teammates.

Exercise

Write a short dialogue with at least two different endings/branches in script format. Afterward, "implement" this dialogue in one of the discussed non–game specific tools (Excel, Articy:Draft, Twine, etc.) to prepare it for an in-game experience.

Reference

J. Schell. 2010. *The Art of Game Design*, Morgan Kaufmann, Burlington, MA, USA.

CHAPTER 9

Cinematics and Dialogue

Brian Kindregan

Contents

Introduction. 106
Prerenders and In-Game Cutscenes 106
Prerenders 106
In-Game Cutscene. 108
Does This Need to Be a Cutscene?. 110
   Is the Primary Purpose Exposition?. 110
   Is It Visual? 111
   Can It Be Ambient?. 111
   Is It Emotional?. 111
   Does It Have Spectacle? 111
Kickoff Meeting 112
Play the Levels before and after the Cutscene. 114
First Draft 114
   The Central Idea. 114
   Theme. 116
   Conflict 116
   Structure. 117
   Dialogue. 118
First Round of Feedback 119
Second Draft 121
   Pacing 121
   Dialogue. 121
   Character 121
   Subtext 121
   Seek Out Help from the Art and Audio Teams. 122
Subsequent Drafts. 123
Animatic 123
   The Director. 123
   Unexpected Changes. 123
Conclusion 124
Exercise 124

Introduction

Cutscenes have been a part of video games since the earliest days. They've taken many forms and have led to some of the most powerful moments in gaming history, as well as some of the most cringeworthy. Since we'd all rather have more of the former, it's worth exploring the ups and downs of making a cutscene.

In this Chapter

- Types of cutscenes, and how to choose which type a cutscene should be
- The steps necessary to create a compelling cutscene
- Defining the central idea
- Working with a team to create the cutscene

As the lead writer of *StarCraft II: Heart of the Swarm*, I am familiar with the thinking that went into the cutscenes of that game, all the mistakes we made, and the lessons we learned along the way. So I'll use those cutscenes as examples, but everything here can apply to any sort of game, and most of the points scale from a large development team down to the three-people-in-a-basement team. There may be fewer marketing concerns at that scale, but the craft of creating the narrative for a cutscene remains the same.

Prerenders and In-Game Cutscenes

All cutscenes fit into one of two categories: prerender and in-game. These two names describe how a cutscene is made, and both have a significant impact on how it is used and what it can accomplish.

Prerenders

Prerenders are produced the same way that animated features, such as Pixar films, are made; characters and locations are modeled, and shots are animated by hand with multiple passes to add in effects and other elements. Each frame is then rendered individually, and when they are assembled in a playback format, they create a high-quality scene of animation. These scenes are then cut together with other scenes to create continuity. A custom scored soundtrack is often added to accompany specific actions on screen.

The result is a highly polished cutscene, with near limitless potential. Something that can easily be used in marketing and advertising venues to achieve the highest levels of hand-crafted cinema, and is either full of action-packed scenes or touching emotional moments.

But prerenders have drawbacks as well. First, they are expensive. A prerender requires a large crew and expensive technology. Second, they take a long time to create—which contributes to their expense. The narrative often changes quickly in game development, even late in the process, yet prerender cinematics must lock in a particular story long before the game's release—in some cases, several years before. Since game narratives can even be changed by postrelease patches, this long timeline is often untenable. The result is a cutscene style that is undeniably impressive, but expensive, slow, and dangerous to use for in-depth storytelling.

I have written a fair number of prerender cinematics, and the most successful ones were those that implied a deep story, but did not go too far, nor get too explicit, in exploring that story.

Prerender Example: Starcraft II: Heart of the Swarm, opening cinematic. If you watch this cutscene, you'll see how it is able to show huge armies fighting on a sprawling battlefield. The setting, characters, units, effects—nothing is ignored in service of the spectacle. But you'll also notice that the story is quite sparse.

The central conflict is simple—two civilizations meet in combat, and one is overwhelming. The only truly narrative moment is at the end. Sarah Kerrigan wakes up on a table in a lab, wondering if she just experienced a memory, a dream, or a prophecy. It's powerful—but also ambiguous and a bit agnostic of the story that is to come in the game. This is what prerenders demand because if you get too specific, you paint yourself into a corner.

Prerender Strengths: Incredible polish, uses for marketing, powerful moments, impeccable timing.

Prerender Weaknesses: Inflexibility, expense, long schedule.

WHAT'S IN A NAME?

Cutscenes go by many names: cutscene, cinematic, in-game or in-engine cutscene, prerender, scripted scene, interstitial, trailer, and a variety of others. These names are often used interchangeably, even though there are technical differences between them. The difference between prerender and in-game cutscenes is significant. The other names listed in this sidebar refer to fairly minor differences.

Cutscene

This is the most generic term and is used here and elsewhere to broadly mean any of the below categories.

Cinematic

This typically refers to the opening cutscene of the game and implies a higher level of polish. For the most part, this means a prerender, which is explained elsewhere. The only real takeaway is that when someone says "cinematic," they mean "this is a highly polished, important piece."

Trailer

This term is also often used to refer to the opening cutscene, although it could also mean a short video edit to be used in advertising. Often, trailers do not have full continuity and are not trying to tell a story. Instead, they are a series of exciting shots and moments designed to entice people into playing the game.

Interstitial

This name simply refers to where the cutscene will play. If a cutscene comes between two important moments in a game—say between Act I and Act II of a campaign, then it may be called an interstitial. All this really means is that it is a cutscene—of any quality, scope, and ambition—that plays between two other important elements.

In-Game Cutscene

The opposite of the prerender is the in-game cutscene. This can also be called an in-engine cutscene or a scripted scene.

An in-game cutscene is rendered in real time by the game's graphics engine. The engine creates each frame of film just as it's needed, based on code and data. Rather than animating by hand and then rendering, developers write scripts or some other indirect function that creates the appearance of a cutscene through a variety of commands. These are typically done by technical or cinematic designers, rather than animators.

For example, a cinematic designer might write scripting commands that tell a particular character to play a walk animation at double speed. At the same time, another command will tell the character to move from point A to point B. A third command will tell a second character to lock their eye line on the head of the first character.

The result is that one character walks from point A to B, very quickly, while another character watches them. If the distance covered is too great or too little for the amount of time allotted for the double-speed walk animation, then the character's feet will appear to slide across the floor, and the tech designer will need to rework the scripts.

This all sounds like a very complicated way to create a cutscene, and the result will almost always be a bit less impressive than that of a prerender. But the benefits are enormous.

- *Immersion*: The in-game cutscene will look exactly like the rest of the game. While a prerender is beautiful and full of textures and effects, it does look and feel different from the rest of the game, which forces the player to acknowledge that they are seeing a cutscene, rather than something that is happening in the game world. But an in-game cutscene maintains the same textures and feel as the rest of the game, so the transition is seamless. Immersion is not broken.
- *Volume*: Designers with the right tools can produce in-game cutscenes faster and in greater volume than prerenders. In some games, such as a Mass Effect or Dragon Age, it's vital to have many smaller but important cutscenes, including interactive conversations. In these types of situations, having a small team of designers dedicated to producing a high volume of cutscenes is vastly preferable to a huge team producing one prerender.
- *Flexibility*: In-game cutscenes are also far more flexible. Because they are the product of script commands, rather than custom animations and textures, they are able to change quickly. Taking from our earlier example, if the character's feet are sliding on the floor, the tech designer can simply change a number in a spreadsheet or script and fix the problem. If, very late in the process, it's decided that the NPC should walk more slowly, a few quick scripting commands can change that element of the cutscene.
- *Verisimilitude*: In RPGs and many other games, the player's appearance may change based on what gear they have equipped, what choices they have made, and where they are in the game's progression. When the cutscene fires, the player will want to see their character featured in it. Not just any character, but theirs, the one wearing the silly green hat or wielding the dread axe that they worked so hard to get. If the cutscene fires and the character is wearing some idealized form of their armor, it will destroy the illusion that this cutscene represents the player's character. This may be the most important thing an in-game cutscene does—the seamless transition, the ability to put the character in the action. Only an in-game cutscene can achieve this.
- *In-Game Example*: An example of an in-game cutscene would be from Heart of the Swarm when Kerrigan confronts a dying General Warfield in his citadel. This cutscene, produced by Blizzard's amazing in-game cutscene team and directed by Ben Dai, looks great and shows the results of the player's actions. Kerrigan can appear in the cutscene as a human, or as the zerg queen, depending on choices the player has made earlier in the game.

  Both versions of this cutscene are available for viewing on the internet, and I urge you to watch both and compare.

- *In-Game Strengths*: Flexibility, quick iteration, the economy of funding and effort, immersion.
- *In-Game Weaknesses*: Less visual fidelity, limited acting/emotional truth.

INITIATING A CUTSCENE

Have you ever been playing a game, and when a cutscene started, you found it incredibly jarring? Or, even worse, disruptive? This usually occurs when the developers haven't taken the trouble to initiate the cutscene properly.

There are certain times that we expect a cutscene to play, such as when we have just killed a boss or finished an act or chapter of a game. However, many games require a greater number, and more varied type, of cutscenes in the course of play. This is where it becomes important to think about how you're introducing your cutscenes.

If the player is traveling somewhere in the game world and crosses an invisible trigger, which in turn causes a cutscene to begin, this will be disruptive. The player may have been going somewhere with a purpose, or they may have been about to open a menu or their inventory to do something important. They may also have been thinking "It's late, I need to save and quit." Now they're stuck in a cutscene and afraid to skip it in case something important happens, and they're unable to watch it again later without replaying hours of the game.

The most straightforward solution to this problem is to only ever initiate a cutscene from a specific player action. So if a player runs down a hallway, avoid putting invisible triggers on the floor that start a cutscene, but absolutely launch a cutscene when the player clicks/activates the door at the end of the hall. The subsequent cutscene would begin with the player walking through the door into a new environment. The player may not know that clicking on the door will start a cutscene but has just taken an action that implies continued engagement and intent to progress.

The key here is to create a shared language with the player about what can initiate a cutscene. Using the same system for initiating cutscenes over and over will communicate to the player, even if subconsciously, that any time they open a door, load into a new area, activate an NPC, etc., a cutscene may ensue.

Does This Need to Be a Cutscene?

The remainder of this chapter will be a walkthrough of the steps involved in creating a cutscene. The very first step is to ask: "Should this be a cutscene at all?" To arrive at the answer, here are a few follow-up questions:

Is the Primary Purpose Exposition?

Are you trying to tell the player something they need to know and this is the only way you can to do it? If so, it should not be a cutscene, as there are other ways to deliver exposition. While exposition is necessary, and most cutscenes will have some, it is hardly compelling. Creating a cutscene to deliver exposition will lead to a terrible cutscene. In turn, this will lose the trust of the player, and they will reach for the escape/skip button as soon as all subsequent cutscenes start.

For examples of other ways to deliver exposition, please see the "Exposition" sidebar later in this chapter.

Is It Visual?

Cutscenes excel at visual storytelling, from a huge space battle to a subtle expression. However, if your cutscene is going to consist of two characters standing in a hallway having a long conversation, you may be using the wrong tool for this job.

There are almost always better ways to present nonvisual story beats. Quests, journal entries, ambient dialogue, mini-games, and a variety of other game features can all convey narrative and character development, albeit in an inherently less visual manner.

Can It Be Ambient?

A cutscene interrupts the player's experience and forces them to watch passively. If there is any way to tell the story in the background and let the player choose whether to listen, that is preferable.

Is It Emotional?

Cutscenes are generally the best way to convey conflicted, complex emotions, due to the extra control of face effects and voice. If you need a scene with that level of emotional depth in your storytelling, it might be a good candidate for a cutscene.

Does It Have Spectacle?

Another good reason to go to a cutscene is because it has a high degree of spectacle or visual drama that would feel underwhelming in the game view. It may seem shallow to suggest that a story moment should be a cutscene simply because it has spectacle, but the truth is that sometimes a moment needs to have that level of visual excitement to sell an important feeling.

If you have a StarCraft II mission set in a base that is being assaulted by Battlecruisers, you could set it up in the game by showing the Battlecruisers in standard gameplay. In that case, you would see small Battlecruisers, viewed from above, shooting at even smaller units below them.

Or you could show the attack in a cutscene, using camera angles to drive home the power and terror of such an attack. To get a sense of what that looks like, I would urge you to find the *StarCraft II: Heart of the Swarm* cinematic called "Get It Together," which is available for viewing on the internet.

However, this cutscene is not simply spectacle for spectacle's sake. Instead, the powerful imagery adds an incredible level of tension to the mission that follows. As the player races their units through the facility, they feel the urgency and danger each time the screen shakes or enemy pods burst through the ceiling. The power of these feelings will be a direct result of the cutscene, which set the tone and pace of the entire mission.

If you're sure that this moment must be a cutscene and that the end result will be a compelling, powerful presentation, then it's time to start the real work, by which I mean … meetings!

WE NEVER USE CUTSCENES!

Over the years, I've encountered a number of developers who have told me of their aspiration or practice to make games with no cutscenes at all. It's an outdated storytelling technique for games. It disrupts gameplay and destroys immersion. They're expensive and unwieldy to make.

These things may all be true, in certain situations, on certain games, and if certain mistakes are made. I'm not a particular proponent of cutscenes, but I'm also not unilaterally opposed to them. My philosophy is "the right tool for the job."

Sometimes, a cutscene is exactly the wrong tool for the job, and the resistance to cutscenes likely springs from the many times they were used poorly in the past. They have been misused to deliver exposition that could have been expressed through gameplay, or for frivolous moments, or just because the developers really wanted a cutscene in that spot for no good reason.

However, sometimes a cutscene is exactly the right tool for the job. A cutscene can still do things no other storytelling technique can, and sometimes it can concentrate the drama, power, and danger of a moment into one experience in a way no other technique can.

You've probably noticed that this chapter contains many steps that precede writing the first draft. All of these steps are designed to help you make sure that the cutscene is the right tool for this job.

If you don't need a cutscene, don't use it. But when the moment is right, embrace the power of the cutscene.

Kickoff Meeting

The next step is to gather all the stakeholders in a room and talk about the cutscene. Even in-game cutscenes require a great deal of work, and it's important to get everyone on the same page early. This includes the directors, artists, animators, storyboard artists who will work on the cutscene, and designers who are working on the levels before and after the cutscene. Depending on the studio and the situation, perhaps marketing, community, or public relations people should be present as well. Even on very small teams, it's a good idea to get everyone in a room and talk it over.

The point of the meeting is simply to discuss the high-level goals of the cutscene. What are the important things that must be accomplished here? Not just narratively, but in every way. What is the scope? How much time and money can be devoted to the cutscene, and how does that square with the creative goals? This is also a useful step from a tactical standpoint. Giving the stakeholders a chance to discuss the cutscene will make them much more likely to buy into the final product later.

A checklist for topics at this meeting might look like this:

- Type of cutscene
- Creative goals
- Marketing goals
- Scope
- Timeline

IN THE SPOTLIGHT

Cutscenes garner a great deal of attention during development. When work begins on a cutscene, people who aren't normally involved in narrative features often attend these meetings. Indeed, sometimes people who are not even directly working on the development of the game will be there, offering many opinions.

There are many reasons for this. For example, cutscenes are among the strongest marketing tools that come out of developing a game, so marketing and public relations professionals may take an interest. At larger studios, high-level franchise development professionals who don't necessarily get into the day-to-day narrative may also wish to be involved, as the cutscene can come to represent an aspect of the entire intellectual property.

Consider the original opening cinematic of World of Warcraft. It was released many years ago and has been followed by much more cinematics from the same game, yet it remains an iconic representation of the World of Warcraft intellectual property.

Another reason for this intense interest, of course, is that telling stories in cutscenes is fun, and seems easy if you don't have to do the actual work. Even so, it's best to approach this intense interest as a helpful tool rather than an annoyance. The differing perspectives that come from the multidisciplinary review will make the final product stronger and more compelling. Many of the people in the room will have a "fresh eye," and if the cutscene is complex enough to confuse them, it's likely going to do the same thing to the part of your audience who pays closer attention to cutscenes than to the overall game narrative.

Play the Levels before and after the Cutscene

If the level/mission/quest that precedes the cutscene is in any kind of playable shape, you should run through it several times. Your goal is to understand the momentum, tempo, and emotional energy that the player will be feeling as they cruise into this cutscene. This is the context the cutscene will live in, and if you don't have a firm grasp on it, you'll likely make mistakes in its execution.

Next, you should play the level/mission/quest that immediately follows the cutscene, for the same reason. You want to have a firm grasp on how the player transitions out of the cutscene and back into gameplay. Do the tempo and energy of the two match? Or are they off?

It's vital that you understand this context, as almost nobody else on the project will have this holistic view. The filmmakers working on the cutscene will be looking at it in a vacuum—their job is to make a great cutscene. The designers who do think about the levels before and after are rarely as involved in the development of the cutscene as you. You are the point of continuity, and so it falls to you to research it, understand it, and make it work.

Keywords for this research: tempo, tone, feel, energy, emotionality.

First Draft

Well, now you've done it. You've gone and committed to doing a cutscene. So what do you pay attention to in writing the first draft? Hopefully, you have some guidance from that kickoff meeting, and some wisdom from your thoughts on whether this needs to be a cutscene.

The Central Idea

As you explore the first draft, working on basic blocking, the conflict that is introduced, rises, and climaxes, there is one question to keep in mind at all times: What is the central idea?

The explanation that follows is the most important concept in this chapter. As a cutscene is developed, various forces will pull and push it—time, money, new ideas, old ideas that rise like zombies, new people, politics, design changes—the list goes on and on. You will fight many battles, and, spoiler alert, you won't win all of them. You may not even win most of them. If you're not careful, the cutscene will get away from you. It will turn out to be something you don't recognize, and you won't even be entirely sure what it's doing here and what it wants.

This is where the central idea comes in. Early on, you must decide what part of this cutscene—what concept, moment, interaction, or beat—is the heart of the matter. Remember when you spent time thinking about why this must be a cutscene? Recall that meeting you had about why everyone cared? Those are part of the equation. Now you need to take a moment and just be a storyteller. Think about what really matters narratively, why you care, and what you (and by extension, the story) need from this cutscene.

This is your central idea. As various pressures exert themselves upon the cutscene, you need to decide where you can compromise, where you can fight back but ultimately retreat, and where you will stand firm, ready to die on a hilltop. As new changes come in, you can evaluate them against your central idea. Does this change or note affect something you like a great deal, but that is not part of the central idea? Then sacrifice it if you must. As one experienced television showrunner once said, "You buy your nos with yeses." That is to say, every time you say yes to a note, it creates a greater understanding that you are a collaborator, someone willing to accept the ideas of others if they are better than yours, or at least as good as yours. So on those occasions when you say no, people notice. They understand that you are saying no because you genuinely believe this new idea would be damaging to the cutscene.

If that new idea or feedback does affect the central idea, then your obligation is to say no and stand against it.

The reason you must define this central idea from the beginning is that your instinct as a creative storyteller will be to fight many of the changes. You will feel that many of them are bad, they damage the original vision, and they are just making the cutscene worse! But it's not true. Some ideas are just as good as your original idea, and you need to find a way to tell the difference. The central idea is the tool that lets you do this. Once you know what the scene is really about, and what it is not really about, everything becomes much simpler.

It is hard to give examples of phrases that represent a central idea because it can be wildly different for each cutscene. Below are a few from cutscenes I've worked on.

Examples:

- Jane represents embracing hope, Frank represents clinging to hate, and that is their central conflict.
- Dredlord Angura must empty herself of anger before she can see the truth.
- Jane has gained great power, and she is going to use it to get revenge on Frank.
- Even as she dies, Dredlord Angura will protect her men.
- Jane cares only about finding Frank, even as destruction rains down around her.

As you can see, the central idea can feel like a trite summary of the cutscene narrative, and that's okay. This is meant to be so bare bones that it helps make clear which changes damage the cutscene and which support it.

Theme

In defining your central idea, you have likely given some thought to the theme of the cutscene. If you haven't devoted thought to the theme, now would be the time. I would take the central idea as your guide since this theme is a core part of the cutscene.

It's important to note that a theme is not a message like "crime doesn't pay" or "no good deed goes unpunished." Your cutscene does not necessarily need a message or moral. The theme is instead the topic that the cutscene is examining.

Example themes:

- Betrayal
- Who has the power in this relationship?
- Passion vs strategy
- New vs old
- Coming home from a long journey

As you can see, many of these are related to the central idea. There is a great deal of overlap, but the central idea is a specific component of this cutscene and is used to keep it on a tight track, while the theme is a statement about the overall feel that the cutscene is examining. The theme can be used to talk to others on the development team and get them thinking about the cutscene creatively.

Conflict

The next question is about the central conflict of the scene. Just like any dramatic scene created in theatre, film, or any other performance media, conflict is the engine that will drive your scene. This conflict may involve giant, sweaty, armored soldiers swinging axes or elite assassins firing guns. Or it may involve nobles sipping tea and exchanging devastating insults veiled as polite conversation. Maybe it's a raised eyebrow at just the right moment. It could be a family fleeing from a hurricane and a child realizing that she's lost track of the family dog. Conflict can take many forms, but you as the writer must always understand a few things about it:

- How is the conflict introduced? Is the conflict already known at the start of the cutscene? Or must it be introduced in the opening moments? If so, how long will it take for the conflict to become clear?
- How does it build? Once the conflict is introduced, the stakes must escalate, and the conflict must develop.
- How does it turn? Simply introducing a conflict and pumping it up is not enough. Instead, the conflict must turn and evolve.

Example:

For the first in-game cutscene of *StarCraft II: Heart of the Swarm*, titled "Hopes and Fears," we introduced a basic conflict early on: Jim Raynor is trying to get access to Sarah Kerrigan, the woman he loves. He faces a series of obstacles along the way—people trying to keep him out of the process and away from her. He overcomes several obstacles and seems to achieve his goal at last—he gets a few moments alone with Kerrigan. Surely, this is victory?

But then the conflict takes a turn. Jim's vision of a perfect future with Sarah is shattered by an insurmountable problem—Sarah does not share his vision. While he envisions a retreat from the greater conflict of the Koprulu sector, Sarah holds tight to a vision of blood-drenched revenge and makes it clear to him that they will never have anything of significance until she has achieved that revenge.

This is the classic conflict turn. After telling the audience "Here's what's at stake and here is what the people in this cutscene care about," you can reframe the entire context. Suddenly everything is worse, the stakes are greater, and the apparent solution is clearly inadequate. This is how you turn conflict.

- How does it resolve? Naturally, the final question is how the conflict resolves. Is there some sort of closure that leads us to feel like this matter is done? One way in which cutscenes are different from other filmic narratives is that they sometimes must not resolve their conflict. That is to say, if you saw a film where the central conflict was not resolved, you would likely feel cheated. But a game cutscene sometimes must introduce conflict without resolving it because that conflict will very likely be a continuing part of the game, and will likely be addressed through player actions.
- If the conflict does not resolve, then how does the cutscene come to a natural end? It can be very difficult to end a cutscene that does not have a natural resolution to the conflict. You certainly don't want the cutscene to feel as if it just stops. Therefore you need to find a way to resolve some other part of the conflict or end in a cliffhanger fashion that can lead into gameplay, or find some other kind of natural end to the cutscene.

Structure

The way I've outlined conflict above suggests a tight structure for the cutscene, and working through the conflict may be enough. But at this point in your first draft, it is worthwhile to take a step back and consider the entire cutscene holistically. You've already thought about how the player will feel going into the cutscene, so how does the structure work with that?

How quickly do we get to the introduction of conflict? Are we taking the time to establish the setting so that it can have an influence on the rest of the scene? Or are we taking too much time? Where in the flow of the cutscene does the conflict turn? In the first, second, or final third? How close to the climax and/or resolution? How quickly can we get out of the cutscene after the resolution or closure? Is the cutscene setting anything up for future story beats, and if so, where in the flow should that fall? As with all things in game writing, economy and tight pacing are always a requisite part of any solution.

Much of this may shift in subsequent drafts, so everything you do during this step-back/holistic look you will need to do again on each draft, as it is easy for the structure to become frayed, or even torn, by multiple rewrites.

Dialogue

Once you have the basic structure of your first draft, it's time to go through and polish all the dialogue.

Wait, you ask, why am I polishing dialogue on a first draft? Aren't I going to end up rewriting all of it? The answer is that yes, you will rewrite most or all of it, but you must do this anyway. The reason is that most people, even some writers, are unable to read "rough" or "first-pass" dialogue without judging it the way they would the final product. And, to be fair, that is a hard skill to develop anyway, as it requires reading something that has obvious flaws, but focusing on bigger issues and not letting those obvious flaws affect your feedback about the overall quality of the piece.

If you send out a first draft to people for feedback and it has temp or rough dialogue, your feedback will be contaminated. Even people who don't openly say that they did not like your dialogue will have problems with the characters and their interactions because they did not like the dialogue.

Even worse, you will likely have this exchange:

> *Note Giver:* I didn't like Dredlord Angura's line in this scene.
> *Writer:* Oh, that dialogue is all temp. Please focus on the structure and themes of the piece. I'll make the dialogue great later, I promise.
> *Note Giver:* Mhm. Well, that moment isn't working, and I'd like to fix it now.
> *Writer:* Maybe you feel like that moment isn't working because you didn't like the line?
> *Note Giver:* No, I'm sure it's because the moment is not working.

Now you're way off track, but whoever is critiquing you is focused on that line and there's no way around it.

So you must polish the dialogue, make it as strong, economical, and punchy as you can so that the feedback you get will focus on the important things—central idea, themes, structure, and conflict.

It is not unusual to become enamored of dialogue after having put a lot of work into it, and that is a good sign, as it shows you care about your work. However, you must be careful at this stage not to become precious or protective of your dialogue, as it has a high likelihood of being changed.

EXPOSITION

Unfortunately, every game narrative requires some level of exposition. These are simply things that the player must understand in order to follow the story and the arc of the game. As mentioned elsewhere, however, this does not make them compelling. And so, we always struggle to find a way to let the player know things that are important without boring them.

You could define expositional dialogue as those lines where a character says something for no other reason than to let the player know that something is a fact.

For example: "Jane, you're my sister and I love you, but you've got to stop doing this." The line is ostensibly to convey that the character wants to confront Jane and tell her to stop. But we all sense that the writer wanted us to know that Jane is the character's sister.

Another example: "As you know, general, we have been at war for six years." Both characters clearly know this, and no one would ever need to say this in real life.

If possible, make exposition ambient or opt-in in some way. If the player decides they don't need to know this and would rather be confused, let them. If you force them to learn something, you're telling them that it is so vital that their entire play experience will be broken by missing it. Very few bits of exposition rise to that standard.

Another key concept when it comes to exposition is importance. One common mistake is assuming that the player needs to know far more than they actually do. Take a look at the information being offered and ask what happens if the player doesn't know it. Will it completely destroy the game for them? Or will they simply keep playing, a bit unsure about a few things? The answer may surprise you.

The other element is timing. Wait until the player absolutely needs to know something. Do they truly need to know it right now? The best way to deliver exposition is to reveal it to the player after they have already started wondering about it. When you crowd the player with information about something they don't think they need to know, it feels intrusive. If, however, something is going on and it doesn't seem to make sense at first glance, the player will begin to wonder about it. Then, when the exposition shows up and reveals the answer, it will feel rewarding and helpful.

The timing of exposition is key. In fact, I would choose to confuse a player before boring them. Obviously, the best way is to do neither, but if a choice must be made, at least confusion can serve as intrigue that will drive the player onward. If they're bored, there's plenty of other exciting games out there to play.

First Round of Feedback

When you're happy with your first draft, or more likely when you've run out of time, send it out for feedback. Once it is out in the wild, find something else to work on, and banish this script from your mind. Don't think about it. This can be hard to do but is necessary to provide clarity in the upcoming round of feedback. You need some distance.

Only when it is time to start getting feedback from others should you crack open the script and give it another read. Hopefully, you've been away long enough to see it with a fresh eye. Glaring problems will sometimes jump out at you, and you won't believe that you did not see these earlier.

You'll think: "Did I really send this out for people to read?"

This is good. It means you're already thinking about how to improve the cutscene, and when people start to give you feedback about that very problem, you'll have already had a chance to think about good fixes.

The proper way to deal with feedback is a much larger topic that encompasses all of game writing, and so is beyond the scope of this chapter, but a few thoughts follow:

Be open to all of it, and remember that all of the professionals giving you feedback have their own filter, based on their particular discipline. This means they may see valid problems that you do not.

Your main goal here is to guide the script through the feedback process, using the opinions and insights of others to improve it, to make it stronger and fix its problems. But also to defend that central idea. It is remarkably easy for that central idea to disappear through multiple rounds of feedback. This is another moment at which having a clearly articulated central idea becomes vital. You should test every solution you or anyone else proposes against that central idea. If a proposed change doesn't violate the central idea, it is safe to implement, if it makes the script better.

The other high-level concept to keep in mind with feedback is that when people say there is a problem, they are almost always right. Something pinged them as they read the script, and there's a great chance it will ping many other people when they watch the final cutscene.

However, when they define what that problem is, or even when they pinpoint the spot where the problem exists, they are almost always wrong. Oftentimes people will say that a beat feels inauthentic, and suggest many changes for that beat. But the reality is that this beat feels inauthentic because the beat that preceded it did not set it up well or did not flow into it well.

When people giving feedback suggest a fix for the problem they've articulated, they are even more likely to be wrong. This is not because they are untalented. Instead, as we discussed in the previous paragraph, they likely have not identified the true source of the problem, so their intended solution won't work.

As the storyteller, it is your job to talk to them about their concern and try to decode what is actually wrong. It's a good idea to let people know you'll be asking them about their feedback to better understand, so they don't interpret your barrage of questions as skeptical defensiveness.

Second Draft

The second draft is your attempt to revise the script in order to address all the feedback that seems relevant. It may end up being incremental changes, or it may be a page-one rewrite. The notes and feedback will determine that. So long as you keep that central idea in mind, and keep that pure, the scale of the rewrite is irrelevant—aside from the amount of work you must put into it.

The second draft also brings a few new concerns to the process.

Pacing

Now that the overall shape of the cutscene is becoming clear, you should consider its speed. How fast does it move? Is there fat you can cut? Does every character need to be present? Do you need all these locations?

I once had a producer cut two of the three proposed locations in a cutscene for logistical reasons. I had to revise the script heavily to deal with this new reality of having one location. In doing so, I think the script got significantly stronger, particularly the pacing.

Dialogue

Yes, once again, you must create polished, sparkling dialogue. This draft, and every draft. However, now that you've got a clear sense of the conflict, you can also take a second look at the dialogue with an eye toward character and subtext.

Character

This is just a simple matter of reading the lines out loud a few times and thinking about how this character expresses themselves. Are there ways that Dredlord Angura would say this line that no one else would? If the current construction of the line feels like it could be said by any character, you can probably do something to make it more specific to the character who actually does say it.

Subtext

Characters are often driven by a deeper emotion or intention than their words would suggest.

Simple Example:

Jane comes home to discover that her roommate, Frank, has not done the dishes when it was his turn. So Jane tears into Frank. In detail. When he shrugs an apology, she thinks it's not enough and attacks again.

121

From this, you may think that Jane takes dish hygiene very seriously. But there are a variety of other things that could be going on under the surface. Perhaps Jane feels that Frank does not pull his weight around the house in general, and the dishes are simply the straw that broke the camel's back. Going deeper, perhaps Jane is regretting her decision to let Frank stay at her apartment, and so, without even realizing it herself, is starting to attack him at every opportunity, in hopes that he'll leave. Perhaps Jane is deeply angry about something else entirely and Frank just happened to be the first target.

For any of those to be clear, the player would need to have further context outside of the cutscene, and they often will. This is why cutscenes are great opportunities to write dialogue with subtext.

I'm not suggesting you try to layer in some subtle subtext to your existing dialogue, because that would require changing many things outside the cutscene. However, much of the dialogue in your first pass may actually be the subtext. That is to say, in your quest to be economical and clear, you may have written a scene in which all your characters say exactly what they mean. The second draft is your chance to revise the scene so that the things the characters said so bluntly in the first draft are revised to feel more natural, with the original meaning still layered in.

Taking from our previous example:

In the first draft, Jane, looking at the dirty dishes, said:

> You're a useless roommate, and I regret letting you move in. I want you gone! Get out!

In the second draft, Jane, looking at the dirty dishes, could say:

> When I let you move in, I didn't know you were the laziest. How hard is it to do the dishes? Are you even trying?

The first line is the subtext of the second. Jane wants him gone, but she says it in a way that is far more natural, and entertaining. The "Are you even trying?" is the telling part, because this is a question that is usually only asked by someone at the end of their rope. This also lets the conflict build a bit more as Frank has a chance to defend himself.

Seek Out Help from the Art and Audio Teams

This is a visual medium, and if you didn't get much feedback from the art team about the visual excitement and visual aesthetic of the script, something is wrong. During the second draft, it is incumbent upon you to seek out some of the artists and discuss how or if the cutscene could be more visual. The same applies to the audio team. These are people who can make the cutscene support your central idea in a much stronger way, and it's a good idea to get them involved and activated as soon as possible.

Subsequent Drafts

When the second draft is ready, send it out as you did the first, and once again, put it from your mind. From this point on, you will be repeating most of the steps of the second draft: incorporate feedback, stick to the central idea, see what you can polish.

Animatic

The final part of making the cutscene that we will take a look at is the animatic. This is a rough version of the film made with hand-drawn storyboards and cut together to simulate the final film. Not all cutscenes get one. Scripted scenes tend to simply have a rough cut of the cutscene itself. But if you are fortunate enough to work on a cutscene with a storyboard team who will create an animatic for it, there are a few things to keep in mind:

The Director

At this point in the process, you and the director should feel like collaborators. But this is the step where the director begins to take more control of the cutscene, and your involvement diminishes. This is perfectly normal, as they have many skills and concerns about how to actually make the cutscene, which have little or nothing to do with narrative.

Hopefully, you have developed a good relationship with the director so they know that if a major narrative change comes up after you've stepped out of the process, they should loop you back in.

Unexpected Changes

As the storyboard artists and director start to flex their creative muscles, they may add new ideas or render an idea in a way you did not expect. At this point in the process, you've lived with the cutscene for a while and have had many discussions about it, and it may feel like people are just changing it with no regard to all the thinking and planning that went into it. This is a good moment to sit back and take a deep breath. See where these changes go.

And remember, the director has been along for this ride with you, so they will also know the areas where it may need to be pulled back. The basic takeaway is to make sure you and the director have a strong bond of trust and mutual respect. That will go a long way toward keeping the cutscene in good shape as it moves through production.

Conclusion

Writing a cutscene can be a quick and simple matter of jotting a few words down or a herculean task that, off and on, takes several months. It may be entirely your vision, or you may spend much of your time in meetings, wrangling diverse opinions.

The key to navigating the process, no matter how vast it becomes, is to take each step by itself and define those key principles that guide you through each of those steps. It is helpful to articulate them to yourself along the way.

The result is going to be exciting!

Exercise

Define a central idea for a cutscene. Spend the time to come up with a well-thought-out and compelling idea. Now write a first draft of the cutscene. Limit yourself to three or four screenplay-format pages.

Now try to write a second draft that uses the same characters, but changes every beat of the plot. Can you retain that central idea, even when everything else is changing? The best way to gauge your success is to show both drafts to others and see if they feel that the central idea of both scripts is the same.

CHAPTER 10

Get This, Kill That, Talk with … Mission and Quest Design

Tobias Heussner

Contents

Introduction to Missions and Quests 125
What Is a Quest? 127
    Quest Design and Motivation 132
    Quest Design and Environmental Storytelling 133
    Quest Design and Exposition 135
    Focus and Progression in Quest Design 136
    A Sample Quest Design Flow 139
        Step 1: The Background 139
        Step 2: The High Concept 139
        Step 3: General Information 140
        Step 4: General Information, The Quest Graph 141
        Step 5: General Information, The Map 141
        Step 6: A First Quest, The Summary 142
        Step 7: A First Quest, Player Information 142
        Step 8: A First Quest, Gameplay Information 142
Conclusion 143
Exercise 143
Reference 143

Introduction to Missions and Quests

Besides writing beautiful dialogues, cinematics and an engaging backstory, one of the most common tasks for narrative designers and game writers is the development of missions, tasks, quests and whatever else you like to call them. Please note that in this chapter, the terms quests, tasks etc. are used to describe general concepts, focusing mostly on the way they are used in RPGs and MMORPGs. For the sake of generalization and to make it easier to follow the content, the fine nuances of quests and missions etc. are omitted.

In this Chapter

- What is a quest?
- How do quests and story relate to each other?
- How can we approach the design of a quest?

TASK, MISSION, QUEST OR WHAT?

Definitions in the game industry are rare and often the terms used depend on a studio's culture and background. I personally like to separate tasks, quests and missions as follows, but, again, that is how I use these terms, and other developers may define them differently. If you're unsure that you and your teammate are talking about the same concept in a conversation … it never hurts to ask and clarify terms.

Tasks are single objectives and the smallest element in quest design. They describe exactly one goal linked to one activity.

Quests are a collection of one or more tasks and provide these tasks with a narrative framework. Quests are given by entities that have the quest giver attribute, in general can be given at any time during the gameplay and usually offer a certain flexibility in how they can be completed by the players.

Missions are a collection of tasks, usually featuring primary and secondary objectives from which only the primary tasks must be completed. They are usually given between gameplay elements and frame the individual gameplay sections. They can be compared to the military missions given to soldiers before they go into action.

Writing and developing quests is a very broad and wide field and, basically, universally always depend on each specific game you're working on and its design and mechanics. Quests will make use of these mechanics and aim, besides creating a beautiful atmosphere, to evoke specific emotional reactions in the players and engage them with the game and its world. It is a complex relationship and not always is it clear where dynamics, as a result of the interactions of the player with the game, drive them and where the plot drives the player. Quest design also always has two key aspects, the mechanical or gameplay aspect and the narrative aspect. While as a narrative designer, your focus clearly will be on the narrative aspect, you cannot ignore the mechanical one, as this is the part that ties your narrative together with the gameplay. Using the same mechanic over and over is just as boring as telling the entire story without showing it. As a narrative designer, your key principle needs to be *Play, don't tell!* You should always seek ways, especially in quest design, of combining game mechanics with narrative elements and to use the identified mechanics to show your narrative elements and engage the players on an emotional journey.

GAME DESIGN FUNDAMENTALS

Even if the actual system design is not the responsibility of a narrative designer, it is always good to know some of the key principles and terms. Two very important game design concepts are mechanics and dynamics.

1. *Mechanics* are the rules of a game and represent the things players can do. In *Super Mario Bros.*, you need to jump, run, collect and fire. This is a very simplified view of the game, but all the things mentioned are the mechanics of the game.
2. *Dynamics* are the things players do with the mechanics and how they try to optimize or use them to maximize their chance to win. In *Super Mario Bros.*, players invented new terms and tactics to achieve the fastest playthrough time. One of them is the "Ricochet Jump," hitting a block while jumping and bouncing back to kill an enemy. Most dynamics are invented in multiplayer scenarios because the social aspect of gaming gives a lot of room for new dynamics and player creativity.

Just like game designers use mechanics (as gameplay) to create and encourage the creation of dynamics, which should result in an entertaining experience, you as a storyteller should use them to drive your story and create the desired emotional reactions.

But if quests so highly depend on the actual design, can we actually ask and know what, in general, a quest is without reinventing the wheel repeatedly? Can we lay down some rules or guidelines, if everything depends on specific mechanics?

Yes, and I hope with this chapter to help you get started with quest design and to share some of the things I have learned over the years. Yet, nothing in this chapter will be the ultimate silver bullet when approaching quest design, and the only one universal rule is: iteration, iteration and iteration. Testing your quests with your co-workers, with the designers and even with friends during board game or roleplaying nights is the key to becoming a better quest designer. Understanding human psychology and leading players without limiting their agency in strict, artificial ways leads to engaging quests. It's always easy to force someone to do something, but the art is to engage them in such a way that they want to do it and they are curious about what happens next.

What Is a Quest?

A common mistake in quest design is to see quests as pure mechanics without any relation to narrative elements. Quests are often designed based on a set of mechanics, and narrative elements are later added as flavor, like frosting on a cake. This disconnection, however, leads also to a disconnected experience, because, as discussed earlier, mechanical and narrative aspects form a symbiotic relationship in quest design. To avoid disconnecting these elements from each other and to understand what a complete quest is, we need to investigate the basic definition of the term "story" and then connect it with the principles of game design.

*A **story** is a directed collection of experiences and adventures of one or more character(s). These characters want something and must overcome obstacles to get it. This journey is told in a linear fashion.*

A WORD ON LINEAR AND NONLINEAR

Today many games are advertised as having nonlinear stories; however, if we look at the definition of the story, we see that linearity is an integral part of a story, so on a first look, nonlinear stories are impossible. Is this true?

Yes and no.

We must consider that stories are the journey/experience of one or more specific characters, the protagonists. In most games, the protagonist is the player as she or he plays the game. The player's experience will be linear as they progress through the plot. They will experience one specific version of the plot per playthrough. This is where we see the linearity of stories come into effect. But, we also see that this experience is bound to a specific player; thus, other players may experience different stories as they take a different path through the plot, if the plot allows multiple paths. This makes the plot, the underlying construct of each story and which is developed by us, nonlinear. So, we can conclude that stories are always linear, while plots, depending on their design, can be either linear or nonlinear.

Now that we have a definition of what story means, we can look at it and identify individual, essential elements. We see that each story needs characters, that it needs experiences or obstacles that lead to these experiences when the characters overcome them and that it implies a structure, a plot, in which the individual elements are sorted.

So how do quests fit into this picture?

Are they characters? No.
Are they the goal of the characters? No.
Are they the plot? No.

They are the obstacles, the tasks the characters must overcome to achieve their goal. This a very generalized view of the story and its relationship to quests. It is generalized because, based on the actual design of a game, the definition of what the obstacles are that the players must overcome can vary greatly. For quest design, we narrow these obstacles down to the ones that the players as characters in a plot must overcome to experience a story. We exclude all obstacles purely based on game mechanics without any relation to the narrative part of the game; for example, opponents and traps in a platformer that the players must overcome by jumping over them, thus testing only the player's skills, are excluded. We look at obstacles you would mention when telling the story of the game in the form of a screenplay.

Another factor that needs to be taken into account is that games usually feature more than a couple of quests. They usually feature a substantial number, keeping the time needed for each of the quests short to fit better to common play session times and thus guarantee that players can enjoy them within one to two play sessions. This leads to networks and chains of quests that can but don't have to relate to each other. It creates additional layers, which can be complete plots in and of themselves, and in the end, it is the combination of all layers that form the overall plot of the game. Depending on the number of layers and how they relate to each other, the role of an individual quest changes.

As quest design is such a complex topic and varies from game to game; we'll consider for the following part a stereotypical MMORPG with a by-now-stereotypical quest system as the basis for our discussion, attempting to define common elements.

In our game, the individual tasks of a quest function like story beats would work in a TV screenplay. The individual quests work like scenes, and a chain of quests works like an episode. The sum of episodes represents a season, and several episodes form the overarching plot of the entire show.

A WORD ON LENGTH

The length of an individual quest and of quest chains can vary greatly and depends mostly on the genre of your game. Some genres allow longer times, while others expect shorter ones. For example, it usually takes one hour to an hour and a half to finish an RTS mission, while most MMORPG quests are way shorter. In general, my recommendation is to consider your expected average play session length and adapt your quests so that a player can finish at least one to two per play session. This usually means that your quests should require an engagement between 15 and 45 minutes. Please note that this is a rule of thumb, not a general one-size-fits-all solution. Tutorial or introductory quests may be a lot shorter, and players can have overarching quests that require several hours or more to be solved. The key is finding the right balance and to keep your players engaged from play session to play session.

The Road

An important concept that all writers need to keep in mind is the concept of the core mechanics, or the road, as it is sometimes called.

The road describes the core activity of a game and its core mechanic; it is the predominant set of mechanics the players use to experience a specific game. Unless you're working on a game where the narrative is part of the core mechanics (Disclaimer: It rarely is, even in the most story-heavy RPGs), narrative elements are usually auxiliary mechanics, which make a road more beautiful, but should in no way block it.

We all love to walk or drive along beautiful roads but usually dislike roads that are cluttered with obstacles. The same is true for game design. The best games have very clear core mechanics, a clear road that was made beautiful using auxiliary mechanics.

The road

A cluttered road

A beautiful road

We see how we can use traditional storytelling techniques to create engagement and emotional experiences without depending too much on the actual mechanics of the game. Knowing how each individual element contributes to the whole is the essence of narrative design, yes, of game design in general. Suddenly, we no longer talk about "get this or that" but see the "a character wants A and needs to overcome B." We even can pull ourselves further away from the individual quests and see the net of scenes and elements that form the layered plot that forms our overarching narrative. We can start asking ourselves for each quest: "Where does it fit in the overarching narrative?" "What does the player know?" "Where does the player need to go?" and "How should the player feel in this moment?"

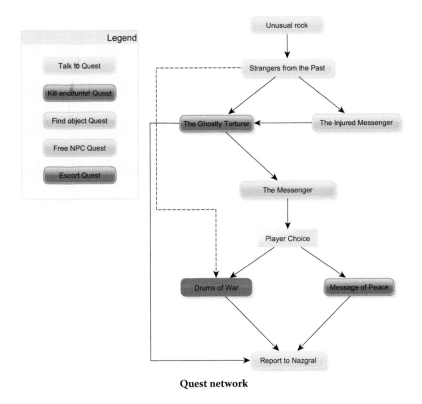

Quest network

Quest Design and Motivation

We have seen how quest design and traditional storytelling are related to each other. We have discovered that quests primarily form the obstacles the protagonist must overcome. However, if we're looking at quests only in the sense of where they fit in the overall narrative and as pure obstacles, we may forget that characters in stories must overcome obstacles because these obstacles hinder them from achieving their goal. This raises the essential question of purpose. We need to answer, "Why does a character have to overcome a specific obstacle?" "Why should the character care?" or "Why is it important for the quest giver to overcome this obstacle?"

Answering the "Why?" question is a powerful tool, as it connects us with the emotional world of a character and with the essence of game design. Game design is about entertaining people with meaningful choices in the context of a game. Knowing the purpose of a quest helps us to support the design of the game with meaningful content. It is in this "Why?" that we find the answer to our quest, that is, how to leave behind the mechanical view of a quest and make even a simple "collect X of Y" meaningful.

Answering the question of purpose leads us to the question of consequences. What are the consequences of choices the player makes as they overcome the obstacles? How does it affect the world? How does it affect them?

We must extend our "Why?" questions to "Why must a character overcome this obstacle and what consequences result from the way the character overcame it?"

Thinking about the consequences not only puts a quest in the plot, it provides clues on how the narrative progresses after a given quest. It helps to better understand the bigger picture and to connect an individual quest or quest chain with the overall multiple paths through this plot, which in the end form the stories the players experience and keep them motivated to continue playing.

Purpose and consequence form the causality of our narrations. Causality as an abstraction of a world's progress is deeply connected to our very own world and our experiences; thus, using it in our artificial worlds and narrations connects these to our own experiences and expectations. This makes it easier for the players to emerge into our worlds, as there are common concepts that connect their experiences with the ones they experience as protagonists in our fictional world. It makes it easier to believe in the role we gave them for our narration and to follow the reasons we gave our characters to be motivated to overcome the obstacles facing them.

Quest Design and Environmental Storytelling

However, no matter how much we focus on the causality of our quests, the experiences are not complete if the surroundings do not support the narration. If we only explain the situation in a dialogue or text without confronting the players with visual, acoustic etc. elements matching the content of the text, the immersion will be broken and the causality of our quests as well, as things become unbelievable.

When designing a quest and before writing any text, we need to study the given environments and speak with the content designers. It is important to understand their vision for a specific area and how they want to bring it to life. Narrative content needs to go hand in hand with the level, audio and visual design. Talking about your plan and listening to their plan leads to a better integration of all elements and better decoration of the road.

The environment is your best and strongest storyteller. It can create atmosphere and immersion without a single line of text. It provides the context for all your narration, can create a believable world and help your players to become a part of your world. Let the environment tell your story. Show, don't tell, is the key principle here, which then is extended to our goal to play, don't tell, with the interactions the players can do.

The fewer words you need to explain what is going on, the more natural the individual situation and quests become. You achieved your goal when it becomes so natural to accept and complete a quest that it is an emotional decision made by your players. If your players want to overcome the obstacles of a quest due to their emotional involvement, you've achieved your goal as a narrative designer; as the players start to feel like their avatar, they start becoming their avatar.

A great example of environmental storytelling comes from *Kingdom Come: Deliverance*. In one of the first moments of the game, right after your home is attacked, the players get the quest to run, get a horse and escape. All around the player is the chaos of the attack as they run towards the horse. If the player character leaves the path, they are likely killed by the attackers, so the path is defined by the environment. Shortly before reaching the horse, the players hear screams from a woman who's being attacked by three men, trying to push her into the house. At this point, the game doesn't give the players any specific quest; the goal is still to get the horse and escape. However, the events in the environment implicitly ask the players if they want to ignore what's going on or if they want to get involved.

If they ignore it, they will later learn that the character feels guilty that he didn't help a woman who was assaulted and whom he knew (the fact that he knew her is revealed in a short scene before the attack).

If they try to help, they receive a quest to help the woman escape and are confronted with three experienced warriors who outmatch him with their combat skills. However, despite being outmatched, the players will be able to save the woman from her attackers and escape and thus complete this optional quest.

The results of their decision, regardless of if they save the woman or not, are noted in their quest journal, thus forming the experienced story for the players based on their decision.

This is an excellent example of how the environment can be used to tell what is happening and to react to a player's decision. Similar structures are usually used in live-action roleplays (LARPs), where the environment and the events surrounding the players are used to tell a story and to involve them. The story progresses based on their decisions, regardless of whether they know that a decision was made. The world doesn't wait for the players to decide in the form of a text window, it moves on naturally based on their action.

This connection of storytelling and environment is not always possible and highly depends on the actual mechanics and genre of the game you're working on. However, at the very least, try to get the environment to tell the backstory of your events and the context of the quest you're giving to the players. This information will not only help players to get immersed in your game world, it will also help environment artists and level designers better understand what they need to design and what the goal of their designs is.

Quest Design and Exposition

Quests, as obstacles that a character must overcome, also serve as the main vehicle besides dialogue to expose information to the audience, to the players. They are, just like dialogue, the interactive element that connects the players with the narration. However, unlike dialogue, quests focus on tasks and activities, on overcoming the mentioned obstacles.

A common mistake in quest design is to put too much backstory and information into the quest texts in the hope of communicating everything that is going on with the players. This leads to overwriting and long texts that are often skipped, as well as unbelievable situations. Just think of yourself … when you have a problem that needs a solution and you ask your friends for help, do you always tell them your entire life story, or do you just ask about what you want?

If you only ask about what you want, why should your fictional NPC act any differently when approaching the hero for help? Does this character always have to fully justify the requests made?

As writers, we usually enjoy writing backgrounds, explaining everything, but, like when writing for a movie, we don't have to include all this information in the text. It is better to use the environment, the action, and the interaction to share these things than to use the quest texts.

There are two kinds of quest texts, those that are spoken by an NPC and those that go into a quest journal. Depending on the type, the length of the text should be selected. An entry in a quest journal can be longer and include more information, as it represents the quests the player character took. These are the notes you would take if you were the hero. The texts that are spoken by an NPC (or similar quest giver) should follow the conventions of traditional dialogue writing; thus, use subtext, avoid on-the-nose text and avoid overwriting. The more natural the dialogue sounds and the better it fits into its surroundings and the events surrounding the NPC, the more believable and immersive everything becomes. Think of it this way: if someone kidnapped the sheriff of a small village and the villagers are concerned, would they tell you all the backstory of the village or simply that their sheriff was kidnapped?

But if we keep our texts that short, where do we put the backstory?

Well, first we need to think what parts of the backstory we really need, and second, we need to think how we can *show* this information to the players. We could reveal information in the way the village is built, how the NPC acts or how they are animated. An NPC cowering in a corner, looking constantly for threats, is more believable than an NPC who stands still and says, "I'm afraid …."

The junction between quest design and exposition is one of the points where narrative design becomes more like directing than simply writing it.

Besides considering how we show the information to the players, we also need to consider the connection of the quests with each other. Not all information needs to be revealed in one quest. Often, it is better to split the information into various chunks, which are then structured as a quest chain. This not only helps to keep the texts of the individual quests short, but it also gives us an excellent tool to escalate situations and implement progression in our quest-based storytelling.

Focus and Progression in Quest Design

Congratulations: you've come a long way. If you have made it thus far, you successfully made it through the theory required to design individual quests. You may have designed a few quests with the techniques discussed, and they are all well located within your narrative, reflected in your environments and fulfill the principles of causality, thus helping to understand the characters' motivations and motivate the players to complete them. However, designing individual quests is only one part of the work. As discussed earlier, quest design is not only about designing great individual quests but making them a part of the bigger narrative, relating them to each other and telling stories with them. Chaining quests works hand in hand with the level of exposition we can have through the quest system and becomes important to keep players engaged with our game.

Jesse Schell discusses in *The Art of Game Design* (2010, Chapter Nine, "The Experience Is in the Player's Mind," pp. 118–122) the importance of focus in game design, as our brains (and our players) can focus their attention selectively on specific tasks. If we're focused on a specific activity, we'll start ignoring less important things. This crucial ability is important for all aspects of game design, including quest design. If we use this knowledge correctly to design our elements, it will help us to deliver an experience to the players that is engaging and will carry them from one challenge to the next. In a way, this is a part of the psychology behind the famous "one more turn" as we know it from turn-based strategy games.

Having a great motivation for one quest is good, and having it for an entire quest chain or narrative is even better, as it will suck players into the stories we try to tell.

How do we get our players to focus on our quests and not on other elements?

Schell discusses what he calls the flow channel (2010, *The Art of Game Design*, Chapter Nine, "The Experience Is in the Player's Mind," pp. 119) as the fine path where the difficulty of a challenge and required skill level to master the challenge are in just the right relationship, meaning that a challenge is not too easy to be solved with the skills the players already have, but also not too difficult.

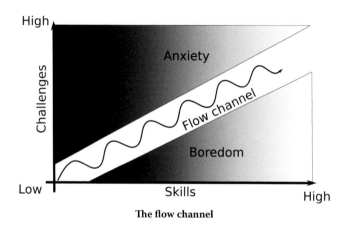

The flow channel

It is a fine balance. This relationship of challenge and skill also applies to our quest design. The challenges that the players must overcome at a given moment need to match the skills they have acquired at this point in the game; otherwise, we would either cause boredom, as the quest is not challenging enough, or anxiety, as the challenge seems impossible to master. Both boredom and anxiety will cause the player to lose focus and eventually quit the game.

To find the right balance, you'll need to talk with the game designers and testers of your game. You may have an idea, but our intuition can be right and wrong and everything in between. That's why you should not only rely on yourself but on any possible feedback you can get. In the end, you'll only find the right balance by iterating and iterating. Experience may help, but even the most experienced designers can be wrong, especially if something is designed late in the development process. At this stage, most of us have acquired a proficiency in our game that only very few players ever will, and it can become hard to scale this down to the real level required to provide an engaging experience. As a rule of thumb, you can ask yourself if your parents would be able to master the challenge you designed and what it would take them to master it. This is just a helpful thought experiment, not a law written in stone, so expect a lot of fine-tuning on your quest to find the right balance for your quests.

To make things even more difficult, the right balance between challenge and skills is not only important for an individual quest, it is what leads us to progression. As the players play our game, they acquire skills and become better in the ones they have already acquired; thus, the difficulty of our challenges needs to increase as well, because otherwise, we would risk leaving the flow channel and end up boring our players.

Luckily for us as writers, we don't have to start from scratch when thinking about progression and the escalation of difficulty. We can make use of well-known story structures such as the three-act structure or heroes' journey and the implied progression systems. From our story writing, we know that an important element of storytelling is to raise the stakes as we progress through the story and move closer to the climax. The same knowledge can be applied to our quest design and, as narrative elements can be layered and are layered structures, remember an individual scene follows the same principles of a three-act structure as the entire story. We can use them as guidance at any detail level, be it an individual quest, a quest chain, a chain of quest chains or the entire narrative. We can zoom in and out and will find the same principles. For the design of our quests, this means that it is best to start with the highest level, the overall narrative, and then zoom in directly to the smallest elements that have a relatable progression, the individual quest chains and their quests, leaving the chains of quest chains for later when we have the design of the elements and can work on the overall connections of the quest chains in light of the overall narrative. In any of these design steps, it is important to remember that we need to raise the stakes as we move forward in the narrative and come closer to the climax. However, story progression, especially in games, is not always about raising the stakes; we also need to allow time for the players to catch their breath. Thus, times of intense action need to alternate with calmer moments while the overall arc of the narrative intensifies.

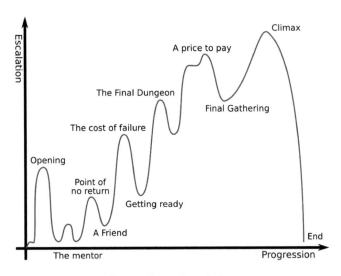

Progression and escalation

In the end, it is at this step, where all the elements are coming together, where we can make the most of our expertise in traditional storytelling techniques. Our quest is completed, and hopefully anyone who picks up the game is drawn into its world and stories and becomes a part of them.

A Sample Quest Design Flow

Wow … this was a lot of theory, and it may be hard to see how all these points play together in practice. So, after all this theory, let us look at a simple, step-by-step example process to design a quest chain for an MMORPG like World of Warcraft. I assume that you're at least somewhat familiar with its core mechanics, so let's assume that our MMORPG uses the same set of mechanics.

Step 1: The Background

Before starting with the design of an actual quest, we need to spend some time with the background material, which is either already available or needs to be written. This background material is your backstory, world story or lore and the overarching narrative that is told by the game.

The reason to do this is, as we discussed earlier, that we need to ensure that our quests are a part of the game world, a part of the overall plot, and that's why we need to know what is going on in our fictional world. It helps to talk with your peers from the lore development team (if your studio has one) and to talk with your fellow writers and designers. The lore team can give you a great overview or help you find the details you need to know, and working together with others on the story helps you develop a collective understanding of the world and to integrate each other's perspectives.

Step 2: The High Concept

After spending some time thinking about the background, it is time to develop the hook for the quest. The hook is the high concept. It is the essence of this narrative piece and should describe the key idea in the shortest feasible way. In general, if you can't summarize your quest idea in one to two sentences, it signals that you don't have a clear idea and that you would most likely confuse others (if you think that's hard, keep in mind that great movies and books can be summarized in this short manner).

The high concept is important, as it not only shows that you have a clear idea of what you're developing, but it is also extremely helpful to communicate your vision to others.

For me the central questions when designing the hook are:

> Why is this quest fun to play?
> What makes it unique compared to other quests?
> What information will the player learn about the lore?
> How epic is this quest?
> What is the purpose of this quest?

The question "Why is it fun?" is the most important one, and you should only design something you like to play, because if you don't enjoy your quest, why should someone else? It's always good to embrace your inner child when designing a quest and to let your mind wander to the places where you would have the most fun. Never forget that you're working on games and your mission is to entertain people.

Serious Games

While most games are made for entertainment and it should be fun to play them, there is also a place for so-called serious games that primarily focus on communicating a message to their players. These games may not focus on fun due to the nature of the themes they deal with and their objectives. In these games, the most important question when designing the quest is not "Why is it fun?" but "How does it help to communicate my message?"

The lines between regular and serious games can be blurry, and there is no rule that a game must be one or the other; however, when working on a specific game or narrative asset, make sure that you clarify your key questions by knowing what kind of game you're making.

Step 3: General Information

Now it is time to start collecting all the general information the quest chain requires to be implemented.

To do so, I usually ask myself the following questions:

How many quests are a part of this chain?
Where does it take place? What locations are involved?
What game regions are involved?
What NPCs/factions are involved?
What items do I need?
Are there any special gameplay mechanics required for this quest chain?

The answers to these questions are critical because ultimately, they give you a picture of how complex the quest chain will be. Also, answering these questions at this point helps to set the limits for the actual design of the quests within this quest chain.

While finalizing this step, it is good to write a short summary about the special content, what makes this quest chain unique and another short paragraph about the background to connect it with the lore, so that it becomes a part of the world and its lore.

Step 4: General Information, The Quest Graph

Now, with all the general information at hand, we can start drawing the quest graph, which shows how all the quests in the quest chain relate to each other. To distinguish the different quests from each other, I recommend either giving them a descriptive name or naming them with their high concept/hook.

For drawing this graph, I prefer using yEd or Articy:Draft, but you can use any tool you like. Just make sure that you use either your studio's standard on the used elements or that you clearly define your symbol set before using it.

Step 5: General Information, The Map

After designing (or sometimes while designing) the quest graph, it's time to start to draw a map of the region where the quest chain will take place, to get a better feeling of the quest flow and to consider any environments needed for your quest chain. This map is usually drawn as "designer art" and is distant from anything that the player will see in the later game, but it helps to get a better understanding of how the player will travel between the different locations while solving the quest chain and to communicate your needs with the level design and other departments.

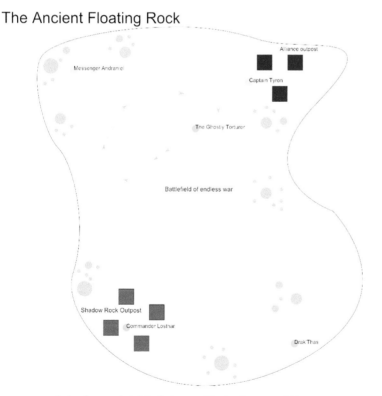

A simple map sketch in designer art to develop a quest idea

It is a great idea to involve them in your design process, as they can help you with tools and material already prepared, especially if you design a quest for an already-designed part of the game.

Now, together with the quest graph, you should already get a rough feeling of how the player will travel across the region to solve the quest chain and how visual, acoustic etc. elements will enrich this experience.

Step 6: A First Quest, The Summary

So far, we have only talked about the general information (or "concept") that is needed to design a quest chain.

Now I'd like to cover some of the things you will need when you create an actual quest. I call this information "in-game information" because most (not all) of the texts from this step on will be visible to the player in one form or other.

As a first step, I prefer to write the short summary that will be visible to the player. The goal for the summary is that the players will know within seconds what their current objectives are. For this text, it is good to be as short and as precise as you can without breaking the imagination.

It is good to make use of clear verbs to describe the actions you expect the players to take.

Step 7: A First Quest, Player Information

This step covers all the texts/dialogues that relate to the quest and will be visible to the player during the quest. Here you can write in prose or whatever style was picked to create the appropriate atmosphere and tone for the game you're working on. You want to apply what we talked about regarding exposition and quest design.

Usually, this is the most fun part of implementing and testing the quest, because you can release your imagination and create with words the pictures that you would like to share with the player.

For me this step consists of at least three different texts: description (the text the players will read, before they accept the quest), in-progress text (the text after they have accepted the quest, but before they have solved it) and the debriefing (the text when they have solved the quest). The first two texts are usually attached to the quest giver entity, while the third one can also be attached to another entity.

Step 8: A First Quest, Gameplay Information

The last step in this design process is the creation of all gameplay information needed for this specific quest. This information block gathers information such as when a quest is unlocked, who the quest giver is, the closing condition (a.k.a. the objective) and so on. It also contains balancing information like the target level range and which rewards the players will receive as soon as they have successfully solved the quest. This is the place where most of the fine-tuning magic happens and where you should talk with your designers responsible for the game's balancing to ensure you stay within the flow channel and that difficulty and required skill level correspond to each other.

Once you finish this step, you return to step 6 and repeat the process until you have designed all the quests of your quest chain.

Conclusion

I hope this chapter gave you some insight into the complexity of quest design. As you may discover, the topic itself is too complex to cover every aspect in one chapter or even one book, but I hope that the information of this chapter gave you some new ideas and concepts to think about. For me, the most important lesson I learned when it comes to quest design is that iteration and observation are the keys to better quests. One helps to improve your ideas and designs, and the other is an excellent source to understand human psychology and storytelling and provides a way to learn from others who have walked the same road before.

Exercise

Design a quest chain of at least three individual quests using the discussed quest design flow.

Reference

J. Schell. 2010. *The Art of Game Design*, Morgan Kaufmann, Burlington, MA, USA.

CHAPTER 11

Planning Your Work

Cash DeCuir

Contents

Schedules and Budgets 146
Setting a Plan 146
Granularity 147
Estimation and Keeping Track of Time 148
Elegance 148
Working with Your Team 148
The Producer 152
Countering Failure. 152
Time Sinks 153
Scope 153
Committing to Your Narrative 155
Iteration. 156
Cutting. 156
An Antidote to Stress 157
A Closing Note 158
An Exercise in Production 158

Scheduling is critical to the success of any creative endeavor. In this chapter, we'll outline a practical philosophy of planning that's useful regardless of your role in the industry. The duties of a writer in an AAA studio are different from those of a creative director, after all; likewise, the responsibilities of a writer in an indie studio aren't those of a solo developer or a freelancer. But the principles of proper planning and the realities that underpin them are universal.

Even if you're a writer who has found success working with less structure than we'll outline here, you need to be aware of the realities creative commercial endeavors face. What's offered here is a set of considerations that will alert you to the pitfalls of production. Not only as artists but as people, we must adopt a healthy and sustainable process for creating our art. It is not worth sacrificing your health to meet a deadline, nor should that ever be demanded of you. Better practice leads to better art. Our industry, famous for its crunch times, will only improve if we band together and force it to improve.

In this Chapter

- How to understand and set plans, schedules, and budgets
- How to track the progress of your project
- How best to work with your team and your producer
- Adapting your plan to the realities of production

Schedules and Budgets

The fundamental truth of production is this: you're not planning based on the talents you and your team possess, you're planning around the time and money that enable you and those around you to work.

Your budget sets your deadlines; your deadlines determine how much time you'll have to work on the project. When deadlines come, and they always do, you'll need to have something to show for it. Otherwise, the deadline goes back and money spreads thin, or you run out of funding and the project must end, whether you want it to or not. Crunch leading up to the deadline isn't a solution, either. You'll produce less work of worse quality and ruin your health besides.

All planning begins with knowing how long your budget will last. Once you're facing that reality, it makes it easier to compromise, and once you start to compromise, you force ingenuity.

Setting a Plan

Preproduction on any project is essential to its success. It's the opportunity to outline exactly what you're attempting to accomplish and why.

On the most basic level, at this stage, you're establishing what the game is, drafting the tasks required to make the game, and ensuring nothing contradicts the reality of your budget. It's now that you must determine what you're working toward. Ask yourself: What kind of immersive experience do you want to create? Does your team have the skills to accomplish it? Can your project be completed in the time your budget allows?

On a more in-depth level, this stage of the project is about being honest with yourself. How much will you be able to complete? How long will it take you to write what you're planning to write? Indeed, this stage is not only establishing how you'll write your story, but also about how the other artists on your team will help you realize it. You are writing for an interactive medium, after all, with a host of other talented individuals lending their own arts.

You must establish how the narrative ties together, as well as how it ties to art, sound design, and so on. Work with your team right from the beginning. Your colleagues are there to assist you in telling your story.

Once you have your plan, stop adding to it. Write down your ideas somewhere; they may prove useful later, if you ever run into a roadblock. Start making the game you've planned for and see how it goes from there.

Remember, a good schedule is a blueprint by which you build a game. It outlines every aspect of its production, from the writing to the programming, the art and the sound design, and all else. But it isn't enough to only outline what you must do. You must break your design down into completable, discrete tasks. Make them granular. Break your cast into characters. Break your narrative into acts, and those acts into scenes. Break your writing into drafting, editing, and reviewing.

Ask yourself how long it will take to complete these granular tasks. Estimate how long it'll take to finish everything. Base it on experience. Guess if you must. But give estimations of how long each task will take to complete, then double it. Can your work be accomplished within the schedule? If not, make compromises now. Start cutting and fusing, making the design as tight as possible so that you don't run over budget. And remember to leave a buffer for yourself, as well: always plan that your work will take 20% longer than you imagined it would. The reality is that the project will be fraught with unforeseen difficulties; sicknesses, unforeseen creative difficulties, whatever have you—these will throw your timing off, so it's best to account for them early.

Granularity

Breaking down your design into its constituent parts can be terrifying at first. Your to-do sheet goes from only a few tasks to dozens. But take heart! Many small tasks are easier to complete than a few titanic tasks.

You may be overwhelmed when first seeing a busy task list, but there's nothing to fear. These are all small, accomplishable tasks. They're also measurable, both by you and your team. As you complete these more modest goals, you'll be able to judge how close you are to completing your larger goals.

Small tasks also help you identify problems sooner. If progress isn't being made on small tasks, it'll be an immediate indication that something is going wrong. One is less likely to raise a red flag on a monolithic task, as it's only natural that tasks of that size take forever to complete. One can become stuck working on a task like this and not realize it until it's too late.

But that's not the case with granular tasks. If you're writing a character that's meant to be finished in three days, and after two days you're not even half finished, you'll know something needs to change in the schedule. Instead of the problem compounding over days and weeks—days and weeks that will no longer be able to go to other work—you adjust the plan.

The time spent on one part of the project cannot be spent on another. Other work will have to be cut or redesigned as a result. But it's better to make those decisions early and work with a revamped design, rather than realize at the end everything is broken and needs desperate fixing in the edit.

Estimation and Keeping Track of Time

When setting a plan, state how long it'll take you to finish any given task. Otherwise, how else will you know if you can complete the work before release?

Every task needs an estimation of how long it will take to complete. If you've done similar work before, use that knowledge to set your estimation. If you have absolutely no way of knowing how long a task will take to complete, then estimate to the best of your abilities. Even if it's arbitrary, it's important to have numbers to plan around. Be honest about your abilities. There's no shame in saying something will take too long to complete.

By now, the tasks should already be granular. Remember, you'll write your narrative in stages. Each stage may require a different amount of time to complete. Ask yourself: How long will it take to write the first draft? How long will it take to revise? Will you go through three drafts? Four? What about player testing—will you show it to anyone and implement their feedback? And remember, the longer your story is, the more time you'll need to edit it later—and the longer you'll need to leave it with your playtesters.

Elegance

Your time is scarce. Simplicity is your ally. Maximize the value of what you can create in your limited time. Keep your cast limited, but tightly knit. If you have 10 characters, see if you can smush them into 5. Reuse set pieces to engender a sense of history in the player.

The less work you can create for yourself, the better off you'll be. This isn't laziness; it's a truth of being an artist. The more you can do with less, the better. Compact your story. Your artists, likewise, will all be thankful that you aren't demanding an epic story of ten thousand characters spread across a hundred miles of realistically rendered, explorable terrain.

Working with Your Team

Once you have your tasks set, talk to your colleagues from other departments about how they can help bring your narrative alive. You'll find your workload lightens. Perhaps your level designers know a few tricks that will reveal aspects of the world you'd struggle to convey otherwise; maybe your character designers will have ideas of how they can communicate nuances of your cast without you having to write a word; likewise, your sound designers may know how to set a specific tone so you don't have to labor over establishing it in writing alone.

Also, the sooner you set your plan, the sooner others can comment on it. If something exists only inside your head, you can make excuses for it. Once it's committed to paper, or to a spreadsheet, or to whatever organizational tool you're using (such as Trello or HacknPlan), then it becomes harder for you to fool yourself—and it becomes nearly impossible to fool your colleagues.

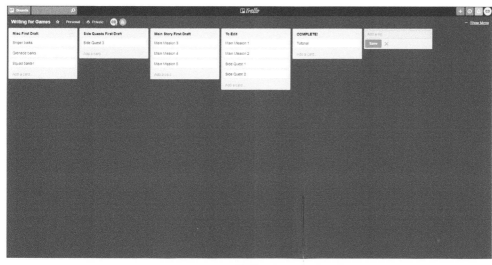

Trello

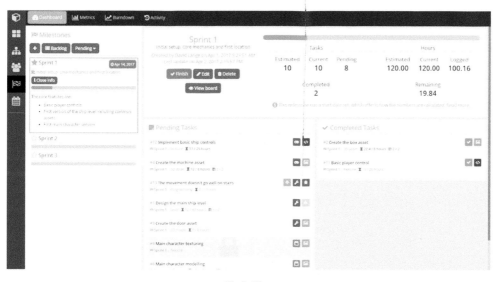

HacknPlan

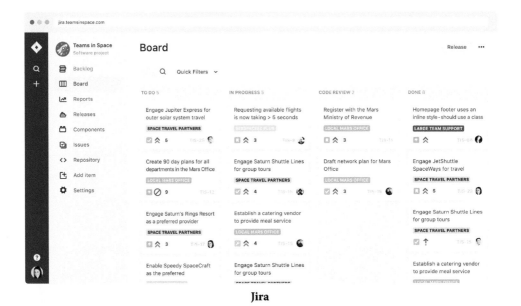

Jira

Hansoft

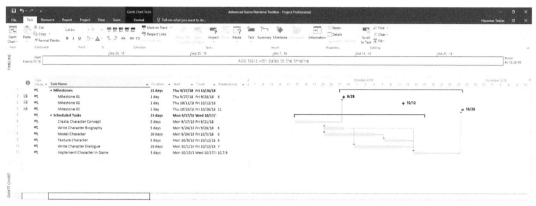

MSProject

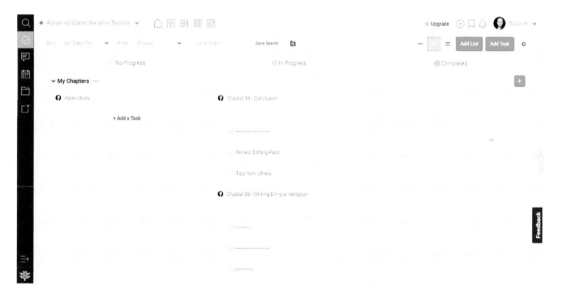

Freedcamp

Your schedules, after all, are reliant upon one another. If you write a character, but they don't model them, or if they model a character and you don't write them, then something has broken down and someone has wasted time. A visible plan also gives you and your colleagues the chance to push back on impractical designs. Perhaps you want more characters than the artists on your team to create and animate. Maybe that level designer has very particular thoughts on why that set piece will be unfun for players.

Communication throughout the project is critical: the team needs to remain in constant discussion, all departments working closely together. As problems crop up, sometimes the best solution is to work with them. More writing isn't always the answer. Plan to work with your team.

The Producer

Every team needs a producer—someone who manages the schedule and ensures the team isn't falling behind. If you have a producer in your company, develop a good working relationship with them. They're there to tell you no—not because they want to cramp your style or stymie your art, but because they want to protect you against your worst artistic urges. There's only so much any of us can do. If something is taking longer than it should, talk to them and work out a solution. If it can be cut, cut; if it can be rethought, perhaps it'll be even better than what you planned initially. Necessity is the mother of invention.

If you don't have a producer on your team, then you must be eternally vigilant. Plan your work. Estimate how long it will take. Time how long it takes. Be honest. If it's going well, report as much to your team; if you're struggling, don't hide it. There's no shame in asking for help, be it from your team, your colleagues, your friends and family, or even the internet. You're vital to the creation of the game. Working yourself into exhaustion won't make the problem any better. It'll damage the project and your health. Work with your producer to set realistic, healthy goals and save yourself—and your game—from harm.

Countering Failure

Your original plan will fail. That's a fact of life. At some point in development, everything you outlined in the beginning will no longer be viable. Maybe a feature is taking longer to implement than you thought it would, or maybe you've taken ill, or maybe your budget suddenly decreases. Whatever the case, your plans will have to change to match the new reality.

Schedules are living documents. Laying out the dates and times is not the end of your planning. Your progress must be updated throughout the project, every day. In the last half hour of work, mark the progress you've made on your tasks. It is a chore, yes, but think of it like flossing your teeth; in the end, it'll be good for your health.

As you mark your progress through your tasks, you'll also develop a record of how long it takes you to complete any given task. This will allow you to better estimate in the future. Likewise, you'll gain a sense of what blockers the future might hold—enabling you to plan for them in advance. If you know you've taken an unusually long time writing barks, you can plan around it. You can budget more time from elsewhere in the schedule, reach out for help, cut how many lines you're writing, bring on extra writing resources, or perhaps some combination of the above or something else entirely!

You don't set schedules to prevent failure. Failure can never be prevented. Every game that ships will be incomplete. Not every feature will go in, not every line will be polished. The reason you set schedules is to prevent failure from compounding. If you have a problem late in development, it's almost always because you had problems at the start. The sooner you can course-correct, the better off the project will be.

Time Sinks

Development is rife with time sinks. If you schedule one working day to write a character but spend the morning on other duties—discussions with your programmers, replying to support tickets, et cetera—then you'll only have half a day to write.

All schedules should plan for these time sinks. Factor them into your schedule early. Every day will come with its own unforeseen demands that pull you away from finishing your scheduled task. If that means blocking out a day a week for support, then that's one week less you have for everything else. If that means shortening your narrative and cutting features, it's best to do that early. One cannot be too careful when it comes to time sinks. They are ever present and potentially fatal to the careless.

As well, the work always takes longer than expected. As a writer, you'll want to put in everything you can. You want to practice your art, relate every aspect of nuance you can, give your players value for their money. But writing takes time; time takes money. The more you write, the more you'll need to edit.

There is no fault in that; it is an art, not a science. As you write, even if you're following a good plan, you'll realize how you can improve it. Ideas will come to you, exciting and new—sometimes even better than what you had before. And while it's occasionally worth incorporating them, they can quickly expand the project's scope beyond what anyone can accomplish.

Scope

A plan is a mission statement. It sets your objective and outlines the work required to complete it. At the start of the project, you set the scope of the project. What can you deliver in the time your budget buys you?

For the writer, this means setting the scope of the story. Establish that up front. Once you have the shape of your narrative, don't grow it; focus on ensuring everything the player will see ties together. Know what your story is and stick with it.

Of course, you can't nail down everything. Epiphanies happen in the process of creation; even when you have a plan, you'll make discoveries about your work along the way. If you've established the fundamentals of your story, however, you'll know what's worth using for this project and what's worth using for the next one.

One must always be cautious with ideas, as a project's scope is always under constant threat of expanding beyond human capability. It's a natural tendency: one good idea often breeds another, which in turn breeds another. Soon, however, you'll have too many good ideas. The work grows easily: a few conversations with a colleague, a good film giving a better idea, a fancy that strikes as you're walking down the hall. It's easy to see these ideas as essential to the project. The more good ideas that are in the game, the better it must be! And before you know it, the project bloats and the ideas meld together. Cutting becomes more painful, because it's attached to other parts of the game. Besides, why would you take a good idea out of the project?

Such ideas will always slip through. You'll strike on a something that should be simple to write and implement. Just a small idea. Maybe it's a theme you want to elaborate on: a background story, a set of conversations, anything. And when you begin to write, the words don't come—but it's a good idea, so you spend a day trying to force them. Or maybe the words do come, but in too great a force—you start to find new ideas, new connections, new aspects that the player should see! And soon, the story grows beyond what it was meant to be. It starts taking longer to implement these ideas, to polish them, to ensure that the player can appreciate them. You lose focus on the rest of the project. You focus in on this one narrow aspect. You revise other content to force the updates in. The rest of the work suffers. And all for a small idea!

Or, on the opposite end, you'll find an idea that—to implement—will require a massive rewrite of what you have already. That takes time, and that's what you don't have to spare. If you're trying to correct a significant error, then perhaps it'll be necessary. That's seldom the case, however. The audience will seldom be able to sense what could have been. Besides, you'll have the idea to use for next time.

And beware! Ideas that seem good on paper can prove disastrous in practice. Some designs, when broken into granular tasks, appear obviously beyond the scope of what you can accomplish. These ideas can be trimmed or cut immediately.

But it's not always obvious that a design is impractical. Again, the sooner you can discover an impractical design, the better off you'll be. The first step to addressing a problem is recognizing it. By keeping a close watch on how your task list progresses, you can find indications of when your schedule is in danger.

Throughout the project, you'll need to be honest with yourself: there's only so much you can do, and it'll neither be good for you nor the project if you lose sight of the whole. There's no shame in cutting, trimming, or holding onto good ideas for another day.

Committing to Your Narrative

If you're writing a branching or nonlinear narrative, planning can save you heartache. If you're not careful, your choices can easily multiply until you have more branches than you can write. At the same time, you need to have enough variation that the player believes their choices matter, and that they have an appropriate impact on the world. These are difficult balances to strike. They're even more difficult if you only try fixing them at the end of your development.

It's easier to avoid these problems by committing to your narrative early on. Careful planning establishes your starting and ending points. If you know where the player comes from, you'll know what they expect to do—if you know where you want them to end next, that gives you an indication of what consequences their actions will have. This limits the possibilities you have as a creator, and that's exactly what you want. When you know what you can't write, when you know what won't fit, you won't waste your time on it.

Video games are not about enabling player freedom, but about giving them a story they're happy to play. If you don't begin with that discipline in yourself, you'll have much more difficulty instilling it in your audience. If you allow yourself those temptations and then cut them off hastily right before release, the audience will sense that there's something they should be able to do and can't. Their illusion of freedom will be broken.

Another boon to committing to your story is that it allows you to better integrate those choices you do write. If you've planned well, you'll find you know how to relate everything. The load lightens. Because you're playing with common themes and story strands throughout, you build a history. As that player familiarity is established, you'll need to say less and less over time.

If you've created a tight narrative, it should be easy for you to identify how one choice can later have an impact. You'll write stories not as individual points in time, but as their evolutions across time.

Planning your story helps you write it faster. Knowing what it's about locks it together. If you know the beats and all that must be introduced, you can write it with that immediate intentionality. You can seed common themes throughout. Over time, your themes will develop. Players will grow familiar with them; introducing variations requires less and less work.

Planning also saves you from writing a disparate story. If you've written several sections of discrete content that don't link together, you'll need to fix them in the edit. Sometimes this can require extensive rewrites. And even if you do give them a few basic links, they'll still feel discrete. Players can sense that failure of intentionality. That's not an easy mistake to recover from, so plan your story and avoid it altogether.

Iteration

Setting a schedule will not limit your creativity. It will encourage it. When you see how much time you have to accomplish your story-telling goals, you'll be forced to make compromises—not only up front but along the way. The earlier you find a problem, the earlier you find a solution; the earlier you find a solution, the more time you'll have to carry its lessons throughout the project.

Build iteration into your schedule. Test your content. If you have playtesters in your office, be sure you utilize them. If you're only able to show a mailing list of players, or a few trusted friends, use them. Their feedback is invaluable. They'll have the perspective of an uninformed public, who's unaware of everything you intend. If you see your story resonating with them, you'll know you're on the right track; if not, you'll know you need to start finding solutions.

Allow yourself time to revise the work based on feedback. The sooner you're able to get the project into testers' hands, the sooner you'll be able to make some of the most meaningful alterations to your game. Perhaps you'll find aspects of your story are confusing or unnoticed by players altogether. Perhaps you'll find they dislike your design or don't understand it. There's no shame in this. It simply means you need to approach it from a different angle.

Seek out this knowledge and use it for all it's worth. All future designs will be informed by the feedback given at the early stages. It will stop you from repeating and compounding your mistakes. That will save you time, allowing you to work on other aspects of the game, instead of having to revisit the broken parts—or worse, shipping a broken project without realizing it.

Cutting

If you're a writer and designer who has trouble reigning in your branching narrative, be ruthless from the start. Establish your goals for the project. What will your story be? Will the player have any control over the narrative—if so, why? And how will they affect it? Is there anything you particularly want to invest in—a conversation system, a romance system? Remember, the effect of freedom is cumulative. The more systems in play, the more you'll have to cover as a writer. Establish from the beginning the type of experience you'll want players to have. Establish how much time your budget allows you to implement them. Establish how you can create that experience with the time you have. Everything else, cut.

But even with this, you'll need to continue reigning your story in. You can't offer the player too much—whether it's too much freedom, too many cutscenes, too many branches of dialogue—or you'll never finish your game. Always know what your endpoints will be when you begin a new task. A few tangents may be okay, but ensure everything leads directly to those endpoints. Save yourself from useless work.

There is one last point to remember when cutting, which may make the exercise easier: if you cut well, no one will know. Your audience will only see that which you present to them. If you've been uncertain in your cuts, they'll sense the hesitation. They'll know something is missing, that something doesn't quite feel right, even if they can't put their finger on it. If your very best idea doesn't fit, players will know it stands out awkwardly. If you cut it well, however, players won't have any idea of what they're missing.

An Antidote to Stress

Planning can also be a bulwark against anxiety. There's horror in facing a monolith. When faced with a task that seems too big to accomplish, it's natural to feel tense. But no project is impossible. Games don't go from concepts to completed features in a single bound. Rather, you'll take countless steps to bring you from your start to your end. A good plan will help you see that. You'll chart your route through the perils of creation. You'll reach milestones along the way and know you're progressing. You'll know the next step. And as those smaller tasks are marked complete, you'll see that there is an end in sight.

It's important to recognize, however, that no matter how well you plan, the plan will be imperfect. As your plan meets the realities of development—as estimations run over, tech doesn't work, bad days slow your input, and all the rest—you plan is bound to change. That's life. That can't be helped. But that doesn't mean one should forswear planning. Even when the schedule needs to be adjusted, that's not an indication of failure. Failure comes when you don't keep track of how long something takes to write and you've overinvested your time. Failure comes when you let the work become more than you can accomplish. Failure comes when you're working beyond your capability, crunching to meet a deadline. What failure is not, is course correction.

And even those failures can be remedied. And even if they can't be—you're still more than your work.

Success, on the other hand, comes when you know a deadline cannot be met and you exercise wisdom in finding something to cut. Of course, if you have the budget to buy you more hours, then that is another matter. But if your time and resources are finite, there will come a day you'll need to make hard calls. A day will come when you'll need to work with less than you expected. That will be when you show your mastery of your craft.

A Closing Note

Scheduling is an imperfect art. You'll make assumptions every project that will be wrong. And again, that's okay. What matters is that you learn from them for next time. What matters is that you adapt. Planning will never prevent failure, but it will signal when you need to correct your course. Good planning won't keep you out of danger; rather, it will provide you a set of outs you might not have had otherwise.

Games are (most of the time!) meant to be fun. You should have fun making them, too. Use your schedule to ensure your goals are healthy and realistic, to try and save more of that fun for yourself.

An Exercise in Production

Practical questions to aid your production:

- How much time does your budget buy you?
- What kind of immersive experience do you want to create?
- Does your team have the skills to accomplish your end goal?
- What are the granular tasks that will need to be completed to finish this task?
- How long will it take you to finish those granular tasks?
- Have you identified what tasks are required for the minimal viable product and what tasks are in a more ideal game?
- Have you identified candidates for cutting?
- Have you added a buffer of 20% to the total amount of time it will take you to finish this project?
- Have you written all of this on paper to show your team or your producer?
- Can all of these tasks be completed in the time you have allotted by your budget?
- Have you been honest with yourself?

CHAPTER 12

Yes, Videogames Need Story Editors!

Toiya Kristen Finley, PhD

Contents

Types of Editing Roles and How They Translate to Games 160
Breaking Down Editing Skills for Game Storytelling 161
Developmental/Substantive Editing (High Level) 161
    Narrative Design and Story 162
    Worldbuilding.. 162
    Pacing 162
    Quests 163
    A Note on Dialogue Systems... 164
    Plot Development.. 164
    Characterization and Character Development 165
    Art Assets 166
    Sound Assets... 167
    Feedback, Budgets, and Time 167
    Sensitivity Reading and Diversity Consulting 168
        Editing *Verdant Skies* 170
Copyediting and Proofreading: Low-Level Editing 171
    Copyediting.. 171
        Accuracy... 171
        Dialogue... 171
        Voiced Dialogue 172
        Unvoiced Dialogue... 172
        Informational/Instructional Texts 173
        Grammar 173
    Proofreading... 173
Modes for Giving Feedback 174
A Feedback Summary 175
Conclusion: The Editor–Developer Relationship........................... 176
Exercise: Developmental Edit 177
Notes 177

Why do development teams need story editors? Storytelling in games is a collaborative effort, after all. Many teams will have at least two people responsible for storytelling, whether that's a narrative designer and game writer, a narrative design team, or a writing team. Since more than one person with storytelling skills is involved, there will be several individuals who can evaluate the game's story. Even if there's only one writer or narrative designer on the project, the creative lead, producer, and/or game designer is going to evaluate their work. While this is true, *all* storytellers need editors. Editors bring an objective perspective because writers are too close to their own material.

In this Chapter

- Why editors are important for your stories
- Types of editors and their daily tasks
- How to work with an editor

Additionally, with the rise in popularity of visual novels and text-based games (especially on mobile platforms), more text means more chances for writing errors. We need more copyeditors and proofreaders to review writing before it's added to builds.

Types of Editing Roles and How They Translate to Games

Before looking at how an editor works on a game story, it's important to understand different editing roles in traditional prose writing.

Types of Editing

There are several kinds of editing in prose fiction and nonfiction. The same applies to games:

- *Developmental/Substantive Editing*: The developmental editor (DE; also a substantive, comprehensive, or structural editor) usually joins a project from its onset and helps with preproduction. A DE provides feedback on all aspects of a story, from plot arcs, character development, structure, and thematic development to style and tone. In short, the DE may analyze any aspect of the story.
- *Copyediting*: Once writers finish a draft, copyeditors review text and visual aids. Copyediting works on overall readability and comprehension, accuracy, structure, consistent formatting, and consistent style. Copyediting can be light, medium, or heavy, based on the needs of the work.

- *Proofreading*: This is the least intensive form of editing. A proofreader corrects typos and misspellings in the main text, visual aids, and menus.

A member of a game-development team can take on *any* of these editing roles. (But writers/narrative designers should *never* edit their own work.) Depending on how story-intensive the game is, you can determine what type of editing your project needs.

If you're joining a project as an editor, your team may not know what type of editing the game requires. Hopefully, this breakdown of roles will help you figure out what kind of editing the project needs.

Breaking Down Editing Skills for Game Storytelling

Editors break down the craft into high-level and low-level issues:

- *High-level issues (developmental/substantive)*: Overall story, character development, and characterization
- *Low-level issues (copyediting, proofreading)*: Consistency of style and tone; word choice for dialogue, informational and instructional texts; consistency in formatting

The high-level and low-level labels aren't indicative of importance. They point to the "big picture" (how all the parts of the story are working together, or not) and the word choice and sentence structure telling that story (low level). With games, the editor is concerned with not just the writing used to compose the story, but also its narrative design. This means the developmental editors need to read documentation as a part of the job—anything that helps them understand how the story and narrative design function in the game: game design document (GDD), bible, character bios, scripts, art character sheets, etc. This will show you the vision the team has for the game. Your job will be to determine if the team has executed that vision in the build, where the execution fails, and where the execution can be even stronger.

Developmental/Substantive Editing (High Level)

If you've edited for other storytelling media, you know that keeping genre and audience expectations in mind are important. The same is true for games. A story editor needs an awareness of what players want and whether the game is being true to its genre as far as gameplay and story are concerned. This doesn't mean the game doesn't have room for innovation or subversion. However, it does mean that we need to assess if the game is going too far afield of expectations.

161

Narrative Design and Story

A versatile story editor for games will also have a strong understanding of narrative design and gameplay. A substantive edit of a game's narrative design analyzes its *story delivery*—how the game delivers storytelling content to the player (narrative design elements, including plot, worldbuilding, pacing, etc.). This may also include comments about art, sound, and other assets used to complement and/or enhance the story's design.

Below are aspects of a game story an editor might tackle.

Worldbuilding

Sound worldbuilding takes research, which means an editor needs to fact-check. It doesn't matter whether the world setting is fantasy, science fiction, or based in reality. For example, the game's setting is the world of piracy in the seventeenth century. The worldbuilding wants to be true to that historical time period. As an editor, you come across a pirate using an idiom that's anachronistic and too modern. Additionally, the pirates use nautical terms, but you do a little research to see what slang pirates used for those same terms. In your feedback to the team, you (1) point out the anachronism and give suggestions for revisions or ask what would be more true to the time period, and (2) you note the slang pirates would use for nautical terms and recommend them for revising lines of dialogue.

But what about worlds not based in reality? Perhaps the pirate game takes place in an alternate history with elemental magic systems, and a prominent location in the game is Libertalia. Major quests along the game's critical path[1] occur here. Libertalia was most likely a myth of a pirate utopia, although whether it existed is disputed. In design documents, Libertalia reads as a realistic place like pirate strongholds Port Royal and Clew Bay. The magical aspect of the game's setting is lost at Libertalia. An editor notes why it's important to use real-world or fictional analogues in the game's worldbuilding, but the team can take more liberties (pun intended) with Libertalia. Because Libertalia most likely never existed, the team can put more of their own interpretation into the island's government and culture, based upon the game's magic systems.

Narrative designers and writers have already done a lot of research to build their worlds. However, this doesn't mean they might not have overlooked some things. As writers commit mistakes such as typos or grammatical errors, they can incorporate worldbuilding inaccuracies.

Pacing

Unlike stories in other media, a game's story pacing can frustrate players because it interrupts gameplay. An ill-timed cutscene can take a player out of enjoying interactive elements. Noninteractive elements can go on for too long, keeping the player from engaging with the game. Additionally, noninteractive elements can be too short. They don't give enough explanation or don't take enough time to communicate whatever the narrative designer is attempting to share with players.

Additionally, story pacing can be a *gameplay* issue. Gameplay is also storytelling and progresses the player from one story element to the next. Gameplay segments between one noninteractive moment to the next can be too short. They can go on for too long, fatiguing players when they need a break. The game's genre is important here. Players expect short gameplay segments in interactive movies and dating sims with mini games. Longer action is characteristic of action-adventure games, RPGs, and platformers.

Of course, issues with pacing will affect players differently. What's too long for one player won't be a problem for another. It's important for story editors to play a build or vertical slice to get a feel for the game's story pacing, as well as to review cutscene scripts.

Important questions to answer about pacing:

- Did a noninteractive element abruptly end gameplay? If so, why should the gameplay be longer?
- Were there gameplay sections that went on too long, and could they benefit from being broken up with noninteractive story?
- Does the pacing of the gameplay and noninteractive story elements make sense for the game's genre?

Quests

Quests progress the story and are often used to develop and characterize player characters and NPCs. They should communicate clear choices and rewards to players. Common quest features are dialogue (voiced or text based) and informational texts to help players understand the choices they're making.

NPCs giving quests should have succinct dialogue that expresses the quest scenario, the action the player needs to complete, and a clear motivation for wanting the player's help. If there's a dialogue tree, the choices players have to choose from should be an honest reflection of what the player chooses. Often in games, the player chooses from words, phrases, or icons that are meant to represent the tone or content of the response. However, the line of dialogue is the *opposite* of what the player wants to say. This leaves players confused, frustrated, and distrustful of the dialogue system.

During a quest's arc, it will often present players with two or more choices. The choices need to be clear to players so that they don't feel tricked or frustrated that the game misrepresented that choice. For example, if the game has a morality system, the player tries to do something evil, but the choice gives them good points.

Quests can have pacing issues, as well. They can feel like they go on too long, or players may feel like they're being strung along if the quest has lots of parts or too many twists. If they're on the shorter end, they may feel unresolved and unsatisfying, leaving players wondering, "What was the point?"

Important questions to answer about quests:

- Is the quest scenario clear?
- Is the NPC's motivation for involving the player character clear?
- Are choices explained so that players understand the decisions they're making?
- Does the quest's pacing work? Why or why not?

For more on quests, please see Chapter 10, "Get This, Kill That, Talk with … Mission and Quest Design."

A Note on Dialogue Systems

I mentioned how dialogue choices can be misleading under "Quests." If the dev team brings on a story editor once it has designed the dialogue system, it will be more difficult to correct confusing and misleading options. While story editors can point out how a phrase or word misrepresents the actual line of dialogue, they won't be able to fix the flaws that are fundamental to that dialogue system. Story editors working with game and narrative designers at the beginning of the design process can help develop a dialogue system that better communicates lines of dialogue through icons, words, or phrases that players choose. If the word or phrase is different for every dialogue choice, they can suggest edits that are more accurate. If words, phrases, or icons are representative of the dialogue's tone or an aspect of the player character's personality, the story editor can work with the design team to make sure that these choices are consistent so that they are always representative of the dialogue choice.

Plot Development

Something that happens to all writers, no matter the storytelling medium, is that they get too "close" to what they're writing. The same is true for game writers and narrative designers creating plot arcs. Even if there's a writing team, all the members of the team can get so familiar with the story that they're not able to step back and see plot holes, contradictions, inaccuracies, or things that don't quite make sense. This is especially true when writers are working with tight deadlines. They don't have opportunities to distance themselves for a period of time and come back to their work with a more critical mindset. An editor has a fresh perspective on the work and can more easily recognize these problems.

If the game has cutscenes and/or cinematics, editors review scripts to see if the storytelling in the cutscenes and cinematics makes sense. Do they advance the plot? Are they confusing? Maybe they are redundant and can be cut. For more on cinematics, please see Chapter 9, "Cinematics and Dialogue."

Additionally, decisions like cutting levels dramatically affect the plot. A character might reference something in level 15 that refers to a major plot point occurring in levels 10–12. The only problem is that the team has decided to remove levels 10–12. Now that comment has no context and doesn't make sense. Removing content from the game (levels, missions/quests, etc.) can create plot holes and inconsistencies, as well. As the game changes during development, editors need to be aware that this can create plot problems and be vigilant in looking for them.

Important questions to answer about a game's plot development:

- Is the game's overarching plot clear?
- If the plot becomes confusing, why?
- Does the story have plot holes?
- Has the team made changes to the game that might create plot issues?
- What suggestions can you make to correct plot holes or inconsistencies?

Characterization and Character Development

Common problems with characters include undefined motivations, inconsistent behavior, and odd word choices for dialogue.

Players need to understand why characters are making choices, whether those characters are player characters, party members, antagonists, or secondary characters. Ill-defined motivations are confusing and lead to players misunderstanding choices they may have to make: "I don't understand why the player character wants to do this. Why am I doing this?" They can also muddy the plot, especially when a plot arc hinges on a character's decision. Character inconsistencies are similar in that the characters' personalities seem to change without a reason from the plot or player decision, and they may say things that contradict their earlier dialogue.

With dialogue, characters may use words that don't fit with their personalities. For example, a calloused cowboy delivering a calf uses clinical language to help the player through the birthing process.

For all three of these issues, editors can identify ways to keep characters' characterization consistent. Focus on characters' personalities, backgrounds, desires, and motivations. What's important to them? How open are they when sharing their feelings? Well-defined characterization keeps their behavior consistent. The cowboy who has no veterinary training will not use the language of a doctor, nor will he have the desire to.

Editors also need to have a sense of a character's development throughout the story. What seems like inconsistent behavior can be explained if the character changes and grows, but the player needs to see and experience this. Is the character's development apparent? What could make it clearer?

The game's characters may have great characterization and development, and the editor can still make suggestions to strengthen them. A game has plenty of opportunities to reveal a character's characterization and development. For example, if a character speaks with a sarcastic and biting tone, the editor can suggest a more cutting word in a scene where the character dresses down her subordinates.

Important questions to answer about characters:

- Can you determine their personalities, desires, and motives through their characterization?
- Do characters behave inconsistently? Why?
- Do characters have a growth arc, and is how and why they're changing clear?
- What opportunities does the team have for better expressions of characterization and development?

Art Assets

Story editors may have opportunities to make notes about art assets. For example, game genres like dating sims, visual novels, RPGs, and interactive-text games use character portraits to accompany dialogue. If story editors are evaluating these types of games, it's important for them to review art assets. Usually, games that use character portraits use a fixed number of art assets per character.

Anthony Washington's emotional states. (*Verdant Skies*, Howling Moon Software, 2018)

Each variation of the portrait expresses the character's emotional state. The emotional state may not fit the tone of the character's dialogue or overall scenario. In these instances, the story editor can suggest an emotional state that would be more applicable. As an editor, when you're familiar with the art assets, you can suggest emotional states and/or poses that you think best represent a character's emotion or what's going on in a scene.

Currently, when he brings up not being "proper," it reads to me as if he feels inferior to Hailey, which is not the vibe I get from the event. So, I'd consider revising his original lines:

[SetEmotion Anthony angry]
Anthony: $Hailey thinks I'm dumb 'cause I don't talk all proper?
[SetEmotion Anthony normal]
Anthony: 'Least I *remember* where I come from ...

When I suggested a revision for this event, I indicated which emotional states would be more appropriate, too.

Sound Assets

It may be useful for the story editor to make notes on music and sound effects. A particular composition may not fit the mood of a cutscene or action sequence, or there may be another theme that's better suited.

If the game uses ambient sound, the story editor can note adding sound effects to a level to aid in its worldbuilding and environmental narrative. Additionally, a sound effect may be tonally off in a particular scenario.

Feedback, Budgets, and Time

A studio looking to make a game with strong narrative design and/or story should include narrative designers and game writers at the beginning of the development process. The same is true if you're looking to work with story editors. Developmental editing best serves both technical and creative processes when the editor is involved from the beginning. The DE helps identify and iterate on narrative design and story issues *before* they're implemented into a build.

Resolving problems becomes significantly more difficult the closer the game gets to release, especially if the story editor gives feedback on a significant part of the plot, quests, and/or assets. These fixes become costly and time consuming—if not impossible.

Developmental editing is important for *any* game with a story, but it's especially important in fast-paced environments. When the narrative designer(s) and/or writer(s) have to produce content quickly, they're more prone to errors, like plot holes and character inconsistencies. A DE working closely with the writing team will spot these holes, notice what's confusing and/or unexplained, and give suggestions for improvement. This gives the team time to iterate on story and get even more feedback to polish the narrative experience.

Sensitivity Reading and Diversity Consulting

More and more developers are hiring sensitivity readers and/or diversity consultants for their projects. Sensitivity readers and diversity consultants analyze the representation of marginalized groups, their communities, and cultures in a work to see if those representations are accurate and if they include any biases or stereotypes. They also review these representations to make sure that they're relatable and positive representations.[2] A developer should exhaust all efforts to find a sensitivity reader/ diversity consultant who has personal experience with the marginalized representations in the game.

As the role suggests, sensitivity readers *read* stories or documentation, while a diversity consultant may review documentation, art assets, sound assets, and any other game components that represent or reflect a marginalized group.[3] Sensitivity reading and diversity consulting, in effect, are specialized subsets of developmental editing because they analyze the content used to tell the story. A game may require a sensitivity reader or diversity consultant when any marginalized group (gender, racial/ethnic, sexuality, religious, with physical disabilities or mental illnesses) is a part of a game.

A DIVERSITY CONSULTANT'S SKILLS

What skills do you need if you'd like to be a diversity consultant/sensitivity reader? As is the case with editing, you don't need to be a writer (or even a game developer!) to be a diversity consultant or sensitivity reader. However, you do need to understand gameplay and game design if you're evaluating a project's narrative design.

To be an effective sensitivity reader or diversity consultant, you'll need the following background(s) and skillsets:

Personal Experience

A diversity consultant/sensitivity reader with a similar background as the marginalized group represented in the game has real-life, lived-in experiences that can speak to the authenticity of a character's portrayal.

Analytical Skills

All editors need strong analytical skills, but diversity consultants and sensitivity readers analyze a game's design from a *cultural* context, not just a storytelling one. Explaining why a piece of feedback is culturally significant emphasizes why an element in the game is problematic or doing something right. Developers need that cultural context to know how to improve their portrayals of characters and cultures and not make the same mistakes in the future.

Education

Certain majors are perfect for this role because of the historical and cultural contexts they can bring to their feedback, on top of their personal experience with the subject matter. These majors have studied how marginalized groups have been portrayed in media and can recognize problematic representations:

- *Sociology*: gives an understanding of societal systems and how they affect marginalized groups.
- *Minority literature*: brings a wealth of knowledge of how indigenous, women, queer, Asian diasporic, African diasporic, and Latin diasporic writers and writers with disabilities write about and represent their cultures and communities.
- *Gender and feminist studies*: includes study of different gender identities and how societal and cultural systems impact people of different genders.
- *Historical studies (especially of minority communities)*: gives contexts for how stereotypes of marginalized communities have developed and why.
- *Pop-culture studies*: understands how marginalized communities have been portrayed in mainstream storytelling media.

Awareness of Where You're Not Knowledgeable

No group is a monolith. You'll be able to speak from your own personal experience and educational knowledge, but it's important for the developer to realize that you can't speak on behalf of *all* members of a marginalized group. Your life can't be representative of the entire group, even if you share similar lived experiences with some members of that community.

Also, it's okay if you lack some knowledge about a certain subject or group. In fact, it's great if you can tell the developer that they'll need additional consultants.

Patience

This last one may sound hokey, but it shouldn't be overlooked. Portrayals of marginalized individuals can be frustrating if not traumatizing, especially when destructive portrayals are prevalent in storytelling media. However, developers working with diversity consultants and sensitivity readers are probably making a good-faith effort to do justice by their marginalized characters and players. They *want* to get it right, and it might take some extra explaining as to what's wrong and how to fix it, especially when they're new to the concepts you're breaking down. These are mistakes they won't want to make again, so they'll need to get *why* they're mistakes.

However, if it turns out that the developer *is not* acting in good faith, don't hesitate to break off that relationship. Nobody deserves to be used.

Editing *Verdant Skies*

I recently worked as a diversity consultant on *Verdant Skies* (Howling Moon Software, 2018), a life sim with a highly diverse group of NPCs. Specifically, I served as an editor for Anthony, an African American NPC. In editing Anthony's content, I did everything from a developmental edit on his quests and characterization to his dialogue word choice.

One of Anthony's most important relationships is with his sister Hailey. While they grew up in the same middle-class family, Hailey and Anthony have very different points of view in how Black people should represent themselves—a very real and passionate debate within the Black community that can lead to mild teasing at best and ostracization and physical harm at worst. Hailey espouses her middle-class upbringing, while Anthony sees her as "proper" and chooses to speak Black English (BE). As I read through Anthony's dialogue and events, I saw that he referred to Hailey as "proper," but there was no context for his comment.

```
385            [SetEmotion Anthony concern]
386   Anthony:   Just 'cause I don't talk all proper like $Hailey don't mean I'm dumb or nothin'.
387            [SetEmotion Anthony normal]
388   Anthony:   I know plenty of stuff.
389            [end]
390   //I remember Hailey from the demo and her formality, so I'm wondering why Anthony's speech is markedly different. They grew up in the same household.
391   //How did their parents speak? How was he raised to speak? Did Anthony pick this up in the military? Additionally, talking/speaking "proper" has a specific
392   //cultural connotation for African Americans. Is this intentional? If so, we'll want to unpack this a bit. The "proper" issue is a sensitive one, with being "proper"
393   //a deeply negative thing for some--acting/speaking "too White" (I was accused of being too proper when I was a kid)--or a positive thing, an illustration of education
394   //and sophistication, as Anthony suggests.
```

Since that term comes with a lot of cultural baggage, I discussed it with Beth Korth, *Verdant Skies*'s narrative designer. She added an event explaining the conflict between the siblings. Now my job as a diversity consultant was to make sure this event struck the right tone, while giving the necessary context for how the siblings viewed each other. This is a sensitive subject, one that's hotly debated in families, and we wanted to make sure the issue in this fictional family was treated with respect.

Always give context for your feedback. The developer needs to understand why you're suggesting a change (as is the case with anything). Here is an exchange I had with narrative designer Korth, as we discussed the event over e-mail:

As for the background of the "proper" comment. Thank you for pointing that out! They were raised in the same household, so that's a fair question that I guess we haven't addressed. I think their parents speak much like Hailey. I think Anthony probably gets his speech from his grandparents who would speak more like he does. I try to do some commentary on touchy subjects in the other NPC's arcs. Such as Emma/Rosie choosing not to get ocular implants to improve her vision because she doesn't see being different as being inferior. "Our differences are beautiful." Ramón discusses mental health openly and compares therapy to going to the doctor. "There's nothing wrong with seeking help for an ailment." So I'd love to be able to use this as a "The way we talk isn't a reason to fight. Neither of us is 'better' because of the way we speak" moment.

If there were an event between the siblings that addresses the discrepancy, do you think it would help? I'm thinking something along the lines of.

Anthony: *You* and our folks always givin' me a hard time 'bout it. I don't wanna be like *you*. I don't need to be like *them*."
Hailey: And *you* do not have to be so much like Grandfather.
Anthony: Least he knows who he is. Where he came from.
Hailey: I refuse to discuss this with you again. Neither of us shall budge on our stance. Regardless of our differences, you are still my brother, my family. I will love you no matter which words you choose to use … or choose *not* to use. Can you not say the same of me?"
Anthony: Awww… Hell, Sis. Ya know I love ya. I wouldn't have come all this way if I didn't.
Then they notice the player and quick go back to their "professional" personas.

This would work. Is this event before or after the "proper" comment? In any case, I think "proper" has to be put in context when Anthony mentions it. The proper issue points to the monolithic argument of "Who gets to be authentically Black?", which comes across in the conversation above. So, if Anthony chooses to be more "real" like his grandfather ("Least he knows who he is. Where he came from."), it means he's judging his parents and Hailey. In this case, the way Anthony and Hailey speak is a point of pride for them. Speaking BE is how Anthony chooses to present himself and a part of his identity.

Currently, when he brings up not being "proper," it reads to me as if he feels inferior to Hailey, which is not the vibe I get from the event. So, I'd consider revising his original lines.

Copyediting and Proofreading: Low-Level Editing

Unlike developmental editors, copyeditors and proofreaders have less of an influence on the way games tell stories. However, they're still important. Copyeditors and proofreaders are refiners; they polish the writing that will eventually go into the game.

Copyediting

Ideally, a copyeditor should review the writing once it's been through at least one revision. The copyeditor checks for accuracy and inconsistencies, revises for clarity, and edits out repetition.

Accuracy

A major part of a copyeditor's job is to check the story's accuracy. This can include correct dates, spellings of real-world people and entities, spellings of scientific and technological terms, spellings of brand names, quotations from people or works—anything based in the real world that might appear in the game in some form.

Copyeditors also check for continuity errors and inconsistencies. A character might reference an event before it happens, or a character talks about a monster's "soulless green eyes," but the monster's eyes are actually purple.

Dialogue

I mentioned that developmental editors focus on characterization. A DE gets more of an overall sense of characters and their word choice, giving recommendations for strengthening their characterization and development. The copyeditor is more detail oriented when it comes to dialogue, focusing on every word writers and narrative designers give their characters.

Copyeditors analyze the word choice characters use and whether it accurately represents their characterization, for the same reasons a DE does.

The copyeditor must keep in mind the game's overall tone, as well as the right tone for characters in each line of their dialogue. Players will notice dialogue that doesn't work with the tone of the game or that doesn't fit a scene. The mood of a cutscene/cinematic, interaction with a specific character, or other purpose for dialogue affects a character's tone. If a mentor character has a playful relationship with a player character, a serious line of dialogue from that character can come across as unintentional dark foreshadowing. On the other hand, if it's *supposed* to be foreshadowing, the change in tone is to get the player's attention.

Copyeditors also identify confusing word choice and repetitive lines. Shorter dialogue is always better, and the copyeditor can revise lines so that they read more succinctly. For example:

Shorter dialogue is better. Copyeditors revise for concision.

A Quick Note on the Technical Benefits of Story Editors

Reducing budget and production time are additional benefits of copyediting dialogue.[4] Editing out lines or shortening them means fewer hours in the recording booth for voiced dialogue. While editors focus on the more creative aspects of a game, their feedback leads to more tangible benefits. Editors trim text. This means that fewer words end up in the game. This cuts production time. They may suggest cutscene/cinematic revisions, meaning less production time for programmers, artists, animators, riggers, and sound designers.

Voiced Dialogue

As I alluded to above, if the game is voiced, copyeditors should review scripts before voice actors go to the recording booth. Copyeditors also identify tongue twisters that can trip up voice actors. Certain words and phrases may seem just fine on the page, but they're a jumble when spoken. Lines with consonance, assonance, and alliteration are potential mouthfuls for the best voice actors, even ones like "She sells seashells down by the seashore."

Unvoiced Dialogue

Unvoiced dialogue has the same problems that voiced dialogue does, but it has another important characteristic copyeditors should be aware of. It's better to not write phonetic representations of accents and dialects into voiced dialogue (like "I'mma," "guvnah," etc.). Voice actors can interpret these as caricaturistic and give an over-the-top performance as a result. It's better to tell voice actors what accent the character has, and let them read that into the performance.

However, phonetic representations for accents and dialects are important in unvoiced dialogue. It's the only way writers can *show* readers what characters sound like. In these cases, the copyeditor needs to keep the accents consistent. Words representing the character's accent should be spelled the same way every time.

Copyeditors and proofreaders may have hundreds of pages to review, and the word may appear less than 20 times throughout. They can check the word against the game's style guide to see how to spell certain words. (For more on style guides, please see "Developing a Style Guide" on p. 174.)

Informational/Instructional Texts

Copyeditors revise all other types of game text, including information on menu screens and directions in tutorials and the UI layout. These texts must be clearly written, since they're explaining controls, gameplay, and mechanics. They must also be succinct. These texts tend to be one sentence or phrase, and not more than two sentences. There is not much room in menus or the UI for lots of words, and players won't have the patience to read them. If the text layout is confusing or difficult to read in other ways (a text box clips a line of text or the spacing makes the text too "crowded"), the copyeditor needs to point this out and/or give suggestions for revision.

Grammar

Sure, copyeditors correct grammatical errors, but that's not why I'm drawing attention to grammar in this chapter. Sometimes it makes sense for writing in games *not* to be grammatical. (Yes, that seismic rumbling of the world was caused by millions of editors shuddering in unison.)

For instance, there are certain things players need to remember. These can be mechanics, items, any number of things. To emphasize this to the player, games use nonstandard capitalization. If players glance through the dialogue, the capitalized word stands out among the rest of the text. One of the studios for which I edit always uses numerals instead of spelling out numbers.[5] The Arabic numeral visualizes the number for the player:

> *Did you find the 6 hostages?*
> *vs.*
> *Did you find the six hostages?*

Whether the game's text will bend grammatical rules is something the team should discuss with the copyeditor, and they should share these decisions with the proofreader.

Proofreading

Proofreading is the last stage of the editing process. While one editor can have the skillsets needed for any of these roles, the person who proofreads a project *should not* be the developmental editor or copyeditor. The proofreader takes the writing that has gone through all of the rewrites and will be implemented into the game.

The proofreader does a final pass for grammatical errors, typos, and punctuation usage. Because production deadlines are often tight, a game can be shipped with a lot of errors that could easily be fixed with proofreading. These are embarrassing, and players will notice them. (And in Let's Plays and walkthrough videos, content creators and influencers *will* point them out to viewers.) Developers should include time in the schedule for a final proofread.

Developing a Style Guide

Every studio—and every project—needs its own style guide. Also known as a manual of style, a style guide establishes best practices for formatting, typography, and spelling. When following the style guide, writers keep spelling throughout a project consistent, making the copyeditor's and proofreader's work easier. Style guides also makes it easier to lay out text.

While studios adopt style guides like Chicago Manual of Style, AP, and MLA, they should consider adapting these depending on a project's needs or developing their own style guides. They can consult with a copyeditor during this process or hire a copyeditor to develop one for them.

It's a good idea for studios to have a dedicated style guide per project. For example, something the UI designer will have to figure out is how many characters (not words or letters, but the number of words, letters, punctuation, and spaces) can fit into a text box. This can affect simple things like how to format ellipses:

- "a…predicament…indeed"
- "a… predicament… indeed"
- "a . . . predicament . . . indeed," or
- "a … predicament … indeed"

If you don't have many characters per textbox, you need to preserve space. The best way to format ellipses would be to not use any spaces ("a…predicament…indeed"). This may seem like a small thing, but it will eliminate … later predicaments when the team realizes it hasn't decided on character limits per text box or formatting issues that might come with them.

Things developers can put in their bespoke style guides:

- Number of lines per menu text box
- Number of lines per dialogue text box
- Number of lines per instructional/informational text
- Number of characters per each type of text box
- Deciding to use bolding, italics, or underlining for emphasis in dialogue
- Listing nonstandard grammatical usage and why
- Listing nonstandard spellings for dialogue and lore

Modes for Giving Feedback

Work in the industry long enough, and you'll find that nothing is standard. Studios have different tools and methods for delivering writing, and this can change from project to project. The same is true of editing, especially since there are so few named roles for editors in the industry. If the developer you're working with does not have an editing process, you might be the individual best suited to help your team establish some best practices.

What kind of documentation is the dev team using? Some documents are easier to edit than others, like Word documents. You can easily use track changes and add comments. For other platforms, you might have to be more creative. A lot of developers generate their scripts in spreadsheets. The editor can use the furthermost columns for notes and make revisions directly into the spreadsheet. Notes can include questions for needed clarity, suggestions, or explanations for an edit. If the writing is in text files, you can add lines with two forward slashes followed by your feedback.

A Feedback Summary

Additionally, a breakdown of your feedback in an e-mail or Word document can summarize all of your granular comments. Categorize your areas of review according to the project's needs (characters, plot, worldbuilding, etc.), and summarize your feedback in each section. This puts your feedback in documents and spreadsheets into an overall context.

Whatever your methods, the most important thing is that your communication is clear, and that the devs you're working with understand that feedback. There's always an initial period where the individuals you're working with have to get used to the way you write and speak. You might have to tweak the way you communicate to suit your audience. Lots of bullet points, short paragraphs, and white space between paragraphs make feedback easily digestible.

A Story Editing Sample

I'd like to include a high-level summary with categories to illustrate the kind of feedback you might give in a comprehensive developmental edit. Or, if you're looking to work with an editor, these are the types of critiques you might request. The following is feedback I gave to one of my students for his Twine game.[6] I've excerpted my comments.

Does each ending feel unique?

To a point. Each scenario feels unique (making it to safety, being taken as refugees, being jailed, etc.). Within each scenario, the results can be more positive or more negative. This is when things start to feel repetitive, especially on third and fourth playthroughs. The endings read the same except for a few different sentences here and there.

Do the game's choices feel meaningful?

The last meaningful choice comes about two-thirds of the way. After this, the player has no control over the story's outcome. It would be good if there were another choice that determined whether the cadets reached safety, were taken as refugees, starved to death, were taken prisoner (and could find some way to escape), etc.

Did the dialogue choices make sense, and did they feel like distinct choices?

Most of the dialogue is to establish the PC's personality and backstory through the game's first and second acts.

There are times when there's very little difference between lines of dialogue. Additionally, sometimes NPCs have no response to a line of dialogue, when it would make sense for them to react. Some lines of dialogue result in the exact same NPC response. For example, in several of the endings, Erhart's response and the PC's subsequent reaction are always the same:

"It doesn't matter anymore, [Rolled Name]. It's over." Erhart murmurs. You sit up, frowning.

These make the choices feel arbitrary.

However, the players' final choices that lead to the ending they get do feel meaningful. They make a decisive decision whether to stay and fight or leave. There's also the authority (or lack thereof) with which they make this decision.

Suggestions for improving the worldbuilding

I think you can pare back on the worldbuilding. At the end of the game, there's a bit of a worldbuilding dump. Names of ruling parties and multiple locations in conflict get namedropped … Since the player must choose between the Northern Principalities and Mercina, it's important to understand what these places are like and why they figure so prominently. What are the cultural differences between the two? How do these differences appear in-game?

Conclusion: The Editor–Developer Relationship

Because editors and writers work so closely together, they develop a collaborative relationship. In games, the editor must also consider a relationship with anyone else who has a hand in making storytelling decisions. It's important that the team trust you as soon as possible and that you cultivate that relationship. Develop your own editing style in the way you communicate feedback. This should be flexible from team to team, as what you need to edit and the people with whom you work change. Whether you're a DE, copyeditor, or proofreader, you're there to make the story in the game better, and any suggestions or edits you make are to the writing's—and the team's—advantage.

Ultimately, trust your own knowledge of what story is and can be, and listen to your intuition. That might sound a little silly, especially for a discipline that follows strict guidelines and rules. But sometimes—just sometimes—you know it might be best to capitalize "Hammer" in the middle of a sentence.

Exercise: Developmental Edit

Watch a Let's Player on YouTube or Twitch play a short story–heavy game or an episode from an episodic game that's 1–2 hours. Pay attention to the game's worldbuilding, overall plot, character growth, player choices, and dialogue.

Part I: Think about the following:

- Do you have a good grasp of the world?
    - Does the worldbuilding make sense?
    - How do the game's narrative design and writing express the world?
    - Is there anything about the world that confuses you?
- How does the game advance the plot?
    - Do you notice any plot holes?
    - Is the story clear in the cutscenes and cinematics?
    - Are there other ways the plot could be clearer?
- How do the characters develop throughout the game?
    - Do their arcs make sense, and can players follow those arcs?
    - Are their characterizations consistent?
    - Do they always behave in ways that make sense for their characters?
- Do characters' individual personalities come through in their dialogue?
    - How could lines of dialogue be rewritten to match the personalities of the characters speaking them?
- Are the choices for decisions or dialogue clear, if the game has branching narrative or dialogue trees?
    - Why are they unclear, if that's the case?

Part II: Write feedback based on your analysis from Part I. How would you communicate your ideas for revision with the team?

Notes

1. The critical path (or critpath) is all of the required elements (gameplay, missions/quests, narrative) a player must progress through to complete a game.

2. By "positive," I'm not suggesting that these characters must be morally good. They should be well-rounded, believable people with strengths and flaws—not harmful, walking stereotypes that are pervasive in media.
3. Additionally, diversity consultants cover technical facets of a game, such as accessibility issues for gamers with physical disabilities (although the technical diversity consultant is beyond the scope of this book).
4. For more on budgetary benefits, please watch Cameron Harris's seminal talk on editing from the 2014 Game Developers Conference: https://www.youtube.com/watch?v=Fg-hpcxRkXl
5. Most style guides state that writers should not use Arabic numerals for numbers 1–9.
6. Many thanks to David Ornelas for letting me reference his work!

CHAPTER 13

Freelancing in Games: Narrative Mercenaries for Hire

Toiya Kristen Finley, PhD

Contents

So, Why Freelance? 181
What a Freelancer Is and Is Not 181
Experience vs. Inexperience 181
    And What If You Don't Have Experience? 181
    But How Do You Get That Experience? 182
Work Is Work 183
Skills Every Freelancer Needs 185
Freelancing Skill #1: Time Management 185
Freelancing Skill #2: Marketing 185
Freelancing Skill #3: Knowing Your Worth 186
    Be Aware of Your Hats, and Get Paid for Each One You Wear 186
    Don't Wear Hats That Don't Fit 186
Freelancing Skill #4: Protecting Yourself 187
Freelancing Skill #5: Networking 187
Freelancing Skill #6: Assessing Client Needs 187
Freelancing Skill #7: Professionalism 188
Establishing Rates and Finding Work 189
Don't Lowball (Seriously, Don't Do It) 189
Lowball, and the Cheapskates Win (Or: Don't Screw with My Money) 190
Establishing Rates 190
Thrive, Don't Just Survive 191
What Are the Going Rates? 191
Minimum, Maximum, or Somewhere in between? 192
Contracts and Clauses 192
Strongly Consider Adding This Clause 194
The Up-Front Payment 195
Finding Work 195
Clients You Want to Work with 197
Evaluating Potential Jobs and Prospective Clients 197

Don't Stare at Your Inbox.. 198
    How to Submit an Application 198
Establishing Professional Relationships.................................... 198
    Make Sure You're in Contact with the One Making the Final Decision 199
Conclusion: Mercenaries for Hire 199
Exercise: Query a Developer 200
Sample Query Letter... 201
References 201

In this chapter, I hope to cover content that will benefit everyone from writers and narrative designers exploring the option to freelance to freelancing veterans. Since freelancing is about running your own business, you'll need to use this information and mold it into what works for you. We communicate differently. We have different skills, strengths, and weaknesses. As far as getting prospective clients* to take you on, all freelancers are tried by fire. You'll discover what works for you, and you'll *always* be refining your techniques.

In this Chapter

- What freelancing in game writing means
- What to do and what not to do when approaching freelancing
- The business side of working as a game writer for hire

You'll read the word "research" several times, and I'm using it very much as a command. If you want to be successful, you've got to research clients, how to present your portfolio, and how to report your taxes, among other things.

I'll share some freelancing skills with you. We don't usually think of these as skills, and they're different from skills you've developed as a storyteller in games. Freelancing skills help you maintain your business and grow as a businessperson. They can also get you work over candidates who have more experience.

Also, I will be giving you some hard truths. I'll be brutally honest—freelancing can be difficult. It can be difficult to find good clients, as vying for freelance work is highly competitive; you might go through a dry month or two … or many. I've been through some very lean times, so I'm subject to those same hard truths, and I'll be preaching to myself, as well. However, I will not give you hard truths without giving you hope.

And here's some hope …

---

* Prospective clients are individuals freelancers identify as good matches to work with in the near future.

So, Why Freelance?

I've been working in games for 10 years solely as a freelancer, and I have never seen so many freelance gigs as I have in the past couple of years. There are fewer and fewer permanent jobs in the industry. Story-based indie projects, narrative-focused franchises from studios like Telltale Games and BioWare, and the white-hot popularity of dating sims and text-based "choose your own adventure" titles on mobile create the need for more narrative designers and writers. The fact is, if you're considering freelancing, you have *so many* opportunities. A lot of prospective clients are looking to make games. A lot of these clients are not game developers. They know they need guidance from people who understand games and game development. There are developers who are looking to subcontract work. Whether you want to telecommute or work onsite, there are gigs out there for you.

What a Freelancer Is and Is Not

Freelancing is a business. A freelancer is an independent contractor. You're self-employed, which means you're your own boss. You determine whom you do and don't want to work with. You can fire your clients. You establish what your work is worth and how much you will be paid. You determine what projects you will and won't take on, and you are responsible for your work schedule.

I can't stress this enough: you are *not* an employee. You are in collaborative relationships with your clients—they're not your bosses. There are freelancers with years of experience who have the employee mindset. You want to avoid this because *you* want to be in charge of your business, not your client. This also means that if you're in the United States, you're not eligible for employee benefits or worker's compensation, and you may not have job security.

Experience vs. Inexperience

A major frustration for people looking for work is their lack of experience. They feel they're shut out of most opportunities because they don't meet the criteria listed on the job posting, whether that's number of years in the industry, number of shipped titles, or both. How can they get the prerequisite experience if they never meet prospective clients' criteria?

And What If You Don't Have Experience?

You'll hear veteran freelancers say you need several years of experience in the brick-and-mortar world before you try a career in freelancing. I don't disagree with them; however, as I've already stated, you have so many freelancing opportunities in games. If you're earning a degree in game development or you already have a degree in game development, you can find smaller writing gigs to gain valuable experience. Prospective clients want to see that you've been able start and complete a project. It doesn't have to be a large one.

But How Do You Get That Experience?

First, you're going to have to build your portfolio.

Prospective clients are going to want see samples of your work. If your work is under NDA, simply ask whomever has the rights to it if you can use it in your portfolio. I've never had anyone turn down this type of request; it's also good advertising for their brand or IP (intellectual property). Showing actual work that was used in a project gives you credibility and proves that you're a professional.

You want to start with smaller jobs or jobs where you don't carry a lot of responsibility because you know it won't be difficult to produce stellar work and finish quickly. For example, an indie studio is working on a nonstory game. The creative lead is doing the coding, game design, and sound design, but she's going to hire an artist. She needs a writer to design three NPCs so she can give the bios and details to the artist. A job like this would take under 10 hours of work, but it would get you an all-important credit.

Please note:

- "Quickly" does not mean "cheaply."
- Even though you won't spend much time on them, you still need to ask for professional rates for shorter gigs (please see "Establishing Rates and Finding Work").

The Online Portfolio

All freelancers need a website where people can find them. Your website should include your contact information, résumé, and any credits you might have. The type of clients you want to attract are going to vet you, so give them a good impression with your website and your online portfolio.

You can get free websites and design them yourself. Research your options. Your website doesn't have to be the most amazingly designed ever; it just needs to contain the information that will give prospective clients a picture of who you are and what you do.

Make sure your writing is error free. Proofread, proofread again, and proofread some more. Have others proofread it. Not every prospective client can identify typos and grammatical errors, but you don't want to take that chance. People will notice clunky, awkward writing.

Watermark and convert to PDFs any documents you post online. Plagiarism is rampant. Portfolio theft is common. While PDFs won't protect your work completely, they make it harder to steal content. And, if people are lazy enough not do their own work, they may not want to mess with PDFs. Alternatively, you can let a prospective client know your samples are available upon request.

If you have social media connected to your professional online presence, don't talk, post, or tweet about things that might make you come across as a liability.

Work Is Work

Do jobs that may not be in games but will get you experience (and cash flow). If you can write for comics, write for comics. If someone needs a substantive editor for their children's book, do it. Or you might have a prospective client who may not need a game designer, but they don't know how to write a game design document. You can end up with a credit as a game-design consultant.

Don't sit around waiting for that job in games when there are viable opportunities for you to use your skills. The experience you gain on these jobs will make you a more attractive candidate for future game jobs, and they build your storytelling and freelancing skills. For example, I have experience writing for children, so that has gotten me work doing narrative design on kids' games.

PLEASE LEARN FROM MY IGNORANCE, PART I

People like to get groups together to make a game for experience. These development teams start out really excited because they can do just about anything they want … and then the team usually falls apart. Nobody's getting paid, they have real-world jobs, and they have other commitments. It's hard to find time and energy to expend on a project that doesn't address the many financial needs of the team. I joined up with such a starry-eyed group once. The project was dead in about a month.

It's better to spend your energy looking for a job that will pay you—something you can put on your CV or résumé.

A Note about "Passion"

Passion's a great thing. Passion keeps you going, especially when you're slogging through a project or you don't know when you're going to get your next job. Passion will make you want to be better at what you do.

And, yet, I see "passion" everywhere, as if it were some kind of secret sauce. I've been to many a convention where eager individuals looking to break in talk about how passionate they are for story in games with great exuberance: "I have a passion for writing, and I've had a passion for videogames ever since I was 5."

As you have probably noticed, I have "passion" in scare quotes.

You have passion? To that I say, "So what?" Does that seem harsh? People will go on and on about their passion because they're just oozing and about to explode with this frustration to make *everybody* understand just how *great* they could be if someone would Just. Give. Them. The. Chance!

WHAT PASSION MEANS TO PROSPECTIVE CLIENTS

But do you know how "I have passion" translates to a prospective client?

- "I have no experience, so I have to sell you on my passion."
- "I'm *soooo* passionate that I just might take over your project and do whatever I want."
- "At some point, I might lose my passion. Wonder if it'll be on *your* job?"
- "Doing something I love is its own reward. You don't have to pay me much (if at all)!"

Passion is an emotion. It's not expertise or a skill.

OTHER PROBLEMATIC BUZZWORDS

- "Aspiring"
- "Student"
- "Amateur" (Yes, people say this.)
- "Looking for Experience"

I've seen all of these in bios, online profiles, or on business cards at one time or another, even from professionals who are "looking for experience" as freelancers.

All of these attract scammers. You'll see notes in job postings that say, "Good for students and people looking for experience." What this *actually* means is "I'll pay you next to *nuthin*, and I'mma probably treat you like crap, too."

When you're developing your profile or bio, don't say things like "I'm a student writer" or "I'm an aspiring narrative designer." You're a writer. You're a narrative designer. OWN IT.

Remember that people are spending money. Their projects are important to them. They're not going to invest in contractors who don't exude confidence and professionalism in what they do.

Skills Every Freelancer Needs

There's another important aspect of experience, and this is the development of freelancing skills. The last time I worked in an office, I was in college. My entire professional life, I've been self-employed with a stint of part-time employment mixed in with my freelance gigs. All of my work has been done from home in front of my laptop. With no supervision, I had to learn how to better manage my time. After several projects, I learned how long it would take me to complete certain tasks. For example, I have a sense for how long it will take me to write story bibles of different lengths.

This brings us to …

Freelancing Skill #1: Time Management

Time management is important because clients are going to want to know how long tasks will take during the proposal stage. They see *you* as the expert on this. They will most likely have their own timetable for a project's completion, which may or may not be a rigid schedule. They may also look to you to help them set realistic dates for deliverables.

Because you'll most likely need to work more than one job at once, time management also helps you figure out how work intensive jobs are going to be and whether you can dedicate your energy to them.

With experience, you also learn what work should and should not entail; your clients may not always know this, and you might have to educate them. If you've been hired as a narrative designer, that does not mean you'll also be doing the lore writing—even if you have experience writing lore.

Experience gives you confidence. When you see a job posting, and it's similar to work you've done before, you know you can do a great job on that project. Your experience also will help you figure out how much a job will cost because you'll know everything that you'll need to do. You'll know how intensive it's going to be, how long it will take you, and how much energy you'll have to put into it.

Freelancing Skill #2: Marketing

As a freelancer running a business, you're always going to have to market yourself and make a good impression. Your online presence is part of marketing, including your LinkedIn profile, Twitter, portfolio, or profile on freelance sites (for more on these, please see "Freelance Platforms"). Any chance you have to speak in person about who you are and what you do is *also* marketing. You want to make sure you always present your business as professionally as possible.

Freelancing Skill #3: Knowing Your Worth

This is understanding the value of your skills and the value that you, with your insight and experience, bring to a project. When you don't know what you're worth, you can get scammed. You can work with clients who treat you as a cheap commodity. You might realize that you've *undervalued* a project, and you're doing a lot more work than what you're going to get paid for. That can make you bitter and stressed. I *way* undervalued some projects when I started out, and it made me miserable. I was not going to get paid for all of the time and energy I was putting in. But this has made me smarter. When you know what you're worth, you're going to attract the prospective clients you really want to work with. They respect what you do, and they'll respect your asking price, even if they can't always afford it. Sometimes, and this has been the case with me, a client will decide to work with me even though they end up paying more than they had allotted in their budget.

Be Aware of Your Hats, and Get Paid for Each One You Wear

The more hats you wear, the more valuable you are. This is true at studios, and you can apply this to your freelancing. My understanding and work as a game designer informs my narrative design. This is a way for me to approach prospective clients.

If I'm working on the game design and narrative design, I should be paid for both.

If I'm hired for narrative design, and I end up doing game design without additional payment, this is *scope creep*.[*]

I had a project where I was hired to establish the worldbuilding for potential transmedia projects. The client later wanted me to take on a writing project, so we negotiated the cost for it and drafted a separate contract. Writing the transmedia was not considered part of developing the worldbuilding.

That might sound obvious, but lots of freelancers take on extra tasks because they believe they've been hired to do them, or they like the client, so they do it for free, or the client guilt trips them into it for one reason or another.

Don't Wear Hats That Don't Fit

Don't try to work outside of your skill set. If the client asks you to do something and you can't, let them know. If you realize the client needs to add somebody to their team or project because there's no one with that skill set, let them know that, too.

---

[*] In freelancing, scope creep is work outside of the parameters you negotiate with your client, and you're never paid for that extra work.

Freelancing Skill #4: Protecting Yourself

Know your responsibilities on a project. Know your contracts. Use the information in your contract to protect you against scope creep and nonpayment. I had a client who subcontracted game design and narrative design work to me. They decided they weren't going to pay me. However, I was in contact with their client, and I let them know that the developer had never had me sign a nondisclosure agreement (NDA),* even after I had offered to. The client was very protective of their IP, so I used not signing an NDA to my advantage.

Freelancing Skill #5: Networking

Don't simply talk about games or what you enjoy about your work. Networking is akin to marketing. During networking opportunities, learn how to discuss your areas of expertise and freelancing skills in the context of prospective client's projects or even when you're sharing with other professionals. Show them why they need you and how you might be a part of their project. This doesn't mean that you jump into a conversation and start talking about what you do and that you're available—you should make this a natural part of the conversation.

Networking can lead to speaking engagements and book projects (like this one)! I've been invited to speak at and attend conferences, which has led to referrals, repeat clients, and contributions to several books. Three of my game projects have come directly from referrals through networking, and one came because of the client's awareness of one of my books. Most jobs in the industry are hidden, meaning they're never advertised, and people ask their friends and colleagues if they know anyone who would be good for specific roles.

Freelancing Skill #6: Assessing Client Needs

Read between the lines of what the prospective client does and does not say. Verbalize what the client cannot. Either it's something they don't understand, and they really *need* to, or it's something they haven't considered because you're the expert. For example, they want you to develop a super-detailed world for a clicker game, but you explain that players don't expect detailed worldbuilding or stories in clicker games. They'll most likely get frustrated with a story interrupting their gameplay. Instead, you explain how you can deliver story through the art and character animations.

I mentioned this earlier, but some of your clients may be nondevelopers. They may not even play games. They don't have the same terminology or knowledge that you do. You may have to be patient with them to help them express what they want.

---

* For a good primer on NDAs, see Reference 1.

Freelancing Skill #7: Professionalism

Be professional in all aspects of your business and communication. If you have a break-up, keep it professional, even if they don't. You don't want a reputation of being difficult to work with.

Dishonest clients may try to blackmail you on freelance websites. They'll promise not to leave bad feedback if you agree to receive less payment or no payment at all. Don't give in to this. Report this behavior. You may have to take a hit to your ratings and in reviews. But giving in teaches clients they can bully freelancers, and it will keep you from hard-earned payments. *NEVER* refund money for work you've done.

Do help clients understand what they need, and don't wear hats that don't fit. You're going to have to help developers and nondevelopers alike understand your role and responsibilities. I worked with a client who didn't know what game bibles and game design documents were. I explained why they were necessary. The client didn't have the funds to pay me to write them, so I gave him some examples, and he wrote the game bible and GDD himself. If the project needs something that you can't provide, be generous with your advice. On that same job, I told the client he needed a level designer, but that level designer couldn't be me.

Remember that, ultimately, it's not your project, and you're not the one putting money into it. You can give advice. Address your concerns. You can try to steer your clients in a certain direction. If they don't agree, don't keep pushing them.

The Freelance Life Is a Research Life (Especially When It Comes to the Legal Stuff)

I am not a lawyer. This is not legal advice but some topics that you will need to explore.

TAXES AND LAWS FOR INDEPENDENT CONTRACTORS

Freelancers are subject to specific tax laws; these are different than the taxes an employee has to file. In the European Union, for example, there's the value-added tax. In the United States, freelancers may make quarterly payments on their earnings throughout the year.

Keep excellent records of your earnings and expenses because you have to report them. These include:

- Invoices sent to clients
- Receipts for travel (plane/train/taxi/rideshare, hotel, meals)
- Supplies

- Equipment
- Professional growth (like conferences, courses, books on games and writing, and videogames)

You might also think about forming a sole proprietorship or private limited company.

Consider the advantages and disadvantages of starting a company and the costs for running it, including business taxes. If you have access to a business advisor or lawyer, explore this with them.

WORK-FOR-HIRE AGREEMENTS

If you are in Japan, the United Kingdom, the United States, or Australia, your job may be work for hire; under a work-for-hire agreement, your client usually will own all rights to the work. Be sure to read up on work-for-hire law!

You must transfer your rights to the client, so your contract will need to specify this (and we'll get into clauses you need in contracts in a bit).

Establishing Rates and Finding Work

And now for that popular question: How much do I charge? I'll tell you what you *don't* want to do first, and that's lowball.

Don't Lowball (Seriously, Don't Do It)

Lowballing is working for a ridiculously cheap rate when the job is worth a lot more. There are contractors who are willing to work for what turns out to be less than $1 per hour, or they'll write 25,000 words for 20 bucks.

Reasons why people lowball:

- They need experience because they're new to freelancing and trying to establish themselves.
- They figure clients will be more likely to hire them if they're cheap; they can build up their experience and then raise their rates.
- They just don't know how much they should charge.

Clients take advantage of these contractors, or they don't know what the work is worth themselves. (In many cases, people think, "Hey, anybody can write! It's not like it's some valuable skill!")

Good clients will equate your skill with the low price. You're cheap, so your work must be cheap, too. Cheap rates = cheap work.

Lowball, and the Cheapskates Win (Or: Don't Screw with My Money)

There are serious dangers to lowballing.

You may find it's difficult to raise your rates, especially if you're on a freelance site, and prospective clients can view your job history and how much you charged. They might be suspicious of you trying to raise your rates on them, when you were so very, very cheap before.

You may lose your repeat clients because they won't be willing to pay you at your new rates.

You screw up everybody else's cash flow—including mine and that of all the other freelancers out there. When clients really don't know what they should be charging, it becomes difficult for others to earn higher rates because clients have grossly unrealistic expectations. (In short, don't screw with other people's money.)

Establishing Rates

Your rates should be determined by your education in the field, your work history in the field (or related fields), your work history with clients, and going market rates.

If you're freelancing full time, or if freelancing makes up most of your income, you need to keep your living expenses in mind. How much do you need to earn in a year? How much do you need to make in a month? What bills do you need to pay? These can include:

- Family needs
- Rent
- Groceries
- Car payments
- Student loans
- Other debts
- Business expenses

The Freelance Hourly Rate Calculator, an online resource, can help you figure out a minimum based upon your goals and expenses: http://allindiewriters. com/freelance-hourly-rate-calculator/.

Please note that you should include in your overall fee any time for research or prep work for the job.

A Hard Truth of Online Freelancing

Many freelancers, including successful, established ones, make less online/virtually than they do onsite, unless their client is a large corporation or a triple-A publisher. That doesn't mean that you can't earn $50/hour or more or make $1000 and up writing documentation.

It's up to you whether you charge by the hour or establish a fixed rate. Freelancers have varying opinions on this. Some only get paid by the hour. Some get paid a weekly rate based on their hourly rate. Others have a fixed rate, especially if the job won't take them very long. As you figure out your financial needs, determine what payment option makes the most sense for you.

Thrive, Don't Just Survive

Independent contractors find themselves in situations where they're living from job to job, and their checking account gets to near zero or even in the negatives. I've been there. That's one reason you don't want to lowball. Make sure that you strive for professional rates. You want to be able to do more than take care of your living expenses and just get by. You want to have fun money. You want to be able to attend networking events. You want to have a cushion if an emergency arises, like an unexpected trip to the dentist or your laptop or cell phone dying.

What Are the Going Rates?

Prospective clients you want to attract expect you to charge professional rates. To figure out what your rate should be, you need to research. Look up the average salaries of narrative-design and game-writing employees with your level of experience. Hang around professional communities for freelancers. What do they suggest?

For example, only the Writers' Guild of Great Britain has suggested professional rates for videogame writers.[2] They say a fair rate is £350–£450 per day. For an 8-hour work day, that equates to about $60–80 per hour.

However, other writers' organizations have suggested rates for copywriting, scriptwriting, and ghostwriting. These are comparable to game writing and narrative design.

The Editorial Freelancers Association says $40–$50 per hour or 20–25 cents per word (fiction writing).[3] Whether the information you find is for game developers or not, you can research similar industries to help determine your rates.

It's a decade old now, but the PDF *Beyond the Basics: How Much Should I Charge?* [4] lists the hourly and flat-fee averages of surveyed copywriters, scriptwriters, ghostwriters, and editors.

Minimum, Maximum, or Somewhere in between?

If you're experienced and have a degree in game design, game development, or a field related to game writing, then you want to aim for the maximum end of the scale.

If you have little or no experience, ask for the minimum, or a little less than the minimum. Prospective clients aren't going to expect you to ask for $75 per hour or $5000 for a GDD. They're going to recognize you're new to freelancing. That's why you should start with smaller jobs and work your way up.

Here's a gauge for determining how experienced you are and where you might fall on the minimum/maximum scale:

Experienced	Have worked several years professionally as a freelancer, employee, or both; have a degree in creative writing, game development, or related fields like film writing; have worked on shipped titles (doesn't matter how large or small they are); or have worked professionally in a related field.
Somewhat Experienced	May or may not have experience as a professional freelancer or employee; may or may not have a degree in creative writing, game development, or related fields like film writing; or have done some work professionally in a related field.
Less Experienced	Little or no experience as a professional freelancer or employee; no degree or working toward a degree in creative writing, game development, or related fields like film writing; or no work professionally in a related field.

Contracts and Clauses

You should always have a contract, and you'll have to provide it if your client doesn't. You may need a work-for-hire contract if you're working in the work-for-hire countries I noted under "Work-for-Hire Agreements." You can go online and find work-for-hire templates. If you have a lawyer, ask to have one drawn up. Your contract needs to clearly state a few things:

- What, specifically, your work entails.
- How you will be credited.
- How much you'll be paid.
- How you'll be paid (check, wire transfer, PayPal, etc.).
- How many free revisions are included if you'll need to make them.
- How your milestones are broken down. (Milestones are dated and indicate when you'll be sending work, when your client needs to get feedback to you, and when you should be paid.)

PLEASE LEARN FROM MY IGNORANCE, PART II

Some writing-related work I did for a very large triple-A publisher only took about a month. It was a lot of fun, and I enjoyed working with the producer … and then the money didn't come. I asked the producer about it. He inquired on my behalf … and then I never heard back from him. So, I kept asking where my money was, and then I finally got an answer from the new producer working on the project. This was about 6 months later. He made some enquiries. Nothing happened. I wasn't near the offices, so I couldn't drop by and do the running back and forth, dealing with the red tape that I needed to in order to get an answer. Finally, about a year and a half later, the second producer learned why I hadn't been paid: the company didn't have my bank account information to transfer the money.

Such a simple. Little. Thing. Just my bank account info! But the first producer didn't know to ask me for this when negotiating the contract because he wasn't in the habit of paying people. And at that point in time, I didn't know to ask how I would be paid and what information they would need from me. *A year and a half.* Did I mention this was during one of my lean periods, and I really needed that money right after I finished the project?

Please, y'all, please. Learn from my ignorance.

Saying in writing exactly what your work entails protects you against scope creep. You can also include a clause that states if additional work is needed, you can negotiate a new rate with the client.

If your work entails revisions, you want to specify how many revisions are included. Don't say you'll keep revising until your client's satisfied. You might find yourself in situations where you're doing endless revisions. Endless revisions mean your payments are delayed. Some clients will ask for endless revisions as a way to keep from paying you.

You want to attach payments to milestones because you don't want to be paid the full amount at the end of the job. You could be working for months. That's a long time to not see any money. You can set milestones so that you're paid at different stages or when you turn something in. For example, you get paid after delivering the script, and you get paid again when you turn in a revision.

Milestones

1. Up-front Payment ($█████)
2. Initial Review, Consultation, and Collaboration
   Payment Upon Completion: $█████
3. First Draft of Universe Bible
4. Feedback on First Draft
   Payment Upon Completion: $█████
5. Second Draft
6. Feedback on Second Draft: ████████████
   Payment Upon Completion: $█████
7. Final Revision:
   Payment Upon Completion: $█████

In this contract, I have a clear description for each milestone

Note: It's also important to set milestones for client feedback. You need this feedback to stay on schedule and to make sure you're delivering what they need. It's difficult to turn something in at the end of a project and find out that the client finds it unusable for one reason or another. Milestones for client feedback put them on notice of their responsibilities to you.

The Writer and Client will agree upon milestones for client feedback. The Client is expected to provide feedback on portions of the Project on or before the feedback milestone date. The Writer will not be held responsible for missing a milestone if the Client has not provided the necessary feedback.

This is language I've used in my contracts

Strongly Consider Adding This Clause

Back to work-for-hire agreements for a moment. This is for anyone working in countries with work-for-hire copyright laws. In the United States, as soon as you put an idea down in a tangible form, you own the idea. If I write three words on a napkin, I own the copyright to those three words.[5] With work-for-hire jobs, you *must* assign the rights to someone else, even if you're creating content for them. Otherwise, the rights stay with you, and you should be making some kind of payment agreement for the client to continue to use your work (which is an unusual arrangement in freelancing). So, make sure you have a clause in your contract that assigns rights to the client, and make sure that the clause protects you.

If you say something like "all rights will transfer upon final payment," it will behoove your client to make sure you're paid *IN FULL*. That final payment milestone is the last one listed in your contract, after you have completed all of the work and received the rest of your agreed-upon payments. If that final payment does not happen, you will remain the copyright owner of the content you produce.

The Up-Front Payment

For my jobs with a flat rate, I charge an up-front fee, especially for jobs that last more than a week. It's a percentage of the overall fee for the job. This is also a milestone payment. Good, serious clients have no problem with you asking for this. It's standard practice. Up-front payment is a retainer for your services and reserves time on your schedule. When you ask for an up-front payment and clients don't balk, you know those clients are serious and professional, and they'll treat you as a professional. But the up-front payment is also a way of protecting yourself. Sometimes you get a weird vibe from prospective clients, and you might be concerned that they'll try to not pay you. Or they might have every intention of paying, but they might lose their funding or go over budget on another project. Projects fall through for all sorts of reasons beyond the client's control. The up-front payment makes these clients you're not sure about bleed a little. They're sacrificing something to prove they're serious, and you won't be left with nothing.

Finding Work

Because of social media and game-development groups online, there are plenty of places to find gigs:

- Posts on Twitter, Facebook, etc.
- Employment search engines like Indeed.com, Simply Hired, etc.
- Game-development communities with job boards
- Crowdsourced campaigns like on Kickstarter or Indiegogo (reach out to projects you find interesting and ask if they need a writer or narrative designer)
- Freelance platforms
- Direct referrals
- Direct contact (a prospective client discusses a job with you in person or contacts you via your website, for example)

Finding good jobs is an art all of its own. There's a lot of chaff out there. There's a lot of soul-sucking work. There are prospective clients who are looking to scam freelancers out of their money, and there are guides online that teach them how to do this. On the other hand, there are wonderful clients with fun, interesting, and sometimes challenging projects.

Some job postings or enquiries you can easily ignore. What they're willing to pay is ludicrously low, or you can tell they're going to be a pain from their correspondence. Sometimes you can't tell exactly what it is the client needs from you, but you're still intrigued.

Never compete with other contractors on price. On some freelance sites, you can see what they're bidding. Some will lower their prices because they think it will give them a better chance of being hired. Whatever the situation, decide what you think the job is worth, and don't waver from that.

Freelance Platforms

Online platforms like Upwork, Guru.com, and Freelancer.com connect freelancers with prospective clients. Prospective clients post their jobs, and they'll usually indicate a budget range they're willing to pay. You can always ask for more. Great freelancers often get above the prospective client's initial budget range. You bid for the job by sending in a proposal and telling the clients what your fee would be and how long it would take. Communication with the client may be done on- or offsite, and you may turn in your work on- or offsite.

While there are many writing jobs on these sites, there are few game-writing gigs, and bidding is extremely competitive. Be aware that writing is often treated as a commodity that anyone can do, individuals who grossly undervalue their work for one reason or another flood these platforms, and there are many predatory clients who pay very little and treat freelancers badly. However, the few clients who treat and pay freelancers professionally often work with the same freelancers on multiple projects.

Important things to keep in mind if you pursue work on a freelance platform:

- Read the Terms of Service (ToS) carefully so that you don't violate them.
- Find out (1) if the site has its own default independent contractor agreement, (2) if you can use your own agreement instead, and (3) what steps you need to take so that the site considers your agreement legally binding.
- Find out how jobs are awarded, and make sure you've been awarded the job before beginning work.
- Understand how the site handles payments.

- Make sure you know how the site guarantees protections for payment. If you don't follow the site's requirements for guaranteed payment, you might end up with the client stiffing you.
- Spend time on the site's discussion/message boards, and read comments from veteran users of the site—both freelancers and clients.

Clients You Want to Work with

Good prospective clients have several ideal characteristics. They want to pay you professional rates. They know they need to pay well to attract and hire the best freelancers. They expect you to know what professional rates are. Sometimes they know what these rates are. Sometimes they have no clue, but they'll expect you to educate them. They believe professionals will behave professionally, and they'll see your expertise and insights as integral to their project.

Evaluating Potential Jobs and Prospective Clients

There's an art to reading job descriptions and queries and identifying good prospective clients. You might have a gut reaction that tells you it's worth it to try to get the client to respond to you. Other times, you're going to feel like you've been smacked in the face with red flags.

Some postings or correspondences are going to be full of information. Some might be only a couple of lines. Lack of information isn't a bad thing. It gives you opportunities to ask questions. Several clients I've worked with didn't have detailed information, but there was a confidence in the way that information was written.

If prospective clients seem like jerks in their communication, they're probably jerks—*period*. If you get warning signs that make you uncomfortable, RUN AWAY. You might need the money, but you don't need the misery. You don't want to be in a horrible situation where the work feels like torture. Your work will probably suffer, and stress will wreck your health.

If the client gives a budget, and you think it's acceptable for what the job entails, perfect. Contact the client or keep the conversation going. If what the client is offering is laughable, don't waste your time. You *might* be able to talk them into raising their budget if it's a little less than what you believe is fair. But I've been contacted out of the blue and asked what I thought something would cost. I gave them an answer, and I never heard from them again.

Freelance websites will allow independent contractors and clients to leave feedback for each other. You can find out a lot about clients through what they say about their past working relationships. Are their comments nasty? Are they complimentary? Do they have a bunch of jobs that were never completed, which should make you ask *why* they weren't completed? What do the freelancers say about them? Are *they* complimentary? If they ran into problems, what were the issues?

Do these clients have an online presence? Do they have company websites? Twitter accounts? Can you find out more about their project by what you find online? Vetting clients lets you find out how legitimate they are. There are scammers out there. But on the positive side, you can get a sense of people's personalities and what's important to them. When you're in a collaborative partnership (and the independent contractor/client relationship *is* a partnership), you want to know that you're compatible. And don't feel like you're spying on someone or snooping around. Prospective clients are looking to invest their money in someone. They're looking up everybody, too. You'll find that they'll visit your online portfolio and your LinkedIn profile because they want to get a better sense of who you are and if *you're* for real.

Don't Stare at Your Inbox

When you send an application or proposal, you don't know when you'll get a response, *IF* you're going to get a response. They may not be interested in what you have to offer. Your message may be swamped under hundreds of e-mails. They may have their job posted on several freelance sites, and they may choose someone from a platform you're not on. Don't wait to hear from them. Keep looking. If you wait, you can be waiting for months. Keep searching for gigs, and send out multiple queries and applications. You don't know what's going to get a prospective client's attention. If you get a lot of offers at once, you can always turn some of them down.

How to Submit an Application

1. Write your proposal or e-mail.
2. Send it off.
3. Forget it.

Establishing Professional Relationships

Once you get that job, make sure you set boundaries with your clients. Let them know when you're available for them to call or schedule meetings. You and your client should agree on your meeting times, and they shouldn't be telling you when you should be working. You'll sometimes have to find compatible work hours, especially if you have international clients.

Make Sure You're in Contact with the One Making the Final Decision

Sometimes your client's client is also your client. Your client may like your work, but *their* client may not. You don't want your work continually rejected because you can't communicate with the ultimate decision maker and find out what they want.

PLEASE LEARN FROM MY IGNORANCE, PART III

I was not in contact with the developer's clients on one game when the developer had subcontracted work out to me. It was very difficult trying to understand what the client wanted because they didn't play games. The project manager and I decided that I would write up a list of questions about their audience, the game's genre, games that were similar to the one they wanted to develop, etc. When I got the questionnaire back, I saw that only two or three of the questions were answered. Communicating with the client was difficult enough. It was even more frustrating when I had to do it through the project manager.

On the other hand, being in contact with my client's client worked to my advantage when the developer refused to pay me. I went straight to the people who were having the game made and explained what was going on, and they pressured the developer. I would have never heard from the developer otherwise and lost out on a significant amount of money.

Always be professional in your communication. I'm not saying don't be friendly. Communication should get a little less formal as you get to know each other. However, relationships can sour, and clients getting nasty isn't unheard of. Stay calm even when you're leaving feedback or addressing their attacks. Arbiters can get involved with client–freelancer disputes. When an arbiter reviews your case, you want the client to look like the problem. Not you.

Conclusion: Mercenaries for Hire

The word "freelance" comes from "free lances," or members of a hired army. Whether they're seasoned developers or nondevelopers wanting guidance while making their first game, plenty of prospective clients are looking for narrative mercenaries to help them perfect their project's stories. They know they need you, and you may have a lot more creative freedom working on certain projects than if you were an employee. Freelancing is not for everyone. It's not always easy, but you'll never have as many opportunities as you do right now.

Exercise: Query a Developer

You find this job listing posted on Twitter.

Identify the following:

- What you know about the job.
- What information you need to have a better understanding of the job and the game.

Looking for a Game Writer

WhoNeeds Games is looking for a contract game writer who'd be fascinated in helping us build a world that uses a magic system based on alchemy.

We will launch *Transmuted* on mobile and PC.

The ideal candidate is comfortable working with a small team and has experience writing for books, comics, and/or film. A degree in writing is a plus but not required. Above all else, we're looking for writing that will give our game the creative spark it needs.

If you're looking for a fun writing experience, please contact janelle@whoneedsgames.com.

What you know:

- The job is for someone who can help with worldbuilding.
- The game has strong fantasy elements.
- The game will be on PC and mobile platforms, which means it won't have a lot of sound or art assets.
- WhoNeeds says what an ideal candidate is, but they don't rule anyone out.
- Janelle is the person to contact at WhoNeeds.

What information you need:

- You don't know the game genre.
- Although the game has fantasy elements, it's not clear what era it's set in.
- You don't know the tone of the game (serious, comedic, etc.).
- You don't know who the player/audience demographic is.
- You don't know if you can work remotely, or if WhoNeeds wants someone in house.

Sample Query Letter

Dear Janelle:

I'm a telecommuting freelance game writer and narrative designer who's developed worlds for titles as diverse as *Little Monster Madness*, *Chocolate Park Chronicles*, and *The Summoning*. Additionally, I have a doctorate in literature and creative writing and have published over 70 short stories in a range of genres. I would love to have the opportunity to work with your team on worldbuilding for a world based on alchemy.

I did have a few questions to get a better understanding of *Transmuted*. What's the game's genre? Whom do you see as your player demographic? What's the tone of the game's writing?

Please find a link to my portfolio and résumé below. I can send along more appropriate samples once I know *Transmuted's* tone and genre.

Thanks so much for your time, and I look forward to hearing from you.

All best,

Toiya Kristen Finley

Schnoodle Media, LLC

References

1. For a good primer on NDAs, see Richard Harroch, "The Key Elements of Non-Disclosure Agreements," *Forbes*, last modified March 10, 2016, https://www.forbes.com/sites/allbusiness/2016/03/10/the-key-elements-of-non-disclosure-agreements/#30756522627d.
2. The Writers' Guild of Great Britain, *Writing for Videogames: A Guide for Games Writers and Those Who Work with Them* (London: WGGB, 2015), https://writersguild.org.uk/wp-content/uploads/2015/02/WGGB-A4-Videogames-2.pdf.
3. Editorial Freelancers Association, "Editorial Rates," accessed May 4, 2018. https://www.the-efa.org/rates/.
4. Lynn Wasnak, *Beyond the Basics: How Much Should I Charge?* (Cincinnati: Writer's Market, 2008), https://www.writersmarket.com/assets/pdf/how_much_should_i_charge.pdf.
5. Betsy Rosenblatt, "Copyright Basics" last modified March 1998, https://cyber.harvard.edu/property/library/copyprimer.html.

CHAPTER 14

Conclusion

Contents

Alexander Bevier 203
Heidi McDonald 204
Brian Kindregan 204
Danny Salfield Wadeson 204
Craig Sherman 205
Cash DeCuir 205
Matt Forbeck 206
Tanya DePass 206
Toiya Kristen Finley 207
Tobias Heussner 207

Congratulations. You've made it through all the chapters. We hope you haven't skipped any and that you have learned something on your journey toward this final moment with us writerlings around the campfire. Game writing and narrative design is a complex topic, and this book only touched on some of the many fields that it includes. We haven't talked about how to deal with existing IPs when trying to revive them or how to support voice recording. We haven't talked about effective critique or how to maintain a universe throughout multiple games and iterations of a game world. All this and much more belong to the daily tasks a narrative designer may have to complete.

Before we now let you continue your journey, we are hoping yet that you'll stay with us at the campfire just a while longer. We would all like to share our personal number-one tip when it comes to game writing.

Alexander Bevier

My largest tip is both simple and broad: learn everything. Effective game writing requires an understanding of entire cultures. This means learning about architecture and about language, and all other forms of design will help create a broad swath of experiences to put into your games. It's also a great way to always be excited about something. Enthusiasm will go a long way.

Heidi McDonald

In conclusion, the single best thing one can do when writing overall, not just writing romance, is to playtest. Playtest with romance fans and non-romance fans, gamers and nongamers. Playtest a queer romance with queer people and a game for teens with teens. Playtest to determine emotional engagement and pacing. Playtest to find out whether your characters are relatable, interesting, compelling, fun, and not offensive in any way. Playtest to find out whether your character dialogue gives players enough opportunities for self-expression. Just … playtest. It's the best way to know whether your writing is having the desired impact on your players.

Brian Kindregan

Most storytelling is an act of control, where an author or filmmaker takes the audience on a narrative journey, calling all the shots and creating powerful moments and themes. Game writing is completely unlike any other form of storytelling in that you, the writer, are collaborating with the player to tell the story. You create the possibility space and some of the big moments, but the player makes choices, even in a linear narrative, that fundamentally influence how that narrative exists in the player's mind and heart. This asynchronous collaboration is pure chaos.

My number-one tip regarding game writing is to embrace that chaos. Use it to make your game narrative resonate with players. There will be a temptation to fight that chaos, because with a little more control you can make the story work just so. Resist that temptation. Player collaboration is the most powerful tool in your toolbox, and it is something that no other narrative medium can do. It's unique to games, and that is true power.

Danny Salfield Wadeson

It's very simple: think of the player. Please note, I did not write think of the "players," plural. If you keep one specific player in mind, a hypothetical fan, you'll both keep yourself sane and have a good Occam's razor.

Whenever you're getting too deep into world-building, you can think of this player. Will they see any of this mad ingenuity you've spent hours brainstorming? Will they care, and will they care at that moment in the game? When you're writing dialogue, again, the same applies—what will the player be thinking? Will they be hoping for information, humor, lore, or characterization? Will you be able to subvert their expectations, or does the genre of game you're writing not have tropes well defined enough for your meta-commentary to actually hit home?

Equally, imagine that one player when integrating your writing or lore-building with the gameplay. Kurt Vonnegut said, "If you open a window and make love to the world, so to speak, your story will get pneumonia." I think that holds true in games to a large extent—if you create a branching narrative to please multiple kinds of players, it's going to be tonally incoherent. Have dialogue or branching narrative choices, sure, but cater to the different whims or sides of one hypothetical player. It's the job of game design to cater to different play styles or author gameplay such that it teaches anyone how to enjoy it best. That's not the job of a writer. That job is to craft a story that will be understood well by one mind, then to put it out into the world, in front of many minds, and let them make up their own.

Craig Sherman

Regardless of what's happening in the game at any particular time, always take a moment to think about your characters' points of view. You've always got to be thinking, "How would they know that?" or "Why would they do that?" If you don't know the answer, something's not right with the story. There's a lot of pressure in game development to move quickly, and sometimes story logic is abandoned in favor of "cool" gameplay moments. However, exciting gameplay and logical storytelling need not be mutually exclusive. I have been faced with many situations as a game writer when designers have refused to make changes regardless of how illogical the situation might be for the game's characters. Of course, in such situations my co-writer and I argue for what we believe is right for the game, and our job is to keep story in mind, but sometimes you lose the argument. These are the moments when you must be willing to throw away all of your preconceived notions and rethink. I'm not always 100% thrilled with the compromises that I've made, but, much more often than not, my partner and I have been able to invent new story elements to explain in-game actions. You have to remember that even if you're getting resistance from other members of the team, your first job is to protect the story. They understand that. In the end, everyone respects a writer who's willing to put in the effort to make the game better.

Cash DeCuir

As I've said before, I'll say again: be a student of the world. Practice your craft, sure, but study life. Better yet, live life. Pursue your interests: read, watch, question, delve. The more experience you have as an individual—or the more thoughtful you can be in your work—the greater your work will be. So, keep reading, keep thinking, keep living, and you'll bring something to your art no one else ever could.

Matt Forbeck

My number-one tip for game writing is this: respect the team.

Most of the time, writing is a solitary venture. It's just you pounding away at a keyboard, trying to fill up the empty space with something compelling that people will want to read. You might talk with people about it, discuss it with an editor, or even have a co-writer involved. But when you sit down to actually write, you can only fit one set of hands on the keys.

When you work on a video game, though, you're part of a team, and often a *small* part in terms of numbers. AAA game development can involve hundreds of people scattered across several studios in multiple time zones and continents. Your job is not to be the auteur of the game but to work with the rest of the team to come up with the best story can you manage within the parameters the team has to work within.

Because of that, you can't get too attached to any part of your work. While you should be advocating for the best possible story at all times, that's not the only concern of the team. Your work has to dovetail with programming, art, design, and—often most importantly—budget issues at every step along the way.

In that way, your job often becomes not "making the best story" but "making the best story possible out of what the team can manage."

While you might feel some ownership over the story, unless you own the company, it's not yours. Even if you do, it's not yours to do with as you wish. Reality places its limits on what you can reasonably pull off with the team you're working with, and you should celebrate that rather than rail against it.

Tanya DePass

My number-one tip for other writers is to be intentional in your work to be more inclusive. Think about the impact your words, combined with the art and mechanics of the game you're working in, will have on players as they traverse the world you're building. Be mindful, and think of what you are putting out in the world not just digitally but in how you are portraying experiences outside your own.

Understand that you'll fail at this, and that doesn't make you a bad person or a bad writer; it's a reminder that you're human and you should take that failure as a learning experience. Repurpose that failure into energy and motivation to do better next time.

The other part of this tip for writers is to take notes on things that may seem inconsequential at the time but could provide a moment of inspiration or bridge a gap between ideas or concepts. Also, when you sit with a consultant, take notes on things that may raise a question for you, and when you get those answers, make notes on how that answer made you feel so you can take empathy into your world-building and writing.

Toiya Kristen Finley

Two of the greatest skills you can have as a narrative designer and/or writer are critical thinking and analysis. Both of these help you break down multiple forms of storytelling, their structures, content, characters, worlds, and audiences. Even if you work on a project in which the genre or world setting is unfamiliar to you, you could study analogous games and quickly learn the mechanics, tropes, and archetypes to help you understand why players enjoy that type of game.

Analytical skills will also help you revise your own work. Instead of thinking about it creatively, you can review if it's functioning in the best way possible for the game's needs.

This may sound hyperbolic, but it's true: critical thinking and analytical skills will keep you evolving as a storyteller over your lifetime as a writer.

Tobias Heussner

Communication, communication, and communication. For me, the single most important skill when it comes to game development and narrative design, especially, is communication. It is essential that you learn how to communicate your ideas in such a way that your audience understands them. If you're talking to an artist, then you'll need to talk like an artist, and if you talk to programmers, you'll need to think like a programmer. It sounds complicated and like a lot of work, but really all it requires is an interest in the other fields and the willingness to listen to others. As writers we should be great at observing our environment; as narrative designers we need to push it a level further by also applying what we observe. The best ideas for games are normally not born in the mind of one brilliant individual, but by combining and filtering the ideas of many, of all that are involved in the development. A common perception of game designers (and narrative designers are game designers specializing in storytelling) is that these are the people with the idea. This image is not accurate … everyone can have ideas and they can be great or not. The job of a game designer is to turn an idea into something playable. The role of a narrative designer is to turn an idea into a playable story that can be experienced and enjoyed by millions of people with all kinds of different backgrounds. This is only possible if you listen to others, learn from their backgrounds to extend your knowledge, and communicate in a way suitable for your audience. If you didn't you read the concept or backstory, it will usually not help when in the trenches of development. What helps is clarity and the ability to communicate an idea quickly and precisely. The best way to practice this is to write one- to two-sentence high concepts, show them to someone you trust, and ask them for their feedback. Quickly, you'll see if they understand your idea or not. Once you have mastered these mini-pitches, you can start working on trying more specific ones, altering your concepts for different groups of people, and observe what happens when you present to them. The better you present and communicate your ideas, the more likely it is that you'll get valuable feedback that will help you to perfect your work.

Thank you again for joining us. If you would like to keep in touch with us, you can browse this book's website or sign up for the Special Interest Group Game Writing from the International Game Developers Association (IGDA). We have a Facebook page and a LinkedIn group, and while you will find the links in the appendix, we also encourage you to join our main mailing list at http://groups. google.com/group/WSIG-Main.

We hope to see you soon, as we gather the stuff from our camp, moving toward the next game developer conference, to ignite the campfire again and hopefully meet you.

Happy writing and happy game development.

All the best,

The writerlings.

Glossary

Ambient dialogue: Dialogue during gameplay spoken by players, AI companions, a voice over a radio headset, or any characters players pass at locations.

Animatics: Still images with text, voice-over narration, and/or a soundtrack, or comic book panels appearing in sequence.

Banter: A few lines of dialogue spoken between two or more characters.

Branching narrative: A narrative in which players make choices that affect individual sections of plot and gameplay.

Cinematics: Fully prerendered in-game movies with no player interaction and high production values.

Combat barks (also soundsets)**:** One-liners spoken in combat situations.

Core mechanics: The mechanics that define the core idea of the game.

Critical path (also critpath)**:** The collection of all the missions, narrative, and gameplay elements that are required to complete the game.

Cutscene: A noninteractive scene, scripted by narrative and usually done "in-engine," that does not allow dialogue options to the player.

Dialogue: Words or utterances spoken in the game.

Downloadable content (also DLC)**:** New game content offered in downloadable formats after the initial game has been released.

Dynamics: Players' applications toward the game's mechanics and how they try to optimize or use the mechanics to maximize their chance to win.

Environmental narrative: Audio, visual, and design techniques in the game's world used to intentionally communicate information regarding the world, its story, and its characters.

Flavor text: Functional in-game definitions given a fictional spin.

Game design: The rules and mechanics of the game.

Game narrative: The story's structure in the game.

Game narrative design (also narrative design)**:** The art of telling a story in a videogame using the techniques and devices available, including gameplay and the sum of visual and acoustic methods, to create an entertaining and engaging experience for players.

Game narrative designer (also narrative designer)**:** The champion of an interactive story, working in the field of narrative design, combining the roles of a writer with that of a game designer.

Gameplay: The set of mechanics, challenges, and story by which players interact with the game.

High concept (also tagline)**:** The game idea condensed into one or two sentences.

Interactive cutscene: An interactive scene, scripted by narrative and usually done "in-engine," allowing the player dialogue options.

Interactive dialogue: Any game system in which the dialogue pauses the action to allow players to select responses from a list, wheel, or any other presentation of multiple options.

Linear narrative: A narrative in which every player experiences the same events in the same order every time the game is played.

Mechanics (also game mechanics)**:** The rules of the game.

Narrative space: The amount of time players allow for a story to be told in a game.

Onomatopes (also grunts)**:** Sounds with no words involved.

Open narrative: A narrative in which players can choose their own order to complete any content.

Player agency: The players' beliefs that their choices and actions are what drive the events of the story.

Quest: A task or group of tasks composing a single, self-contained storyline that may be a part of, or alongside, a larger plot in a nonlinear story.

Quest texts: Structured text boxes that include a short dialogue, a description of the task, a summary of the task, and the rewards players will receive upon completion.

Retcon (also retconning)**:** The process of making a change to a game's world or story in a way that strives to be true to what's already published about that game.

Schedule/project plan: A document outlining all of the desired delivery dates for the content of the game, for purposes of ensuring that everyone knows when tasks need to be completed. This plan is usually synced with many different departments and may change during the development, so make sure to always look at the latest version so as not to miss any important deadline.

Sidequest: An optional quest in the game, which players do not have to complete to advance the story.

Storyboards: Illustrations and/or images displayed in sequence as part of the preplanning process for animations or other interactive sequences.

Task: Any goal a player needs to accomplish through gameplay, if in reference to game content. It also refers to the work of an individual developer that needs to be completed, if in reference to the development schedule.

Transmedia: The telling of several or many stories from the same fictional universe/world in various media, including prose fiction, comics/manga, film, animation, and games.

Voice-over: Narration not accompanied by a visual of the speaker.

Wireframing: The process of structuring the hierarchy of an information flow.

World-building: The development of details of the world where a story takes place, including its history, geography, peoples/races, governments, science/technology, religions, and languages.

Resources and Groups

Organizations and Groups

International Game Developers Association (IGDA)

Website: http://www.igda.org

Twitter: @IGDA

The IGDA is a nonprofit membership organization for game-industry professionals, students, and individuals interested in the industry. The IGDA has local chapters worldwide, where developers from the community get together to discuss game development and issues that affect game developers. IGDA meet-ups are great places to network and share ideas.

IGDA Game Writing Special Interest Group (SIG)

Websites: http://www.gamewriting.org and http://www.igda.org/writing

Google Group: https://groups.google.com/d/forum/wsig-main

Facebook Group: https://www.facebook.com/groups/119570501396639/

Twitter: @IGDAWritingSIG

The Game Writing SIG is a community of narrative-design and game-writing professionals, students, and individuals interested in evolving and promoting narrative within the industry. Anyone can join the SIG; you don't have to be a member of the IGDA. The Game Writing SIG discusses game-writing and narrative-design theories and best practices, shares diverse personal experiences, and chats informally about favorite stories in games.

IGDA Game Editing SIG

Website: http://www.igda.org/group/game-editing

Google Group: https://groups.google.com/forum/#!forum/game-editing

Facebook Group: https://www.facebook.com/groups/game.editing

Twitter: @GameEditing

The Game Editing SIG is a community of professional editors working in games, aspiring editors, and individuals interested in game editing. Nonmembers of the IGDA can join the SIG. While not focused specifically on narrative design and game writing, the Game Editing SIG is concerned with ways to improve story through editor/narrative designer/writer relationships and editing best practices.

Writers Guild of America, West (WGA)

Website: http://www.wga.org

The WGA is a professional union representing film, television, radio, and new media writers. Writers Guild of America, West recently started a program to support videogame writers with the goal to integrate game writers in the future.

Writers' Guild of Great Britain

Website: http://www.writersguild.org.uk

The Writers' Guild of Great Britain is a union for professional writers in the United Kingdom. It features support programs for narrative designers and game writers, including negotiating rates. Membership is available to writers of all experience levels.

Online Communities

GameDev.net

Writing for Games Forum: http://www.gamedev.net/forum/32-writing-for-games

GameDev.net serves game developers at all stages of their careers with news, developer journals, informative articles, and community forums. This is a good place to network, share ideas, collaborate, and look for feedback.

Other Communities

Coding programs and languages like Unreal, Unity, Ren'Py, RPG Maker, and GameMaker have their own community forums. Like the GameDev.net forums, these are great places to connect with other game developers, discuss narrative techniques, and get feedback.

Also, more and more groups open Discord servers that are free to join, such as the Unreal Slackers (a huge Unreal Engine 4–related Discord group). The various Discord channels and mod websites like Nexus can be a good starting point to look for mod groups looking for members if you would like to try your skills in a mod project.

Online References

Game Writing Samples, hosted by the Game Writing SIG

Website: http://www.gamewriting.org/game-writing-examples

This is a repository for all kinds of game-writing documentation, featuring submitted samples from members of the SIG. Documents included will give you some ideas of how you might format your own documents, whether you're working on a project or creating portfolio pieces.

Game Pitches

Website: http://www.gamepitches.com/

Game Pitches hosts the pitches and concept documents of games like *Bioshock*, *Fallout*, and *Fallout 2*. Looking over these, you'll get ideas of how different studios format their pitch documents. It's also interesting to note how much the finished game changes from the initial pitch. Game Pitches also has many game-design documents (GDDs), which will be of interest to readers who want to see how core mechanics and narrative design are explained in GDDs.

GDC Vault

Website: http://www.gdcvault.com

GDC Vault is a subscription-based database that contains most presentations held at past Game Developers Conferences (GDCs). Some sessions are free, but most require a paid subscription or an all-access pass to the conference. The database also includes many sessions from GDC's Game Narrative Summit.

Game Conferences

Game Developers Conference (GDC)

Website: http://www.gdconf.com

Game Narrative Summit: http://www.gdconf.com/conference/gamenarrative.html

There are several GDC conferences worldwide, but the largest is the five-day event in San Francisco during early spring. GDC in San Francisco is also home to the Game Narrative Summit, held the first two days of the week. A large community of narrative designers and writers meet at GDC each year. Attending the conference is a great way to become a part of the community. The community is friendly, welcoming, and always looking to support new members.

East Coast Games Conference (ECGC)

Website: http://www.ecgconf.com

Narrative Track: http://www.ecgconf.com/tracks/

ECGC is held in Raleigh, North Carolina, during the spring. It's a two-day conference that also features a Narrative Track dedicated to game writing and narrative design, and it's developing its own narrative community. While ECGC is a much smaller conference than GDC, its passes are more affordable.

Index

Note: Page numbers followed by *"fn"* indicate footnotes.

A

AAVE, *see* African American Vernacular English
Accuracy, 171
AD, *see* Authentic diversity
Advanced narrative design techniques, 2
African American Vernacular English (AAVE), 21
Alonso, Antonio, 94–97
Ambient dialogue, 111
Ameritrash, 53
Analytical skills, 168, 207
Ancillary romance, 29
Android Netrunner (A:NR) (game), 60–61
Animatic, 123
Arms in world-building, 41–42
Art
    assets, 166–167
    talking, 93–97
Articy:Draft, 91, 99, 103, 141
Art of Game Design, The, 136–137
Assassin's Creed (movie), 76
Assassin's Creed Odyssey, 66
Authentic diversity (AD), 13–14
    dangers of stereotype usage, 17
    diversity consultants, 16–20
    examples of failure in games, 14–17
    research, 17–20
Authenticity, 35
Autodesk Maya, 93–94

B

Bad dialogue, avoiding, 27–28
BE, *see* Black English
Belief systems/mythology in world-building, 40
Betrayal at House on the Hill (game), 59
Bevier, Alexander, 3, 203–204
Beyond Good and Evil (game), 15
BioWare (studios), 181
Black English (BE), 170
Blueprint, 91
Board games, 52–53
    case studies, 58–61
    connection with narrative content, 57–58

    embedding narrative content, 54–57
    future, 62
Branching narrative, 156, 205
Brave New World (game), 8
Breaking down editing skills for game storytelling, 161
Budgets, 146, 167
Buzzwords, problematic, 184

C

C# (programming language), 90, 92
C++ (programming language), 90
Campaign Cartographer, 99–100
Card art, 56
Card games, 54
Cause-and-effect scripts for NPCs, 55
Central romance, 29
Character, 121
    development, 165–166
    inconsistencies, 165
Characterization, 165–166
Chronicles of Riddick: Escape From Butcher Bay,
    The (movie), 75
Cinematics, 4, 79–80, 108, 125, 165
Clauses, 192–195
Client needs, 187
Collectible card games (CCGs), *see* Card games
Communication, 100
    in world-building, 42–44
Conflict
    in first draft of cutscenes, 114
    in world-building, 41–42
Content designers, sample domains of, 88
Contracts, 187, 192–194
Copyediting, 160, 171
    accuracy, 171
    dialogue, 171–172
    grammar, 173
    informational/instructional texts, 173
    unvoiced dialogue, 172
    voiced dialogue, 172
Core mechanics, 130–131
Countering failure, 152–153
Crimson (hand cannon), 42

Critical path (critpath), 162
Critical thinking, 207
Cutscenes, 106, 107
    animatic, 123
    emotional storytelling, 111
    exposition, 110–111, 119
    first draft, 114–118
    first round of feedback, 119–120
    having Spectacle, 111–112
    in-game cutscenes, 106
    initiation, 110
    kickoff meeting, 112–113
    playing levels, 114
    prerenders, 106
    second draft, 121–123
    subsequent drafts, 123
    visual storytelling, 111
Cutting, 156–157

D

DE, *see* Developmental editor
DeCuir, Cash, 6–7, 205
Deep immersion, *see* Narrative flow
DePass, Tanya, 8–9, 206–207
Destiny series, 41–42
Detroit: Become Human (game), 15
Developmental edit, 177
Developmental editing, 160–161, 167
    art assets, 166–167
    characterization and character development, 165–166
    dialogue systems, 164
    feedback, budgets, and time, 167
    narrative design and story, 162
    pacing, 162–163
    plot development, 164–165
    quests, 163–164
    sensitivity reading and diversity consulting, 168–169
    sound assets, 167
    world-building, 162
Developmental editor (DE), 160
Dialogue, 118, 121, 171–172
    systems, 164
Dialogue writing, 87
Diversity, 14, 16
Diversity consultants, 14, 16–20, 31
    skills, 168–169
Diversity consulting, 168
    analytical skills, 168
    education, 169
    knowledge, 169
    patience, 169
    personal experience, 168

Domestic abuse, avoiding, 27
Dominant forces in world-building, 39
Dragon Age: Inquisition (game), 15
Dragon Age: Origins (game), 15
Dragon Age (game), 40
Dynamics, 127

E

Economy in world-building, 39
Editing, 160–161; *see also* Copyediting
Editor–developer relationship, 176–177
Editorial Freelancers Association, 191–192
Elder Scrolls, The (game), 40
Emotional storytelling, 111
2017 Entertainment Software Association (ESA) report, 15
Environmental narrative, 167
Environmental storytelling, 38, 46, 133–135
Escalation, 138
E. T. The Extra-Terrestrial (game), 77
Eurogames, 53
Exposition, 110–111, 119, 135–136

F

F&F, *see* Flora and Fauna
Factions in world-building, 44
Falcon, Marcos, 91–93
Feedback, 167
Films, 75
Final Fantasy VII (game), 15
Final Fantasy X (game), 41
Finley, Toiya Kristen, 9–10, 207
First draft of cutscenes, 114
    central idea, 114–115
    conflict, 116–117
    dialogue, 118
    structure, 117–118
    theme, 115
Flavor text, 41–42, 56–57
Flexibility, 109
Flora and Fauna (F&F), 39–40
Flow channel, 137
Forbeck, Matt, 7–8, 206
Forced romance, 27
Freedcamp, 151
Freelance Hourly Rate Calculator, 190
Freelance Platforms, 196
Freelancer, 181
Freelancing in games, 180–181
    application or proposal, 198
    clauses, 192–195
    contracts, 192–194

experience *vs.* inexperience, 181–183
hard truth of online freelancing, 191
independent contractors, 191
jobs and prospective clients, 197–198
life, 188
lowballing, 189–190
minimum/maximum scale, 192
professional relationships, 198–199
rates, 189–192
skills, 180, 185–189
up-front payment, 195
work, 183–184, 189, 195–197
Friendship, romance *vs.*, 28

G

Game design, 7, 10, 13, 34, 44, 47, 57, 127
Game design document (GDD), 161
Game design fundamentals, 127
Game development, 86
Game narratives, 107, 119
Gameplay, 24–25, 27, 35, 46, 79, 82, 111, 163
    information, 142–143
Game rights, 65–67
Game storytelling, breaking down editing skills for, 161
Game to movie, 80–82; *see also* Movie to game
Game to novel, 71–72; *see also* Novel to game
    taking criticism, 72–73
Game writing and implementation
    common formatting, lack of, 86
    implementation, 87–89, 102
    preparation, 98–101
    scripting, learning, 89–93
    scripting, word on, 89
    talking art, 93–94
GDC Online, 11
GDD, *see* Game design document
Geopolitics in world-building, 44
Gloom (game), 60
God of War (game), 40
GoldenEye 007 (movie), 75
Google doc, 47
Grammar, 173
Grand Theft Auto (game), 39, 77
Granularity, 147–148
Guild Wars 2 (game), 15

H

HacknPlan, 149
Hansoft, 150
Headcanon, 35–36
Heterosexual romance, 30

Heussner, Tobias, 10–11, 207–208
High-level issues, 161
High concept, 139–140
High level editing, *see* Developmental/substantive editing

I

IGDA, *see* International Game Developers Association
Ill-defined motivations, 165
Immersion, 35, 109
In-game cutscenes, 106, 108–110
Inauthentic diversity, 14
Independent contractors, 191
    taxes and laws for, 188–189
Informational/instructional texts, 173
Inkscape, 99–100
Intellectual property (IP), 182
International Game Developers Association (IGDA), 208
Interstitial, 108
IP, *see* Intellectual property
Iteration, 156
iThrive Games, 4

J

Japanese roleplaying games (JRPGs), 24
Java, 92
Jira, 150
Jobs, 197–198
Journal entries, 111

K

Key programming, 90–91
Kickoff meeting, 112–113
Kindregan, Brian, 4–5, 204
Kingdom Come: Deliverance, 134

L

Language in world-building, 42–44
LARPs, *see* Live-action roleplays
Legacy games, 62
Lego Movie, The (movie), 76
Length of individual quest and chains, 129
Linear stories, 128
Lingua franca, *see* Pidgin
Live-action roleplays (LARPs), 134
Lore creation and deployment, 45–46
Low-level editing, 171–174; *see also* Developmental/
    substantive editing
Low-level issues, 161

Lowballing, 189–190
Lua (scripting language), 90–91

M

Mario series (game), 77
Marketing, 185
Masquerada: Songs and Shadows (game), 41
McDonald, Heidi, 3–4, 204
Mechanical function, 57
Mechanics, 127
MIDA Multi-Tool (scout rifle), 42
Mini-games, 111
Minimum/maximum scale, 192
Missions, 125–127
MMORPG quests, 129
Mobile Games, 76
Monster Hunter World (game), 40
Movies, 79
    adaptation, 81
Movie to game, 76–80; *see also* Game to movie
MSProject, 151
Multiple simultaneous romantic and/or sexual
        relationships, *see* Polyamory

N

Narrative commitment, 155–156
Narrative content
    board games connection with, 57–58
    embedding board games with, 54–57
Narrative designer, 52
Narrative flow, 35
Networking, 187
Nomenclature in world-building, 36–37
Nondigital games, 52–53
Nondisclosure agreement (NDA), 187
Nonlinear stories, 128
Nonplayer character (NPC), 24–25, 27, 31, 37
    actions/interactions, 35
    cause-and-effect scripts for, 55
Novel to game; *see also* Game to novel
    analysis, 67–68
    approvals, 69–70
    consulting with creators, 69
    getting game rights, 65–67
    making game, 70–71
    observing central traits of subject, 68–69
NPC, *see* Nonplayer character

O

Online portfolio, 182–183

P

Pacing, 121, 162–163
Pantheons in world-building, 40
Passion, 183–184
People of color (POC), 16
Pidgin, 43
Pixar films, 106
Planning, 145
    antidote to stress, 157
    countering failure, 152–153
    cutting, 156–157
    elegance, 148
    estimation and keeping track of time, 148
    exercise in production, 158
    granularity, 147–148
    iteration, 156
    narrative, 155–156
    producer, 152
    schedules and budgets, 146
    scope, 153–155
    setting, 146–147
    time sinks, 153
    working with team, 148–152
Player agency, 37
Player collaboration, 204
Player information, 142
Playtest, 204
Plot development, 164–165
POC, *see* People of color
Polyamory, 31–32
Prerenders, 106
Producer, 152
Professionalism, 188–189
Programming, 93
Progression, 138
Proofreading, 160, 173
Prose or fiction writing, 87
Prospective clients, 180*fn*, 182, 184, 197–198

Q

Query Developer, 200
Quests, 111, 125–131, 163–164
    design and environmental storytelling, 133–135
    design and exposition, 135–136
    design and motivation, 132–133
    focus and progression in quest design, 136–139
    graph, 141
    map, 141–142
    sample quest design flow, 139–143
Quest texts, 135

R

Recreation in world-building, 41
Representation in romance game, 30–32
Research in narrative design, 17–20
Responsibilities, 187
Retcon, 36
Rigid gender roles, 27
Roleplaying games (RPGs), 24
Romance game, 23–25
  representation and sexuality, 30–32
  satisfying and dissatisfying romance, 26–28
  workflow of romance, 29–30
Royalty on game's earnings, 66

S

Sample Query Letter, 201
Scheduling, 146, 158
Scope creep, 186
Scripting
  languages, 90–91
  learning, 89–93
  word on, 89
Script writing, 87
Second draft in cutscenes, 121
  character, 121
  dialogue, 121
  help from art and audio teams, 122–123
  pacing, 121
  subtext, 121–122
Sensitivity reading, 168–169
Serious games, 140
Settlers of Catan, 54
Sexuality in romance game, 30–32
Sherman, Craig, 5–6, 205
Shinobu's Vow (Hunter class gauntlets), 42
Slang, 43
Social hierarchy in world-building, 40–41
Sound assets, 167
Spider-Man 2 (game), 82
Sport in world-building, 41
Starcraft II: Heart of the Swarm, 107, 112, 117
Story, 128
  delivery, 162
  editing sample, 175–176
  story-based indie projects, 181
Storyboards, 123
Story editors, 160
  breaking down editing skills for game
      storytelling, 161
  developmental/substantive editing, 161–170
  editing roles and translating to games, 160–161

low-level editing, 171–174
modes for giving feedback, 174–175
technical benefits, 172
Storysense, 37
Storytelling, 87–88, 204
  environmental, 38
  in games, 160
  as mechanic, 57
Stress, antidote to, 157
Style guide development, 174
Substantive editing, see Developmental editing
Subtext, 121–122
Super Mario Bros (game), 80, 127
Super Street Fighter II (game), 15

T

Talking art, 93–97
Tasks, 126
Taxes and laws for independent contractors, 188–189
Telltale Games (studios), 181
Terms of Service (ToS), 196
Theory crafting, 35–36
Time, 167
  management, 185
  sinks, 153
Tomb Raider (game), 77, 81
Trailer, 108
Transmedia, 4, 11, 186
Trello, 149
Tropes, avoiding, 28
Turn orders, 55
Twine, 91, 99

U

Uncertainty, 55
Unvoiced dialogue, 172
Up-front payment, 195

V

Value of skills, 186
Verdant Skies, 170
Verisimilitude, 109
Video games, 23, 51–53, 55, 77, 79, 106, 155
  film adaptations, 81
  romances in, 30
Visual scripting, 91
Visual storytelling, 111
Voiced dialogue, 172
Volume, 109

W

Wadeson, Danny Salfield, 5, 204–205
Warriors, The (movie), 75
Wayne's World (game), 76
Wireframing, 87
Witcher, The (game), 40
Work-for-hire agreements, 189
World-building, 34, 37, 47, 162
 on creating and deploying mysterious lore, 45–46
 headcanon, 35–36
 practical tips, 46–48
 principles, 34–35
 theory crafting, 35–36
 toolbox, 39–44
 toolkit, 38–39
 workflow, 44
 worst case, 36–38
World of Lexica for Amplify Education, The, 3
World War Z: An Oral History of the Zombie War (novel), 78
World War Z (movie), 78–79

Y

YEd, 99, 141

Z

Zelda series, 37